ROYAL MURDER

Marc Alexander

FREDERICK MULLER LIMITED

*First published in Great Britain in 1978
by Frederick Muller Ltd., Victoria Works,
Edgware Road, London NW2 6LE*

ISBN 0 584 10446 4

Printed in Great Britain by
Arrowhead Publishing Limited, Kingsley

For my friend and partner
DAVID LEADER
who has always tried the game again

Acknowledgements

For assistance in the preparation of this book the author wishes to thank the British Library and its reading room staff at the British Museum, the Colindale Newspaper Library, the Harrow Civic Centre Library and the Radio Times Hulton Picture Library. For permission to take photographs which appear in this book thanks are due to the Dean and Chapter of Canterbury Cathedral and the Dean and Chapter of Winchester Cathedral.

Sincere thanks are also due to Richard Aldrich, Marie Alexander, Paul Alexander, Barbara Cheeseman, Susan Lamb and Anne Williams.

The picture opposite the title page is a stained-glass portrait of Thomas Becket in Canterbury Cathedral. It is believed to have been the work of a contemporary of the martyr and therefore could be an accurate likeness.

All photographs are by the author.

Contents

Illustrations

Introduction

And tell sad stories of the death of kings:
How some have been depos'd, some slain in war,
Some haunted by the ghosts they have depos'd,
Some poison'd by their wives, some sleeping kill'd;
All murder'd: for within the hollow crown
That rounds the mortal temples of a King
Keeps Death his court, and there the antick sits,
Scotting his state and grinning at his pomp . . .

Thus wrote Shakespeare appropriately in *Richard II*, and it is the sad stories of murdered kings — and the equally sad victims of royal murderers — on which this book concentrates. Until the Twentieth Century all royal deaths, ranging from the ludicrous to the noble, are a fascinating study. They not only signalled the passing of a mortal to whom blind destiny gave extraordinary advantages and burdens, but they usually triggered a convulsion through the everyday life of the land, sometimes marking the end of an era for good or ill. How much more significant, therefore, was royal murder. Those familiar with English history will be aware of the shockwave of horror which swept Europe at the judicial murder of Charles I. Even today it is possible to appreciate something of what was felt in the past; I am sure there are many like me who will remember the announcement of President Kennedy's murder as the most stunning newscast ever heard in their lives.

The first King of England to be chronicled as a murderer was Athelstan, a grandson of Alfred the Great, who ascended the throne in 925. He was the son of Edward the Elder and his mistress Egwina about whom a curious story survives. The daughter of a humble shepherd, she one day fell asleep while guarding her father's flock and dreamed that a great globe of light 'resembling the moon' shone out of her body, miraculously sending its rays throughout the country. Later she recounted her dream to the woman who had nursed the baby who was to become Edward the Elder. Seeing a divine omen in the girl's vision, the royal nurse had her taken from her lowly surroundings, groomed and educated, and introduced into court life where she was purposely put in the company of Edward, with the result that he fell in love with her and she bore him three children, the eldest being Athelstan.

When he became king, Athelstan faced hostility from the clergy and men of influence who objected to his illegitimacy and preferred his younger half-brother, Prince Edwin, who had been born in wedlock. The new king's first task was to secure his kingdom against the Scots and the Danes, who had settled in Northumbria. Following this, he turned his attention to a more domestic threat to his crown. An ambitious member of his household, hoping to profit from his tale bearing, warned Athelstan that Prince Edwin was plotting against him and the king, only too conscious of the weakness of his position, was ready to believe the charge. Edwin was brought before his older brother, but denied any conspiracy against him to the end.

Fearing the effect of the public execution of the young prince, and not wishing to technically stain his hands with family blood, Athelstan ordered that Edwin should be placed in a small boat without provisions, oars, sail or rudder; towed out to sea and cast adrift so that the prince would perish by natural causes. Faced with a death by thirst, Edwin preferred to jump over the side and drown himself.

When this news reached the king the full impact of his action struck him, and as a sop to his conscience he founded the Abbey of Middleton in Dorset where masses were said daily for his brother's soul. And in looking for someone to share his guilt Athelstan's kingly wrath fell on the courtier who had sown the seeds of suspicion. It happened one day when the man, who was the king's cupbearer, lost his balance when one foot slipped while standing by the high table. Nimbly he used his other foot to save himself, joking, "See how one brother helps another."

This remark cost him his life; the king read much more into it than the cupbearer had intended, and had him summarily executed.

The first English monarch to be murdered was Athelstan's younger brother, Edmund, who succeeded him in 940. He was eighteen at the time, and his enthronement was the signal for rebellion by the Danes of Northumbria and Mercia, and much of his short reign was spent in restoring order to his kingdom. In these troubled times he observed that the accepted system of fines for robbery was having no effect as crime was generally committed by those who had nothing to lose, except their lives. He therefore instigated a law which stated that the oldest member of a robber gang should be hanged, and this was the first English law which made death a penalty for theft.

Too many centuries have passed, too many shifts in the nature of the English character have taken place, for us to hazard whether Edmund's murder was as straightforward as the chroniclers record, or whether it was the result of a conspiracy. Today one cannot see who would have gained by his death, yet it seems strange that the outlaw Leolf should enter the king's hall so blatantly. Most probably we shall never know more than Holinshed's brief account of what happened on May 26, 946. The chronicler wrote: "On the day of Saint Augustine the English aspostle as he was set at the table, he espied where a common robber was placed neere unto him, whome sometime he had banished the land, and now returned without licence, he presumed to come into the kings presence, wherewith the king was so moved with high disdaine, that he suddenlie arose from the table, and flew upon the theefe, and catching him by the heare of the head threw him under his feet, wherewith the theefe, having fast hold on the king, brought him downe upon him also, and with his knife stroke him into the bellie, in such wise, that the kings bowels fell out of his chest, and there presentlie died. The theefe was hewn in peeces by the kings servants, but yet he slue and hurt divers before they could dispatch him. This chance was lamentable, namelie to the English people, which by the overtimelie death of their king, in whome appeared manie evident tokens of great excelencie, lost the hope which they had conceived of great wealth to increase by his prudent and most princlie government. His bodie was buried at Glastenburie where Dunstane was then abbot."

So many hundreds of years later it is hard to sense the tragedy of these early murders; the victims are now ciphers in a chronicle, their lives and passions dried to ink, yet the pathos of the next royal murder to my mind survives the passage of the centuries, perhaps because it was the result of a love affair, and all great love stories have unhappy endings.

Ten years after King Edmund was disembowelled by Leolf, his son Edwy was crowned upon the King's Stone* at Kingston-upon-Thames following the death of his uncle Edred. Surnamed "the Fair" because of his pleasing appearance, he was only fourteen years old when Odo, the Archbishop of Canterbury, anointed him. And immediately he had the misfortune to fall foul of Dunstan who had been the power behind the late king's throne.

This remarkable prelate, the son of a West Saxon nobleman, was educated at Glastonbury Abbey before spending some time at the court of King Athelstan — until he was banished for practising "unlawful arts". One of the reasons for his being denounced as a magician was the construction of a harp which could play itself; today it is thought that it was some form of Aeolian harp. If the future saint was not a magician, he was certainly a clever conjurer for his career was packed with convenient miracles.

*Still to be seen

When Edmund became king he recalled Dunstan and made him Abbot of Glastonbury in 945, and from this position he began his life-long work of making the Church the supreme power in the kingdom. To this end he was aided by Edmund's successor Edred who made him his High Treasurer, and who was so much under his influence that he allowed himself to be scourged by the abbot as penance for his sins. The death of this complaisant monarch must have been a bitter blow to Dunstan's plans, and he determined to get the upper hand of his successor. Naturally monkish chroniclers were biassed when writing about their patron, and they made much of an incident at the coronation of Edwy who, despite his youth, appeared to be of a far more independent mind that his predecessor.

"On the verie day of his coronation," wrote Holinshed "as the lords were set in councell about weightie matters touching the government of the relme, he rose from the place, got him into a chamber with one of his neere kinswomen, and there had to doo with hir, without anie respect or regard had to his roiall estate and princelie dignitie. Dunstane latelie before named abbot of Glastenburie, did not onlie without feare of displeasure reproove the K. for such shamefull abusing of his bodie, but also causing the archbishop of Canterburie to constreine him to forsake that woman whom unlawfullie he kept."

The new king's "neere kinswoman" was his beautiful cousin Elgiva with whom he was deeply in love, and he never forgave Dunstan for the abuse he poured upon her and her mother (who was present at their meeting), and for the way the abbot dragged him back to the hall by force.

Despite the opposition of Odo and Dunstan, Edwy planned to marry Elgiva. The clergy professed themselves shocked because it would be a marriage of cousins. The king, angry at the clerical party's opposition and still resentful over the humiliating scene at the coronation, refused to be cowed by the clerics and struck back by calling Dunstan to account for the vast sums of money which the previous king had entrusted to him. The abbot refused to give any accounts, merely saying that it had been given to him for religious purposes and he was answerable only to God.

In the end Edwy summoned up all his royal authority and banished him. Dunstan fled to a monastery in Flanders from where he incited the monks in England to oppose royal authority at every turn and mount a whispering campaign against the young king, whose morals were loudly deplored by the clerics when he defiantly married his cousin Elgiva. Their happiness was to be as short-lived as that of any classical star-crossed lovers.

A revolt, inspired by the clerical party, flared up in Northumbria and Mercia in favour of the king's brother Edgar. The distant hand of Dunstan can be detected when the nobles of Mercia were considering their choice of leader; a mighty voice from heaven commanded them to choose Edgar as their sovereign, on another occasion a statue of Christ miraculously spoke on behalf of Dunstan's policies. Not content to see Edwy's kingdom whittled down to Wessex, Archbishop Odo and Dunstan conspired for the young king to be parted from his queen.

Elgiva was kidnapped from a royal residence, branded on the forehead and sent to Ireland to be a slave, but when she was recognised as the Queen of England she was released and, when she was cured of her wound, returned with honour to England. She was travelling with a small party to rejoin Edwy when she was set upon by armed men in the vicinity of Gloucester. She was badly mutilated with sword thrusts, then, having been hamstrung, she was left to die of her wounds.

The priestly persecutors of the royal couple must have been delighted at the effect of the murder, for when King Edwy heard the news of his wife's ghastly end he fell into a state of melancholia and died, it was said, of a broken heart in 959. He was by no means the last king of England to suffer through falling out with powerful princes of the Church, and even out of Edwy's death Dunstan was able to make holy capital. On returning to England, where his protege Edgar was now in full control, he revealed that he had had a vision in which he saw Edwy's soul being borne away by devils, but as a result of his prayers they had to release it and thus the late king was saved from Hell.

Chronicles written by monks have portrayed the next king, Edgar, in the best possible light because under his reign the Church became more powerful than ever before. As soon as he was established, he recalled the exiled Dunstan and made him Bishop of Worcester and then of London, and on the death of Odo he became Archbishop of Canterbury. In effect he was the real ruler of England and was responsible for the restoration of many monasteries and the banishment of married clergy.

The reign was a quiet one as the Vikings left England alone and in consequence Edgar was known as "The Peaceful", but as a person he was said to be cruel and selfish, and his treatment of his friend and favourite courtier Athelwold bears this out. The king, wishing to marry for a second time, heard of the beauty of a certain lady named Elfrida. To assure himself that she was as beautiful as rumoured, and that she would make a suitable consort, he dispatched Athelwold to her father's hall in Devonshire to make a report.

Athelwold found that the glowing accounts of Earl Ordgar's daughter had been in no way exaggerated, and within a short while he was in love with her himself. Luckily he had not told Ordgar or Elfrida the real reason for his visit, and it was easy to claim that he sought her for himself. As far as his master was concerned, he dispatched a letter to the royal court at Winchester informing the king that the girl had not lived up to her description and that she would be unsuitable as a queen because she was simple-minded.

The earl agreed to the marriage, and after the wedding Athelwold took his bride to his estate at Wherwell in Hampshire, where he was so in love with her that he could not tear himself away from her to visit the king. Elfrida wondered why he did not take her to the court — and so did Edgar the Peaceful. Soon a courier arrived at Wherwell to announce that the king was hunting nearby and planned to spend the night at the hall of his old friend.

Once more let us turn to Holinshed for an account of the drama which he culled from earlier chronicles: "Some say, that the woman kindled the brand of purpose: for when it was knowne, that the king would see hir, Ethelwold willed hir in no wise to trim up hir selfe, but rather to disfigure hir in fowle garments, and some evil favoured attire, that her natiue beautie should not appeare: but she perceiving how the matter went, of spite set out hir selfe to the uttermost, so that the king upon the first sight of hir, became so farre inamored of hir beautie, that taking hir husband foorth with him on hunting into a forrest or wood then called Warlewood, and after Horewood, not shewing that he meant anie hurt, till at length he had got him within the thicke of the wood, where he suddenlie stroke him through with his dart. Now as his bastard son came to the place, the king asked him how he liked the manor of hunting, wherto he answered; 'Very well if it like your grace, for that that liketh you, ought not to displease me.' With which answer the king was so pacified, that he indevored by pretending his favor towards the sonne, to extonaut the tyrannicall murther of the father. Then did the king marry the countesse Alfred (sic), and of her begat two sonnes, Edmund which died young, and Ethelred."

When Edgar the Peaceful died in 975 Queen Elfrida desired her son Ethelred to be proclaimed king. Dunstan, however, favoured his elder brother, Edward, and it was Edward who was duly enthroned at the age of fifteen. Elfrida, just as ambitious as when she had betrayed her husband and bewitched the old king, remained determined that nothing should stop her son from ruling England.

One evening in the fourth year of his reign, Edward was hunting in Dorsetshire. As he was riding near Corfe Castle, where his stepmother resided with young Ethelred, he decided to pay a visit being very fond of his half-brother.

As he rode up to Corfe's Gate in the twilight, thanes from Elfrida's household came out to greet the young king and his small party of huntsmen. As Edward reined his horse these servants milled round him with cries of joy while Elfrida appeared with a smile of greeting on her face. Her cup-bearer held up the traditional wine horn of welcome and, as he did so, a man seized the king's hand and pulled it down as though to kiss it as a sign of loyalty. At the same time a man on the king's left held his other hand.

"What are you doing?" laughed the unsuspecting Edward. "Breaking my right hand?"

At these words the conspirator on the left buried a knife in him. The king wheeled his horse and used his spurs, but as it galloped away from the castle he fainted from loss of blood and reeled from the saddle. In falling his foot remained caught in the stirrup and the dying sovereign was dragged over the rough ground. His huntsmen finally came upon his mutilated body by following the trail of blood. They buried him privately at Wareham on March 18, 978.

The country was shocked by the assassination. The *Anglo-Saxon Chronicle* said: "No worse deed that this for the English people was committed since first they came to Britain. . . men murdered him but God honoured him. In life he was an earthly king, he is now after death a heavenly saint."

Edward's body was translated to Shaftesbury Abbey with magnificent ceremony in 980, and it was soon reported that miracles of healing were occurring at the tomb which became a famous shrine with the result that Edward was revered as a saint and officially styled a martyr in 1001.

The twilight of Saxon England deepened when Ethelred, the son of murderous parents, came to the throne in 979. The boy was only ten years of age when he stood by his mother's side and saw his beloved elder brother murdered. It made him cry so bitterly that Elfrida beat him unmercifully with a big candle until he thought she was going to kill him and for the rest of his life he refused to have candles carried in procession before him.

Dunstan is said to have forecast on his coronation day that his reign would be an evil one because he had come to the throne through the murder of his brother. Through history he has been known as "The Unready", but in his day he was nicknamed "Ethelred the Redeless", which means lacking good counsel. For a while this boy king was greatly under the sinister influence of his ambitious mother, but as he grew up this declined and finally she retired to a nunnery she had built at Wherwell in which she spent her remaining years in prayerful repentance.

After the Norman Conquest information on royal murder becomes more detailed though contemporary chroniclers often remained understandably circumspect, while those who came later were inclined to slant their histories to avoid offending the ruling house. Tudor writers — with Shakespeare prominent among them — were particularly prone to present history to the advantage of their royal masters. Thus for for centuries the last Plantagenet king has been regarded a homicidal monster as a result of writings by those whose interest it was to make the Tudor seizure of his kingdom appear justifiable.

There is no doubt, however, that the Plantagenets were the most murderous — and the most murdered — of our kings. The legend that they had the blood of the Devil in their veins must have found few disbelievers in their day. The story went that an Angevin ancester was married to a strange lady who would always leave the mass before the host was elevated. This disturbed her husband who one day tried to prevent her leaving, with the result that she seized two of her children and *flew* out of the window never to return. St Bernard once remarked of Henry II, the first Plantagenet king of England, "From the devil he comes, to the devil he will go."

Murder at court ceased with the Plantagenets, not that the Tudors were less bloodthirsty but they had a passion for the law — they saw no need to prepare poisons or send secret assassins when enemies could be removed legally by a stroke of the headsman's axe or, if religion was involved, by being burnt at a Smithfield stake.

When Henry VIII fell in love with Jane Seymour he disguised the murder of Queen Anne Boleyn behind an elaborate legal charade. Early in May, 1536, she was accused of incest with her brother Lord Rochfort and of adultery with three gentlemen of the Privy Chamber and a musician. Three days before her hearing her four alleged paramours were condemned to death for high treason, which meant that the queen's case was already judged before she was tried. One of the peers who pronounced them guilty was Anne's father, thereby implying the guilt of his daughter. When she and her brother appeared before twenty-six peers, each gave a verdict of guilty. One of the witnesses was Rochfort's wife, but she could not be regarded as very reliable as she was later put to death for helping Catherine Howard in her intrigues. Anne's uncle, the Duke of Norfolk, passed sentence on them and an ecclesiastical court ruled her marriage to the king invalid on May 17, the same day her brother was decapitated.

Two days later Anne was led to Tower Green where she declared to the assembled nobility and the London aldermen that she accused no one of her death and, while not acknowledging the charges on which she had been condemned, expressed submission to the law. The manner of her death was a novelty for the spectators as an executioner had been brought from Calais to strike off her head with a sword, a French custom then unknown in England.

Sir William Kingston, Constable of the Tower, was so moved by the courage with which she faced her execution that he wrote: "This lady has much joy and pleasure in death."

There was a curious phenomenon about the quiet acceptance of death on the scaffold by Henry's victims. While there was an occasional protestation of innocence, there was never a suggestion that a sentence was illegal or unfair. When it was Thomas Cromwell's turn to place his head on the block he declared: "I am by the law condemned to die. I have offended my prince, for the which I ask him heartily forgiveness." And Lord Rochfort, whose guilt like his sister's has been greatly doubted, remarked that he had not come to preach but "to serve as mirror and example."

Perhaps these sentiments were the fruit of the king's method of making everything conform to law, though a more chilling suggestion was that such behaviour was the price of an easy death in the days when victims were frequently "drawn". Tyndale wrote in *The Practice of Prelates:* "When any great man is put to death, how his confessor entreateth him, and what penance is enjoined him, concerning what he shall say when he cometh unto the place of execution, I would guess at a practice that might make men's ears glow."

* * *

Apart from the question of Queen Elizabeth's famed virginity, the greatest puzzle during her reign was whether the wife of her lover had been murdered. On September 9, 1560, Amy Robsart, the neglected wife of Robert Dudley, Earl of Leicester, was found at the bottom of a staircase in Cumnor Place with her neck broken. The suspicion that she had been assassinated so her husband would be free to marry the queen not only swept England but the whole of Europe.

The most curious and sinister aspect of the tragedy was that prior to September there was a general expectation that Amy Robsart was doomed, a sacrificial victim to the queen's passion and the earl's ambition. It was expected that Elizabeth and Dudley would marry, the queen had practically announced it herself, yet all knew that the match would be out of the question as long as Dudley's wife was alive.

Following Amy's death reports that the wedding was about to take place caused English ambassadors at foreign courts to send urgent messages to London, imploring the Council to halt it as Dudley was regarded by the world as his wife's murderer, and there was little doubt about the queen's aquiescence in the affair. If they were to wed it would be taken as an admission of guilt. As it turned out Queen Elizabeth's head ruled her heart and she did not make the same mistake as Mary Queen of Scots who lost her kingdom through marrying the man who had engineered the death of her husband Darnley.

When Elizabeth inherited the throne in November, 1558, one of the first to offer his homage was Robert Dudley who galloped to her residence at Hatfield on a snow-white horse. The new queen and the earl were already friends; together they had been prisoners of the late Queen Mary in the Tower of London, and now she rewarded his devotion by making him her Master of Horse. When she made her magnificent entry into London on November 28 it was Dudley who escorted her.

Although the new queen proclaimed, "This shall be for me sufficient, that a marble stone shall declare that a queen, having reigned such a time, has died a virgin," she made no attempt to hide her feelings for her dashing Master of Horse. Though he was married he spent all his time with the queen while his wife lived a life of unofficial banishment at Cumnor Place in Berkshire — the house of Anthony Forester who has been described as "a creature of her husband's". Honours were heaped upon the young earl by his doting queen; he was made a member of the Council, the Order of Garter was bestowed upon him, as was the lieutenancy of Windsor Castle and a highly profitable licence to export duty free wool. The queen also gave him a handsome mansion at Kew.

Elizabeth's infatuation with Dudley was the talk of court and kingdom, and its development was reported to the Continental sovereigns by their ambassadors who saw political implications in every kiss and tiff.

The Spanish ambassador Bishop Alvarez de Quadra wrote to the King of Spain in November, 1559, "I have heard from a person who is accustomed to giving me veracious news that Lord Robert has sent to poison his wife. Certainly all that the Queen will do with us in the matter of her marriage is only keeping the country engaged with words until this wicked deed is consummated."

By the middle of the following year Sir William Cecil, the queen's chief secretary, returned from Scotland to find that his royal mistress seemed to be completely infatuated by Dudley, to the point that she neglected state business while the object of her affections became increasingly powerful, being referred to as "the king that will be".

In a remarkable conversation with de Quadra, Cecil revealed his anxieties about the queen's behaviour. "He begged me for the love of God to warn the queen as to her irregular conduct and to persuade her not to abandon her business as she did," wrote the ambassador. "Then he repeated to me twice over that Lord Robert. were better in Paradise. And finally he said they were scheming to put Lord Robert's wife to death, and that now she was publicly reported to be ill, but she was not so, on the contrary was quite well and taking good care not to be poisoned."

This meeting between the secretary and the ambassador

took place on Friday, September 6, at Windsor. The next day the queen told de Quadra that "Lord Robert's wife was dead or nearly so", but asked him not to speak about it.

On the Sunday a trusted servant in Robert Dudley's household by the name of Thomas Blount left Windsor for Cumnor Place. On the journey he encountered another servant named Bowes who was hurrying towards Windsor with the news that his mistress Amy Robsart had been found that morning at the foot of the staircase with her neck broken. He had no explanation as to how the accident had occurred, she had been alone in the house when it happened. For some inexplicable reason she had insisted that everyone in her household should visit the Abingdon Fair.

Elizabeth ordered Dudley to stay at his house at Kew until the verdict of the inquest was known. This was the expected "death by misadventure", but it did nothing to stem the rumours. One of the most persistent of these was that assassins employed by Dudley — and the queen — had poisoned the unfortunate woman and then thrown her down the stairs in the deserted house in order to make it look like an accidental death.

What has always remained a mystery was why she should voluntarily empty the house on that fatal morning. Was she expecting a visitor whom she did not want her servants to see, or had she planned an elaborate suicide in order to revenge herself by casting suspicion on her husband and the queen? What seemed to be the most damning fact in the case was Elizabeth's remark to de Quadra about Lord Robert's wife being "dead, or nearly so" a few hours before the event. Had there been a delay in the timetable of the murder?

Ironically the death of Amy Robsart prevented the marriage which it should have made possible. Elizabeth must have been shocked at the allegations and suspicions which turned not only her own countrymen against her but became powerful political weapons for the Catholic kings across the Channel. It seems that the day had come when royal murder could no longer be overlooked. Elizabeth knew that if she married Dudley it would be construed that, even if she was not involved personally, she was condoning the Earl who was regarded as the instigator of the plot — yet if she did not marry him it would appear that she doubted his professed innocence. Her solution was to do nothing. Dudley remained the honoured favourite and behind the scenes the faithful Cecil worked to repair the damage caused by the scandal.

* * *

After the Amy Robsart affair murder was not associated with our monarchy until the establishment of the House of Hanover. Prior to assuming the crown of England George I was — as we shall see further on in this book — suspected of being responsible for the assassination of his wife's lover. Later in England a son of George III was involved in a curious case of attempted murder, though at the time it was hinted that the would-be assassin was actually the victim.

Born at Kew in 1771, Ernest Augustus, Duke of Cumberland, grew up to distinguish himself as a soldier with the Hanovarian Army before returning to England in 1796. Here he remained until he became King of Hanover when that state separated from Britain on Queen Victoria's accession. In the first battle of Tourney the duke had lost an eye and was severely wounded in the right arm in hand-to-hand fighting. Later he was conspicuous for his personal bravery in the sortie from Nimeguen when he lifted a French dragoon from his horse and carried him a prisoner back to his lines.

In 1810 the duke was unexpectedly wounded again. The *Dictionary of National Biography* states: "On the night of 31 May 1810 the duke was found in his apartments in St James's Palace with a terrible wound on his head which would have been mortal had not the assassin's weapon struck against the duke's sword. Shortly afterwards his valet, Sellis, was found dead in his bed with his throat cut. On hearing the evidence of the surgeons and other witnesses, the coroner's jury returned a verdict that Sellis had committed suicide after attempting to assassinate the duke. The absence of any reasonable motive caused this event to be greatly discussed and the democratic journalists did not hesitate to accuse the duke of horrible crimes, and even hint that he murdered Sellis."*

A differing version of the events was given by J. Heneage Jesse in his *Memoirs of the Life and Reign of George III,* published in 1867. He wrote: "The murder took place early on the morning of the 31st of May. At about half past twelve the duke, after dining at Greenwich and attending the benefit of the Royal Society of Musicians, entered his apartments overlooking Cleveland Row. He retired at one. His sleeping room which was dimly lighted by a lamp which stood behind a screen in the fireplace. On the sofa by the duke's military sabre which his favourite valet, Sellis, a Piedmontese, had recently repaired and sharpened. At two thirty the duke was aroused by a blow on the head, followed by a second blow. He thought a bat had got into his apartment. The light, however, gleamed on the sabre, he at once saw the extreme peril of his situation. He felt for the bellrope but it was not there. Now receiving a third stroke, he sprang from his bed and rushed to the door of the apartment of the page Neale who was in attendance. His assailant pursued him. He opened the door but not until he had received a wound in the thigh and other injuries. The assassin, having dropped the sabre, now made good his retreat. In the meantime the duke, with the assistance of the page Neale had succeeded in alarming his Royal Highness' household.

"The duke asked for Sellis and some people, dispatched to summon him, found the door of his apartment fastened. To their repeated exclamation that the duke had been assassinated no answer was returned. They then went through another entrance by the principle staircase, opened the door of Sellis' apartment and were appalled by the most horrifying sight of Sellis sitting half undressed in a reclining position on

In 1813 Henry White was sentenced to fifteen months' imprisonment and fined £220 for suggesting the duke was responsible for Sellis' death. In 1832 a pamphleteer named Joseph Phillips stated that the "general opinion was that His Royal Highness had been the murderer of his servant Sellis." The duke prosecuted Phillips who was found guilty without the jury retiring and sentenced to six months' imprisonment.

2 *The murder of Edmund by Leolf*

3 The Rufus Stone in the New Forest glade where William II was killed by an arrow

Right: 4 The tomb of William in Winchester Cathedral (The author wishes to express his thanks to the Dean and Chapter of the cathedral for permission to photograph it).

5 *The gate where Edward the Martyr was stabbed at Corfe Castle*

6 *The death of Amy Robsart*

THE STATESMAN.

LONDON:
THURSDAY, MAY 31, 1810.

ATTEMPT to ASSASSINATE his Royal Highness the DUKE of CUMBERLAND.

A base attempt to assassinate his Royal Highness the Duke of CUMBERLAND was made at an early hour this morning, by one of his domestics. According to the report which has reached us, this horrid attack was committed by the Royal Duke's Valet, who, it is said, entered his Master's bed-room about three o'clock in the morning, and endeavoured to stab him in bed with a sword. We understand that he struck two blows at his Royal Highness—the second of which fell upon his wrist, his Royal Highness having awoke and raised his arm to guard against this barbarous attempt. His Royal Highness then raised himself up, and the Valet withdrew. His Royal Highness however came to the door and called for assistance. It was at first thought that robbers had entered the house, and a serjeant's guard was called in.— The serjeant and his men proceeded to search the house, and on coming to the Valet's apartment they found there the perpetrator of this atrocious transaction with his throat cut. It appears that the wretch, on seeing his Royal Highness move, had retired to his own room, and immediately destroyed himself. The razor with which he committed the act of suicide was found near him by Serjeant CURTONTON. As his Royal High-

7 The newspaper report on the attempted assassination of the Duke of Cumberland, later there were suggestions that the affair was not as straightforward as this account suggests

his bed with his throat cut from ear to ear with life extinct. His countenance was not only composed but was said to have worn a smiling expression. On a chest of drawers near the bedside lay a razor and a basin containing water tinged with blood. It was suggested that after having attacked his master he rushed back to his own apartment with the intention of washing the duke's blood from his hands and getting into bed as soon as possible. The approach of the persons sent in search of him told him that detection was inevitable and he committed suicide.

"The fact is worthy of mention that Sellis was a left-handed person whereas it was the conviction of one of the physicians who examined his body after death that the wound must have been inflicted with the right hand."

In the *Diaries and Correspondence* of the Rt Hon George Rose, we find the following account: "It was noticed, that there was a smear of blood on the *left hand* side of the doorcase, from the duke's bedroom, to the state apartments — between four and five feet from the floor — and some unfavourable inferences seem to have been drawn from this. Sir Thomas Dyer told us that he saw Sellis' body in the room, exactly in the state it had been found; that he sat, lying back upon the bed, his hands on each side, and his face composed, and with rather a smiling expression. That his coat was off, and hanging on a chair, as far as could be from the bed in so small a room. He observed that it gave proof that the blood had gushed from the wounds while it was warm; for that the left sleeve, between the shoulder and the elbow, was soaked with blood, which must have streamed on it from the sabre held in the right hand. One of his half-gaiters was off, and the other half unbuttoned; in short he had the appearance of having been interrupted in undressing, and of having thrown himself hastily onto the bed. When it was observed that the blood on the sleeve accounted for that on the doorcase, he said, he had not seen it, nor had he heard it noticed; but afterwards remarked on inquiry that Sellis could *not* have taken his coat off and placed it where it was after having cut his throat."

Colonel Willis, a gentleman who was well known in Court circles, wrote at the time what he thought might have been Sellis' reason for attacking his master, declaring: "I strongly suspect that the motives which activated Sellis in his attempt to assassinate the Duke of Cumberland were the taunts and sarcasms the duke was constantly, in his violent, coarse manner lavishing on Sellis' religion, who was a Catholic (sic). This conduct, in addition to the part the duke had notoriously taken to prevent the extension of entire toleration of that religion, appeared to be very sufficient motives to induce a bigot to commit this most desperate action."

Was Sellis a bigot? At the inquest servants who worked with him complained that he was irreligious. At this inquiry the jury heard evidence for four hours, debated upon it for an hour and returned a verdict of suicide against Sellis. The body was interred in the "high road" in Scotland Yard.

Those who disagreed with the finding claimed that it was unlikely that in the throes of agony after cutting his throat Sellis would have been able to place his razor on the chest of drawers, it would have been more likely to have fallen to the floor or remained in the dying man's convulsive grip. Another point was that according to a doctor the gash had been made by an instrument held in the right hand, yet Sellis was said to be left-handed. If he was this raises doubt about the Rt Hon George Rose's remark that the blood on the left hand sleeve of the coat must have "streamed on it from the sabre held in the right hand." It is also doubtful if enough of the duke's blood would have adhered to the blade to "stream".

Some authors have written that when the physician Sir Henry Halford was summoned to the duke's apartments he found him with his shirt stained with blood. Cumberland explained that he had been set upon and injured but Halford only found a cut on his hand.

Others who did not agree with the official version of the events suggested that in a fit of temper the duke killed his valet with the newly sharpened sabre, then laid his body on the bed and cut himself with the dead man's razor to give credence to the attack-and-suicide story. This theory is as open to question as the coroner's and unless some over-looked clue comes to light the affair will remain a minor mystery.

The Duke of Cumberland was not the only Hanovarian about whom rumours of gory murder spread. After Jack the Ripper terrorised gas-lit London in 1888, it was inevitable that among the extraordinary collection of suspects assembled by the ripperologists there should have been a member of the royal family — Albert Victor, Duke of Clarence and Avondale, the eldest son of the Prince of Wales and a grandson of Queen Victoria. His alleged involvement with the ghastly murders has become part of modern folklore and like most myths has several variations.

The most bizarre of these appeared two years ago in the book *Jack the Ripper — The Final Solution,* by Stephen Knight, which was based on information supplied by Joseph Sickert, the natural son of the artist Walter Sickert. He claimed that his mother was the daughter of a shop girl named Annie Crook and Albert Victor who secretly married her in the 1880s. When news of this reached Queen Victoria, and the Prime Minister Lord Salisbury, it was arranged to have the couple abducted from Annie's rooms in Cleveland Street, London. Albert Victor was forced henceforward to behave in a way that would have won his grandfather's approval while poor Annie Crook was taken to Guy's Hospital where Sir William Gull, the Queen's surgeon, performed a brain operation upon her which left her insane.

More horror was to come when the woman who had looked after the child of the star-crossed couple confided the story to some East End prostitutes who saw in it a means for profitable blackmail. Fearing the political disaster which would follow the story becoming public, Salisbury persuaded Sir William Gull to eliminate the wretched women. This he did under the guise of the Ripper, assisted by a coachman and Walter Sickert.

It was a sensational solution to a sensational case, but just as this book was about to go to press *The Sunday Times* of June 18, 1978, carried the news that Joseph Sickert had admitted that his story about the Ripper murders was a hoax. Yet the fact that the story is a fabrication will not kill it. Over the past two years thousands of copies of the book were sold and many people who read and believed it will never know of Sickert's confession, thus the myth of the Queen's surgeon slashing prostitutes to preserve the Duke of Clarence from a scandal will be perpetuated.

Soon after Sickert's admission of the hoax news came of another royal 'ripper' book by an American ex-detective named Frank Spiering. In his *Prince Jack* he revives the old rumour that Albert Victor was the Whitechapel murderer, and embellishes his account with the "thoughts" of the duke as he disembowelled his victims.

In fact no real evidence has ever been produced to link murders with royalty, but as so much is still being written on this theme I feel that it deserves examination in a book such as this. Therefore I am grateful to Colin Wilson, who as well as being a philosophical author is an acknowledged authority on the Ripper, for providing the final chapter on this subject.

In writing the following accounts of royal murder I have tried to show that each one described is only the final link in a long chain of events. While some of the actual killings may provide a certain morbid interest, it is the complex patterns of behaviour prior to them wherein the fascination lies. And if in the past our crown has been tarnished with blood it must be remembered that the old kings, cast by divine right in the centre of the historical stage, were seen to express their human traits in terms of Olympian drama, personifying nobility, piety, ambition or greed. The words of Alexandre Dumas should also be remembered: "The king is but a man, royalty is the gift of God."

CHAPTER ONE

The Murder of William Rufus

". . . departed in the midst of his unrighteousness . . ."

". . .thereafter on the morrow was the King William shot off with and arrow from his own men in hunting."

This terse statement in the *Anglo-Saxon Chronicle* refers to one of the classic puzzles of English history — the violent death of William II. When his body was found by a charcoal burner named Purkiss in a New Forest clearing, no one mourned the dead monarch or cared whether the arrow had struck him by accident or had flown from an assassin's bow. It was left to Purkiss to transport the royal corpse to Winchester on his cart, tradition asserting that it left behind a trail of blood which the king's spectre returns to follow on each anniversary of his death.*

The universal detestation for William was expressed thus by a contemporary English chronicler: "Though I hesitate to say it all things that are loathsome to God and earnest men were customary in this land and this time. And therefore he was loathsome to wellnigh all his people and abominable to God . . . he departed in the midst of his unrighteousness without repentance and expiation."

The dead king was interred in Winchester Cathedral without ceremony — no bell tolled, no prayers said for the repose of his soul and later when the roof collapsed the accident was blamed on the evil which clung to his remains.

*See Phantom Britain *by Marc Alexander, published by Frederick Muller.*

It is understandable that the Saxon population should feel no grief over the death of the son of the harsh Conqueror, and the antagonism which existed between William and the Church could explain the monkish author's pious criticism, but the complete lack of ceremonial for an anointed sovereign could have had other connotations — to have mourned the victim might have appeared as disrespect to the man who gained the throne as a result of the murder.

Born between 1056 and 1060, William was only the third of William the Conqueror's sons, yet it was he who gained the crown of England on his father's death. It was eleven years after the Conquest that history first takes note of William, when hostility grew between his eldest brother Robert and his father. Soon after 1066 Robert had been nominally invested with the Duchy of Normandy but as he grew older he resented the way his formidable father refused to allow his sons any real say in the governing of his realms. With some encouragement from his mother, Queen Matilda, he began to intrigue against his father, but in the resultant disputes the king was supported by his sons Richard and William. In 1079, the latter was wounded in Normandy when the Conqueror was attacking a castle held by Robert. This shedding of blood on his behalf endeared the youth to William.

Two years later there befell a tragedy for the Conqueror which the Saxons saw as an act of supernatural retribution. While hunting in the New Forest — a vast game preserve the king had created by demolishing the hamlets of the vanquished — his most promising son Richard was gored to death by a stag. Thus, when King William lay on his death bed six years later in the Priory of St Gervais in France, he brooded on the disloyalty of his first-born and, with Richard dead, decided to make the dutiful William his successor in England. The day before he died he sent him to England with a letter for Archbishop Lanfranc requesting him to crown William "if he deemed it might be justly done." In England William's first astute action was to race to the royal treasury at Winchester where he seized the keys and found that his father's fortune amounted to £60,000 in silver, gold and jewels.

Possessed of this basic necessity for royal power, he persuaded the archbishop to crown him on September 26, 1087.

In appearance the new king had a broad forehead, blond hair, eyes of "varying colour flecked with white" and a ruddy complexion which caused him to be known as Rufus or the Red King. He was of middle height, and, like his father, of stout build. His greatest love was for hunting, spending so much time at the chase that he earned the additional cognomen of the Wood-Keeper.

He had been reared as a typical Norman lord to hunt and fight and, like the knights of his time, he had a schizophrenic outlook which reconciled brutality with the principles of chivalry. It was his ambition to become the most famous knight in Christendom, an ambition which it seems he fulfilled.*

The only men he had respect for were Norman warrior knights. For the clergy he felt contempt while his subjects seemed to have inspired no feeling at all. Nor, it seems, did he have any serious feelings for women. He was the only adult English king never to marry, nor did he father bastard children, with the inevitable result that some historians have suggested that he was homosexual. Earlier chroniclers, who had little sympathy for him, never went so far as to accuse him of what was then regarded as a blasphemous vice, though William of Malmesbury did write of the "troops of pathics"† as well as the "droves of harlots" which followed his court. The same author probably gave the best summing up of him as a king, and in the final words there is the suggestion of reckless arrogance: "His greatness of soul was obscured by excessive severity and the world doubted for long to which

---

Lines in the Roman de Rou *refer to him thus:—*

> *Li Reis Ros fu de grant noblesce*
> *Proz fu e de grant largesce*
> *N'oist de chevalier parler*
> *Ke de proesc oist louer,*
> *Ki en son brief escrit ne fust*
> *E ki par an del suen n'eust.*

†*A word meaning a "sodomite's minion".*

side he would incline: but at last the desire after good grew cold – for he feared God but little and man not at all."

Yet through chinks in the criticism of the chroniclers we do get glimpses of the man within the armour of kingship, a man who enjoyed cracking jokes with his heroes when out of the public eye and who had some amusing character traits. Of one of these William of Malmesbury wrote: "He was a man who knew not how to judge the value of goods – the trader might sell him his commodity at whatever rate he pleased. He was anxious that his clothes should be extravagant, and angry if they were purchased at a low price. One morning .when putting on some new boots he asked his chamberlain what they had cost, and on hearing three shillings, he cried out in a rage, 'You son of a whore, how long has the King worn boots of so paltry a price? Go, get me a pair worth a mark of silver.' The chamberlain went and, bringing him a much cheaper pair, told him falsely that they had cost as much as he had ordered 'Aye', said the king, 'these are suitable to regal majesty.' "

In the new reign the forest laws were enforced even more harshly than they had been under the Conqueror, and this was to earn William the hatred of the common people. No dogs were allowed to be kept within miles of the royal reserves except mastiffs which were used to guard households in those uncertain days. Even these animals had to be crippled by amputation of three claws of the forefeet so they could not run after deer. A special Court of Regard was held every three years to ensure that no one had a dog fit for hunting.

No Saxon Englishman dared approach the accursed hunting domains unless he was some desperate dispossessed wretch whose hunger drove him to poaching. If caught, he knew he would be hanged on the spot with his own bowstring. The evidence required for such rapid execution was impressed into the minds of the peasants by this doggerel:

> *Dog draw – stable stand,*
> *Back berand – bloody hand!*

This means: *Dog draw,* holding a dog by a leash; *stable stand,* standing concealed with a drawn bow; *back berand,* bearing away a dead deer, and *bloody hand,* obviously hands stained with deer blood.

William exploited the love of the English for their forests when, three months after his coronation, he learned that his uncle Odo, the Bishop of Bayeux, was plotting to replace him with his more tractable brother Robert.

"When the King understood these things and what treason they did towards him . . . he was greatly disturbed in his mood," states the *Anglo-Saxon Chronicle.* "Then he sent after the Englishmen and set forth to them his need and prayed their help and promised the best laws everywhere in this land and that he would forbid all unjust taxation and give them back their woods and their hunting."

It was to prove an empty promise, but in London enthusiastic crowds flocked to the Red King's standard and marched behind him to attack the strongholds of the rebels in Kent. The campaign was successful, Odo was banished but the forest laws remained and popular disillusion with the king grew.

Next William prepared to invade Robert's dukedom of Normandy. The following campaign was not a success and uneasy peace was made between the two when they agreed to attack their third brother, Henry. He had used part of his inheritance to buy some territory from Robert, and into this the brothers marched while Henry locked himself up in Mont Saint Michel on the French coast.

At one stage of the siege Henry's water supply became dangerously low. Robert, the most good natured of the Conqueror's sons, not only allowed Henry's men to get more, but sent wine from his own table. At this William was furious, but Robert said, "What! Shall we let out own brother die of thirst? Where shall we get another when he is gone?"

The Red King had great faith in his royal authority. One day he rode out alone along the shore, looking at the castle held by Henry, when a small enemy party came stealthily over the dunes and overpowered him. As one was about to stab him he cried out, "Good knave, do you not recognise the King of England!" At these words the man-at-arms dropped his dagger and respectfully helped William to his feet.

William showed his chivalrous side when he haughtily demanded who had brought him down, and when a knight admitted that he had done it the king used his favourite oath, declaring, "By the Face of Lucca, you shall be mine. Your name will be written in my book and you shall receive the reward of good service."

Unable to hold out indefinitely, Henry left Mont Saint Michel and William returned to England. In 1092, he carried out what has been described as the one good act of his reign. He went north to the ruins of Carlisle, which had been razed by his father, where he restored the city and built a castle there. Then he went south and sent many "churlish" folk to occupy the city and recolonise the district which, under the Conqueror's mailed hand, had been made into a wilderness.

Two years later William was once more at war with his brother Robert. Bribes and the payment of mercenaries had emptied his coffers and the crippling taxes imposed on his reluctant subjects were slow in coming in. Then he had a novel idea for replenishing his funds. An army of 20,000 Englishmen was ordered to assemble at Hastings, prior to embarking for the Normandy war. Each shire had to send a required number of men and supply each with ten shillings to cover his expenses. When the army was assembled the king's favourite minister, Ranulf Flambard, collected each soldier's ten shillings and sent him packing to his shire. The £10,000 thus raised was dispatched to William who used it to bribe the King of France to withhold support from Robert, and to pay his barons to continue the war while he returned to his kingdom.

The fighting remained inconclusive and in 1096 Robert, having "taken the Cross", and needing finance for his crusade, pledged Normandy to William for 10,000 marks. The need to raise this comparatively small sum gave William a fine excuse to levy so many taxes that even the barons were forced to extract every possible penny from their tenants. When some clergy protested that the common people were being driven to despair, they were told they could lessen the burden by selling Church treasure and adding it to the fund. They dared not refuse this royal suggestion and even jewellery which had adorned holy statues was tossed into the melting pot. William was soon able to go to Normandy, pay his brother and take temporary possession of the dukedom.

In June, 1099, William was setting out to hunt in the New Forest when a messenger arrived with the news that the French had occupied Le Mans. He immediately galloped to Southampton and leapt on to the deck of the first ship he reached. He ordered the master to cast off, but the frightened mariner pointed out the unseaworthy state of the old vessel and the fact that a storm was blowing up in the Channel.

"Cast off," William ordered. "Kings never drown."

The leaking craft wallowed through the gale and the Red King won back Le Mans.

In the summer of 1100 news came that Robert was returning from the Holy Wars to reclaim his dukedom. William, treacherously determining to hold on to it, ordered the construction of a fleet to carry a vast army to Normandy. During these preparations he went to Castle Malwood, a royal hunting lodge in the New Forest.

* * *

It was the end of July when the royal cavalcade of over a hundred members rode merrily out from Winchester along the 20 miles of road and dappled forest track to Malwood. Around the king were his special companions for the hunt – his brother Henry (old quarrels apparently forgotten now Robert was the enemy), Robert Fitz-Hamon, William's most trusted friend, and William of Breteuil, Keeper of the Treasury at Winchester. There were also the barons Gilbert de Laigle and William de Monfichet, and Earl Gilbert of the House of Clare and his brother Robert. With them was their brother-in-law Sir Walter Tirel of Piox who, according to the contemporary historian Geoffrey Gaimar, was a stranger at court.

The scene is set, the actors are assembled, and now is the time to consider Count Henry, brother of the king and destined to become Henry 1 of England, and already qualified to be listed as a royal murderer.

When William the Conqueror died his youngest son Henry inherited £5,000, of which he used £3,000 to buy territory, including Mon St Michel, from his brother Robert. It was said that he ruled the land he bought with zeal, an expression which has a slightly ominous ring about it.* In 1090 the citizens of Rouen revolted against Duke Robert in favour of William Rufus, and Henry went to Robert's aid. The insurrection was suppressed and its leader, a man called Conan, was brought before Henry who took him to the top of the castle tower where he told him to look out over the fair dominion he had tried to seize and which he had now lost.

The rebel appealed to Henry for clemency, only to be told to prepare himself for death. He then begged to be allowed to be shriven, but in a sudden burst of fury Henry murdered him by pushing him through the tower window, shouting after him, "By my mother's soul there is no mercy for a traitor."

For a while Henry managed to hold the territory he had bought by skilfully playing his brothers off against each other, but when the two joined forces against him he was forced to quit Mont St Michel and wander like some landless pilgrim in Brittany and the Vexin, accompanied only by three men-at-arms, a knight and a clerk. The latter gives us a clue to his complex character as from an early age he had been fascinated by learning which earned him the nickname of Beauclerc. No doubt after the loss of his land his feelings towards his brothers were deep and bitter, though his wanderings came to an end in 1094 when he was invited to the English court where he remained.

He must have realised, when the news reached England that Robert was returning from the Holy Land to reclaim his realm, that with his arrival he would lose any chance of claiming the English throne should his brother William die.

On the fatal day of August 2 the usual hunt was delayed because the king had been taken ill the night before, prob-

*He was always strict over the carrying out of justice and he punished offences against the state or individuals by blinding or castration. As a result England became very law abiding during his reign and he became known as the Lion of Justice.

ably with a severe stomach upset. In those days any sudden royal sickness was usually given the most sinister interpretation, but on this occasion the chroniclers made no allusion to poison perhaps because they were too engrossed in looking for portents of divine displeasure.

During the night William awoke with a great cry which brought his attendants running and which was said posthumously to have been the result of a nightmare in which the dreamer saw himself die in a welter of blood. The king sat up for several hours, then went back to bed and slept late, and when he did wake in the middle of the morning he was still so agitated that it was obvious he was unfit for the chase.

A visitor to his chamber was his friend Robert Fitz-Hamon.

"There's a monk outside who begs to give you a warning."

"How like a monk," William answered. "He's dreaming of money. Give him a hundred shillings and tell him to go away."

If William had been in a mood to heed the premonition it is possible the history of England might have followed a different course.

During the afternoon the king had a private conversation with Sir Walter Tirel, which has given rise to much speculation. Only the last words of the meeting were overheard in which William told Sir Walter to remember what he had been told and to carry out the necessary action, to which Tirel replied he would. An extraordinary view of this was given by the famous anthropologist Margaret Murray in her *God of the Witches* by suggesting that William Rufus had instructed the knight to slay him in a forest glade as the culmination of some ancient magic ritual. From what is known of the Norman kings in general and William II in particular the idea of such a sacrifice is out of character.

As the afternoon wore on the king must have felt better for he had a meal with his guests in the hall, and it was recorded that he ate and drank more than usual, suggesting that his appetite had returned and he was making up for having missed his breakfast. And, although it was getting late, he decided to go hunting after all, though Robert Fitz-Hamon tried to talk him out of it. It was now around six o'clock,

37

which meant it would be possible to hunt for a couple of hours at that time of the year. While a servant was attending to the king's hunting boots a fletcher offered six new arrows to his lord.

The king took them and selected two which he handed to Sir Walter Tirel saying, "It is right you should have the sharpest, you can fire deadly shots."

Soon afterwards the hunting party mounted with the customary jokes and laughter at the prospect of killing deer, and was about to ride off when a travel-weary monk arrived with a letter for the king from Serlo, the Abbot of St Peter's Abbey at Gloucester. Impatiently William listened while the letter was read to him for he was illiterate as were most of the nobles of his day. Serlo's message was that one of his monks had experienced a terrifying dream which involved Jesus Christ and the Holy Virgin and which was seen as a warning that the king was in danger.

At the conclusion William spurred his horse forward, shouting, "Does Serlo think that I believe in the dreams of every monk? Does he think I am an Englishman to put my trust in old wives' tales?"

One wonders whether it was a genuine dream or whether Abbot Serlo had got wind of a conspiracy and, wary of making dangerous accusations, had invented it as a pretext for putting William on his guard.

Heedless of the warning, the king rode off at the head of the party to take up positions for shooting the deer when the beaters drove them through the trees. William of Malmesbury wrote that "the party split up in the woods and the king was left alone with Tirel." In the lurid light of the sinking sun the two men unslung their bows and waited in the glade where the "Rufus Stone" stands today, a short distance from the A31 near Stoney Cross.

No one knows what happened next, but a traditional version is that the king and Sir Walter were in some bushes opposite each other when a beautiful stag bounded between them. William raised his bow but the string snapped.

"Shoot, Walter, in the Devil's name," shouted the king. The knight obeyed, but the arrow missed, glanced off the bole of a tree and thudded into the Red King's chest.

It is doubtful that an arrow, unlike a bullet, would still have killing power when deflected from its course. In his *Gesta Regum*, William of Malmesbury described the death of the king thus: "The sun was setting when a stag passed near by; and the King, drawing his bow, loosed an arrow which hit the mark but failed to kill. Slightly wounded, the animal ran off to the west while the King watched intently for some time, raising a hand to shield his eyes against the rays of the sun. Just then another stag passed by. Tirel shot at it and missed, but the arrow flew on and, by mischance, struck the King beyond. Clutching at the shaft where it protruded from his breast, the King fell forward, breaking the arrow in his body as he hit the ground and dying instantly without having uttered a word."

What we do know is that when Sir Walter saw the body of the king lying on the grass he immediately fled from the spot and crossed the Channel to claim the protection of the French king. He declared that King William had been struck by an arrow fired by an unseen bowman and, knowing that he would be the obvious suspect, he had made his escape.

* * *

Legend says that after Henry joined his brother William Rufus at the fatal hunt in the New Forest, the string of his bow broke. Retiring to a forester's hut to mend it, he encountered a witch-like hag who prophesied that soon he would be wearing the crown of England. Dramatic proof of her words came with breathless hunters who announced that the Red King was dead. Henry afterwards related how he had been so smitten with grief that he kept a sorrowful vigil in the glade where the mysterious arrow had transfixed his elder brother.

In reality, he galloped to Winchester where he demanded the keys of the royal treasury. His brother's example had shown him how important it was for a claimant to the throne to first make sure he had his hands on the country's finance.

William of Breteuil, the Royal Treasurer, refused to hand

over the keys, saying that Henry's brother Robert, at present returning from the Holy Wars, was the Conqueror's eldest son and therefore the rightful successor by primogeniture.

Henry's furious shouts brought attendants running to support the treasurer, but Henry settled the matter by unsheathing his sword. William of Breteuil unlocked the treasury and on the third day after the death of the Red King, Henry was crowned at Westminster Abbey.

Two points in particular are raised by the chroniclers' accounts of William's death. The first is the way the body was abandoned in the glade. The unpopularity of the king with the people and the Church has been explained by these writers, but surely this did not extend to the members of William's hunting party, made up of personal friends, Norman lords with the same stern outlook as himself, and his brother, Henry, whom he had entertained at his court for the past six years. One imagines that they would at least have borne the corpse back to Castle Malwood, that they would have shown some respect to the body of their anointed king. Instead there was a stampede to get away from the place. Orderic Vitalis wrote that the dead king's brother "immediately hurried to Winchester Castle where the royal treasure was kept." Was it because the delay in the hunt caused by William's indisposition had upset some secret schedule?

Secondly, what stands out is the speed with which Henry acted to secure his succession. Despite his story that he remained praying in the glade — and if he was so concerned for his brother's soul why did he allow his body to be taken without a guard of honour on a peasant's cart? — he must have quit the scene of the "accident" within minutes in order to be able to leave the forest in the failing light and get on the Winchester road. There could have been no time lost in shocked confusion, no time wasted searching for the assassin or in trying to find Sir Walter Tirel who must have been the prime suspect. Instead Henry and the party rode straight to Winchester without even pausing at Castle Malwood. If Henry had not been prepared for the event, he showed remarkable coolness when it happened.

Again it seems a remarkable feat of organisation for the

Manuscript portrait of William II

9 St James's Palace where the Duke of Clarence's would-be assassin cut his own throat in mysterious circumstances. Left 10 Ernest Augustus Duke of Cumberland and later King of Hanover (By courtesy of the Radio Times Hulton Picture Library).

11   *A romantic engraving of the murder of the Red King*

12   *Statue of William II in the choir of York Cathedral*

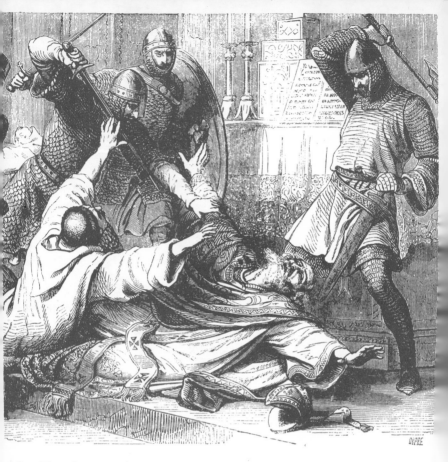

13   *The slaying of Archbishop Becket in Canterbury Cathedral*

new king to be elected and the coronation to be held so quickly after the death of the old one.

"On the following Sunday (William Rufus died on the previous Thursday evening), before the altar at Westminster, Henry vowed to God and to all the people to abolish all the injustices which were prevelent during his brother's reign," states the *Anglo Saxon Chronicle.* "Thereafter, Maurice, Bishop of London, consecrated him King."

* * *

Wisely the new king secured his popularity by issuing a charter stating that the laws of King Edward were to be restored and, by consent of the barons, laws relating to the forests were to be as they had been in the days of the Conqueror. This charter, and the release from the Red King's tyranny were greeted with joy by the people, who were further pleased by the fact that Henry had been born in England and was therefore not regarded as a foreigner.

Later Henry was to reorganise tax gathering methods and the English judicial system. He also reformed the coinage and saw to it that quick justice was meted out to forgers. Death and mutilation were the punishments for wrongdoers, and though Henry's rule was harsh, it brought order and security to the country. He established the length of his arm as the universal unit of measurement.

Meanwhile there was the problem posed by his elder brother Robert, newly returned from the Crusade. At Whitsun in 1101 rumours swept England that he was preparing to follow his father's footsteps by invading the country. On July 21 he arrived with his fleet at Portsmouth and Henry's army waited for him at Alton in Hampshire. Here Henry went to parley with his brother and as a result of their conversation the battle did not take place. Instead it was agreed that Henry would relinquish all rights to territory in Normandy and Duke Robert would renounce his claim to England. The Norman army sailed away and Henry methodically eliminated the nobles who had plotted against him on behalf of Robert.

The feuding between the brothers was not yet over. On the pretext that he wanted to save the Norman people from Duke Robert's misrule, Henry crossed the Channel and finally on September 28, 1106, a famous foot battle was fought outside Tinchebrai. This time it was the Norman banners which drooped in defeat.

Duke Robert was captured and confined to a royal castle. One day, while being allowed to exercise on a horse, he attempted to escape. Galloping away from his attendants, he rode into marshland and his mount got trapped in a bog. After this he was taken to Cardiff Castle where he was locked in a foul cell. There is a story, probably apocrypal, that the king had him blinded with the rim of a red hot metal bowl.

Whether this is true or not, Robert lived out the rest of his life in lonely misery.

So that he could understand his simple jailers, he learned Welsh and passed many of his solitary hours writing poetry in the style of the Welsh bards. This fragmentary translation of one of his poems, written to an oak tree, tells of the despair he must have felt in his long captivity.

> *Oak, placed in the midst of the woods*
> *which cover the promontry*
> *from whence thou see'st the*
> *waves of the Severn struggle*
> *against the sea; Misery to*
> *him who sees that which is*
> *not death.*
>
> *Oak, which has lived through*
> *storm and tempests in the*
> *midst of the tumult of war*
> *and the ravages of death;*
> *Misery to the man who is*
> *not old enough to die.*

Duke Robert's release came in death at the age of eighty — thirty-four years after his brother had met his unmourned fate in the New Forest.

CHAPTER TWO

The Murder of Thomas Becket

"What a parcel of fools and dastards I have nourished in my house. Not one of them will avenge me of this one upstart clerk."

IF EVER ENGLAND was in desperate need of a strong ruler it was after the "nineteen long winters" of King Stephen's reign. In his successor the groaning country found one. Henry Plantagenet was twenty-one when he and his wife Eleanor were crowned at Westminster on December 19, 1154. Within twelve months he brought peace and order to his new kingdom with a vigour that made him one of England's outstanding sovereigns.

He was not just king of an island realm. Earlier his mother had given him her Norman dominions, at nineteen he inherited Anjou from his father, Geoffrey Plantagenet, and soon after, his marriage to the ex-Queen of France brought him Aquitaine. Thus his "empire" stretched almost to the Mediterranean.

Henry's queen, Eleanor, Duchess of Aquitaine in her own right, was fifteen when she married Louis VII of France. She joined the Second Crusade with him, and her huge baggage train and army of servants were almost as famous as her many love affairs which, according to scandalous legend, included a black slave in Jerusalem.

Back in France she began an intrigue with Geoffrey of Anjou, "the most accomplished knight of his day" and the father of Henry. Soon after Geoffrey's death the French king, wearied of her infidelities, divorced her.

Although young Henry had been warned against the wanton by his father, he married her — no doubt with an eye to her territory which spread between the Loire and the Pyrenees. Despite her reputation she was a popular queen in

England. Henry, too, was hailed as a popular monarch by people weary of civil bloodshed and the tyranny of local nobles who held the power of life and death within their domains.

This approval of Henry was also due to his Saxon blood traced to one of his remote ancestors, Alfred the Great. The fact that his great-grandfather had been William the Conqueror was inclined to be overlooked. Immediately after his coronation he began the restoration of Crown lands and the dismantling of the unlawful castles of rebellious nobles who had "filled them with devils". The barons had minted their own money as they needed it, but now the only legal coin was to come from the royal mint. To great jubilation Stephen's mercenaries were dismissed and royal justice was restored.

The new king's energy was reflected in his appearance. In a contemporary account, Peter of Blois wrote: "His eyes are full, guileless and dove-like when he is at peace, gleaming like fire when his temper is aroused, and in bursts of passion they flash like lightning. He has a broad, square, lion-like face. . . His broad chest and muscular arms show him to be strong, bold, active man. His hands show by their coarseness that he is careless and pays little attention to his person, for he never wears gloves except when he goes hawking. Although his legs are bruised and livid from hard riding, he never sits down except on horseback or at meals. He always has weapons in his hands when not engaged in consultation or at his books. When his cares and anxieties allow him to breathe, he occupies himself with reading."

So we glimpse the king as a man of action with an active mind. His household was always in a state of upheaval which he never seemed to notice, being more interested in reading or debating with the scholars who flocked to his court. It was said of him that he loved reading only less than hunting, and he and Queen Eleanor enthusiastically encouraged the wandering Provencal poets.

In England it had been the custom for the king to wear a stately robe, but the young Plantagenet arrived at his coronation in such a short cloak that he was nick-named Curt

Mantle. To the dismay of his courtiers, Curt Mantle cared nothing for comfort. Always on the move about his kingdom, he would sleep rough wherever darkness overtook him. It seemed that he could never be idle. During council sessions he would sit listening to speeches while repairing his hunting gear.

At times he gave way to almost insane outbursts of passion in which he would hurl himself to the floor and gnaw the rushes, shout blasphemies and even bite his attendants. According to Gerald of Wales, St Bernard said of him: "From the Devil he comes, to the Devil he will go." This refers to the odd legend that there was Satanic blood in the royal veins.

After restoring order, Henry revived his grandfather's system of sending judges on circuit. In their work they were to be assisted by twelve local men sworn to tell the truth and thus trial by jury was firmly established. He also began the abolition of trial by combat and trial by ordeal. In the latter the accused had to seize a piece of red hot iron or plunge his hand into boiling water. If his skin healed within a week he was considered innocent.

Men who felt they had been wrongly treated had recourse to the royal court of five judges — the King's Bench — which established a great reputation for impartial justice.

In this work Henry was greatly helped by his boon companion Thomas Becket, who he made Chancellor soon after his coronation. In 1162 the king suggested that his Chancellor should become Archbishop of Canterbury for, with his friend in control, Henry felt he would be able to limit the vast power of the Church in England.

Thomas Becket, the son of a Norman-born merchant who traded in London and a Saracen princess, was a good scholar, an experienced soldier and an immensely rich man of the world. When he was sent to France as an ambassador the magnificence of his train was such that the people cried out: "How splendid must the King of England be when this is only his Chancellor!" He had little desire to give up his sumptuous way of life even if it meant becoming the chief cleric in the country, and he warned Henry: "You will take your favour from me and our love will become hatred."

But the king insisted, and in May, 1162, Thomas was consecrated. Its effect on him was dramatic. From a jovial soldier-statesman, he became an ascetic priest ready to defend the Church against his old friend.

The first major clash between the two came when Henry wanted to retain the royal right to appoint bishops and, more importantly, have clerics tried in civil courts. In those days a cleric was anyone in holy orders and subject only to Church law. No matter what the crime, a Church court could only sentence a cleric to be degraded. Therefore any villain could escape the King's Justice if he could prove he was one. The only requirement for this was for him to be able to read a Latin text, which became known as "neck verse".

The question became of great importance when a priest in Worcestershire committed a foul murder which aroused indignation throughout the country. Henry demanded that the man should be handed over for a civil trial, but the archbishop refused and kept him in a Church prison.

On his side Thomas claimed various estates from nobles as being rightful Church property, and required the king to give up Rochester for the same reason.

Henry was full of wrath. Instead of looking after his interests, Thomas was challenging him on behalf of the Church. In an assembly in Westminster Hall he demanded that all priests found guilty of a crime by their bishops be handed over to civil courts for sentence. Thomas, seeing it as a whittling away of Church privilege, refused.

Then Henry turned to the clergy and demanded they should obey the laws of the land. Each replied in the words of Thomas, "Saving my order!" This meant they would obey laws which did not interfere with the rules of their own denominations. The lion face of the king was dark with anger as he stormed out of the hall.

Many of the clergy began to fear that Thomas was going too far in challenging Henry. Another council was held at the Palace of Clarendon, but again Thomas replied to the king's demand: "Saving my order!" Nobles implored, and priests with tears in their eyes begged the archbishop to be reasonable, and finally he relented. The Constitutions of Clarendon, which put clerks within civil law, were agreed, though later Thomas bitterly regretted it.

The quarrels of State and Church, personified by Henry and Thomas, continued. In October, 1164, the king summoned the archbishop to a great council at Northampton where he accused him of misappropriation of £20,000. The bishops advised Thomas to give up his feud with the Crown and resign his office, but he went before the assembly carrying a large cross which he held before him during the proceedings as though warding off evil.

Furious at his old friend's behaviour, Henry retired followed by the rest of the assembly. At last the Earl of Leicester led the court back and read out Thomas' sentence for treason. The archbishop's reply was to deny the power of the court and walk out proudly. Some of the assembly were so irritated by him they picked up the floor rushes and flung them at him.

That night Thomas opened his house to the common people, shared a Last Supper with them, and then fled to Flanders where he put himself under the protection of the Pope.

Henry wrote to the English bishops: "You are not ignorant, reverend fathers, of the injurious treatment which I and my Kingdom have received from Thomas, Archbishop of Canterbury, and how basely he has fled the country. I command you, therefore, to cause all his clerks who remained with him after his flight to be prevented receiving any of the proceeds of their benefits. . ."

Following his departure all who had supported the Constitutions of Clarenden were excommunicated. Henry's reply was to have the English coast and ports watched so that no letters of Interdict could be brought into the kingdom. And so the quarrel continued for the next six years.

In 1170 the king decided to have his eldest son Henry crowned to remove any future problems over the succession. Thomas objected because, as Archbishop of Canterbury, he was the one who should perform the ceremony. But the coronation went ahead with Roger, the Archbishop of York, performing the service assisted by the Bishop of London and six Diocesan bishops. Thomas let it be known the Pope would excommunicate those concerned, and Henry wrote to Gilbert, Bishop of London: "I have heard of the outrage which that traitor and enemy of mine, Thomas, had inflicted on you and other of my subjects, and I am as much displeased as if he had vomited forth his poison on my own person."

Thomas Becket had powerful allies in Europe, as well as the Pope, and in the same year a meeting was arranged between him and Henry in France. The final outcome of these political manoeuvres came in a letter from the king: "I remit to the Archbishop of Canterbury and to his adherents who are in exile with him. . . all my anger and offence, and I forgive the same all previous quarrels whatsoever that I may have had against him. . . and I restore him the Church of Canterbury."

In December, 1170, Thomas returned to Canterbury to be joyfully received by the common folk. On Christmas Day he preached in the cathedral, and announced the excommunication of the Bishops of Salisbury and London.

Henry had hoped that, with Thomas restored, he would have some peace from his one-time companion but, when the news of the excommunications reached him at his Christmas court in Normandy, in fury he shouted the fatal words: "What a parcel of fools and dastards have I nourished in my house? Not one of them will avenge me of this one upstart clerk!"

Taking his words literally, four knights — Reginald FitzUrse, William Trach, Hugh de Morville and Richard Brito — galloped from the court. On December 29 they reached Canterbury and entered the cathedral to find Thomas calmly waiting for them. What happened next was given in an eye-witness account by a monk, Edward Grim:—

" 'Absolve,' they cried, 'and restore to communion those you have excommunicated, and the functions of their office to the others who have been suspended.' He answered, 'There has been no satisfaction made, and I will not absolve them.' 'Then you shall die this instant,' they cried, 'and receive your desert.' 'I, too,' he said, 'am ready to die for my Lord, that in my blood the Church may obtain peace and liberty: but in the

48

name of Almighty God I forbid you to harm any of my men, whether clerk or lay.'

"Then they made a rush at him and laid sacrilegious hands upon him, pulling and dragging him roughly and violently, endeavouring to get him outside the walls of the church and there to slay him, or bind him and carry him off prisoner, as they afterwards confessed was their intention. But as he could not easily be moved from the pillar, one of them seized hold of him and clung on to him more closely. The Bishop shook him off vigorously, calling him a pandar and saying, 'Touch me not, Reginald; you owe me fealty and obedience; you're acting like a madman, you and your accomplices.'

"All aflame with terrible fury at this rebuff, the knight brandished his sword against the consecrated head. 'Neither faith,' he cried, 'nor obedience do I owe you against my fealty to my lord the king.' Scarce had he uttered these words than the wicked knight fearing lest he should be rescued by the people and escape alive, suddenly leaped upon him and wounded the sacrifical lamb of God in the head, cutting off the top of the crown. . . and by the same strike he almost cut off the arm of him who tells the story."

Benedict of Peterborough related what happened next:—

"While the body lay still on the pavement some of them (the townsfolk of Canterbury) smeared their eyes with blood, others brought bottles and carried off secretly as much of it as they could. Others cut shreds of clothing and dipped them into the blood. At a later time no one was thought happy who had not carried off something from the precious treasure of the martyr's body. And indeed with everything in such a state of confusion and tumult, each man could do as he pleased. Some of the blood left over was carefully and cleanly collected and poured into a clean vessel and treasured up in the church. The bishop's pallium and outer vesture, stained with blood, were the discreet piety given to the poor to pay (sic) for his soul, and happy would it have been for them, if if they had not with inconsiderate haste sold them for a paltry sum of money."

The martyrdom of Thomas Becket sent a shock wave

through the Christian world. Henry ". . . grieved more terribly, more than it was possible to say: for three days he would eat nothing nor speak to anyone, and for five weeks his doors were closed and he led a solitary life."

Pope Alexander threatened excommunication unless he would yield unconditionally to the demands of the Church. Henry's response was to take an army of 4,000 to Waterford on October 18, 1171, to conquer Ireland. He left an order that no man should follow unless he was summoned, and thus he ensured that no letters of excommunication would reach him.

Isolated from the rest of the world, Henry subjugated most of the country which until then had been independent of the Church of Rome. When the Irish clergy made formal submission to him at Cashel, Henry was in a position to offer the Pope the loyalty of the Irish. He then went to Normandy, where he did penance before papal legates and was absolved. In the death of Thomas the Church had gained not only a saint but a hold over the King of England, and Ireland was brought into its fold.

CHAPTER THREE

The Murder of Prince Arthur·

"Is it my fault that I was Geoffrey's son?"

WITHIN THE GRIM walls of the Castle of Chinon Henry II lay huddled on his sickbed and brooded bitterly on his star-crossed destiny. Spasms shook his body as his fever increased in virulence; the suppurating abcess in his groin was a throbbing obligato to the mental suffering which transcended that of his body. The first Plantagenet King of England, his empire stretched from Hadrian's Wall almost to the Mediterranean, but now it was crumbling on account of a damnable alliance between his lion-hearted son Richard and Philip II of France. Not for the first time it must have seemed to the king that his beloved children had inherited the satanic blood of the Angevins, that he had sired a devil's brood.

Eager to rule his vast dominions before they inherited them by his death, three out of his four sons had openly waged war on him — enthusiastically encouraged by their mother Queen Eleanor.

His eldest son Henry had acquired a taste for power as temporary ruler of England while his father was in Ireland after the murder of Becket. When the king returned, he demanded a kingdom for himself on one side of the Channel or the other. When this was refused the plotting began, and King Henry learned of his danger at Toulouse when a Count Raymond, kneeling before him in the usual act of homage, whispered: "Beware of your sons and your wife." The warning came just as young Henry left for Paris and — in company with his brothers Richard and Geoffrey, the King of France, the King of Scotland and various barons on both sides of the Channel, declared war on his father. Only his youngest son John, who had no territorial prospects and was therefore nicknamed "Lackland", remained uninvolved.

Henry's energetic response to this wholesale treachery was amazing. He arrested Eleanor as she was fleeing in a man's disguise to join her rebellious sons, and had her imprisoned at Winchester for the next 16 years. He recalled troops from Ireland, spent every penny he could raise on mercenaries, and set about crushing his enemies one after the other. The French king was defeated on the Normandy border, rebellion in Brittany was stamped out and Aquitaine subdued.

Then, on July 7, 1174, Henry crossed the Channel in a fierce gale to save England. The Scots had swept down from the north, Flemish forces were ready to invade the east coast and followers of rebel barons were rioting in London. The king went straight to Canterbury where he entered the cathedral barefoot and in pilgrim's rags to do public penance before the tomb of Thomas Becket which had become a famous shrine.

He spent a night long vigil before it, and was scourged by the 70 monks of the chapter. At dawn he left for London where, four days later, news reached him that King William of Scotland, pinned beneath his horse, had surrendered to one of Henry's loyal knights when the English king was on his knees at Canterbury. On the same day the Count of Flanders had called off the invasion as adverse winds had held back his fleet so long he no longer had any money to pay his troops.

Henry Plantagenet had triumphed. England was at peace, his frontiers were secure and the Pope was friendly. During the following years his reforms prospered and his influence abroad was so great that when kings quarrelled he was called upon to mediate. His support of the Pope against his enemies brought peace in Europe.

But the disloyalty of his sons had been a bitter blow, for Henry loved them more than anything else. To pacify Richard he made him Duke of Aquitaine and Geoffrey became Duke of Brittany, but the Plantagenet family quarrels were to continue. Sometimes the brothers fought each other and it was said they were united only when they joined and fought against their father. Only the youngest, John, seemed to be loyal, and Henry loved him most.

In 1183 young Henry rebelled against the king, and William

of Newburgh related: "Having made an alliance with his brother Geoffrey, Count of Brittany and some magnates from Aquitaine, he provoked his father by his warlike movements . . . Shortly after, by God's judgement, the younger Henry was stricken with fever. His malady growing more serious and his physicians despairing of his life, he was smitten with remorse and sent to his father, humbly confessing his fault and begging as a last favour from his affectionate father that he would condescend to visit his dying son. On receipt of this message his father's bowels yearned over him but, being persuaded by his friends that it would not be safe for the King to trust himself to those wicked conspirators who were about his son's person, although it would be a fatherly act to visit him in his sickness, their timid counsels prevailed and the King did not go. Instead he dispatched to his son a familiar ring as a token of mercy and forgiveness and a pledge of his parental affection. On receiving the ring the son kissed it and immediately expired."

The death of Henry made Richard the heir apparent, but the satisfaction he may have felt was soon soured when he saw that the king wished to provide for his favourite John at his expense. Matters became more complicated three years later when Prince Geoffrey was unsaddled in a tournament and battered to death beneath the hooves of the charging horses.

At the death of Geoffrey, Philip Augustus, the new French king, as suzerain of Brittany, claimed the custody of his son Arthur — a claim which Henry as the king's grandfather emphatically rejected. Richard, fearing he might be dispossessed in favour of his younger brother John, aligned himself with Philip and by the end of 1188 was at war with his father.

Henry had few troops in Anjou, the home of the Angevins, to match the combined forces of his son and the King of France. By the middle of 1189 his town of Le Mans had fallen and, stricken by fever, he sought refuge in Chinon where he heard the terrible news that Tours, the city of his birth, had fallen to his hereditary enemy and his rebellious son. It meant that he had no other option but to agree to their demands, though when Richard arrived to negotiate and received the traditional kiss of peace from his ailing father, Henry was heard to mutter, "May the Lord never let me die until I am avenged on you."

One of the terms Richard and Philip insisted upon was that Henry would officially pardon all the rebels who had plotted against him. In order for him to do this he had to know who they were, and a list of their names was brought to his sick chamber. As the king sat up in his bed and glanced at the scroll he went white, uttered a groan and, throwing himself back on to the mattress, turned his face to the wall.

The very first name on the list was that of his best-loved son John, the only one Henry had believed had always been true to him.

"Let things take their course," he said to the wall, "I care no longer for myself or anything in this world."

On July 6 one of England's greatest monarchs died of fever and a broken heart, his last words being "Shame, shame on a conquered king!"

Prince John had given history the first proof of his character.

* * *

Rightly it has become the trend for serious historical authors to re-evaluate the characters who have played significant roles in the past. "Unreliable" tradition is dismissed and the bias of contemporary chroniclers is queried, and thus some of our blackest villains are seen in a new and more sympathetic light – a striking example being Richard III. One almost senses a spirit of competition between writers to discover redeeming features in the most unlikely subjects.

Bad King John, for centuries regarded as one of our most evil monarchs as any reader of the Robin Hood legends knows, is now frequently portrayed as a maligned victim of monkish chroniclers who invented vile anecdotes about him in retaliation for his treatment of the Church. Now he is described as "an intelligent and hard-working ruler who distinguished himself as a general, diplomatic and justiciar." And when it comes to the question of his cruelty we are told to judge him against the background of his age and not by the civilized standards of the 20th century. (Will historians several centuries hence suggest that our spectacular tyrants such as Hitler and Stalin should be seen in the context of their day?)

But, having stated that the traditional view of John is inaccurate and that in reality he was a "progressive ruler", his most enthusiastic vindicators have to admit he was treacherous to his brothers and his father, that he lost most of the Plantagenets' Continental possessions, that he disastrously antagonised the Church, his subjects and his nobles — hence the Magna Carta! — and that at the end of his reign the Dauphin of France was in England, having been invited across the Channel to replace him. And then, of course, there is the tricky question of murder . . .

* * *

John, the youngest son of King Henry and his remarkable queen, Eleanor of Aquitaine,* was born at Oxford Palace on December 24, 1167. As he gew up he was known as "Sansterre" or "Lackland" because of the claims of his three elder brothers to the various Plantagenet dominions. His father did what he could for John who became his favourite, proposing to make him King of Ireland and crown him with a "diadem of peacocks' feathers", but, though Pope Urban gave his consent, the coronation never took place. True John went to Ireland in April, 1185, but after eight months he returned, his lordship of the country having been a complete failure.

The chronicler Gerald of Wales, a chaplain at King Henry's court, was in John's entourage and later wrote: "John, being himself young and little more than a boy, followed the counsel of young men whom he took with him, who were utterly unknown in Ireland and themselves knew nothing, whereas he rebuffed the honest and discreet men whom he found there, who knew the customs and habits of the

*For the life of this extraordinary woman see "The Outrageous Queens by Marc Alexander, published by Frederick Muller Limited, in 1977.

country, treating them as though they were foreigners and of little worth."

Not only did he rebuff them, he and his friends were so amused at the long beards of the Irish chieftains when they came to welcome him that they had an uproarious time tugging them. So outraged were the various kings of Ireland by this insulting behaviour they went so far as to agree to stop feuding amongst themselves in order to unite against the English prince.

The following year John's prospects brightened briefly when his brother Geoffrey was killed, but when his widow bore a posthumous son who was christened Arthur, John's hope of becoming Duke of Brittany evaporated. And with the arrival of this child was the knowledge that he was closer to the throne of England than John. When Richard Coeur-de-Lion and Philip of France went to war with Henry II and although John went to Normandy with his father and was given a division to command, he secretly came to terms with them — a secret which Henry only learned on his death-bed.

John may have broken his father's heart but the superstitious believed that it was Henry's wrath against Richard which lasted beyond his death. Gerald of Wales wrote that when Richard entered the Abbey of Fontevraud where the king's corpse lay and "approached the bier his father's face lay unveiled, the cloth that had covered it having been lain aside. To all of them it appeared still to retain its colour and wonted look of fierceness. The Count gazed on it with real and strong emotion and knelt down before the altar in prayer remaining there however scarcely longer than the space of a paternoster. But at the very moment he had entered the church as those present saw there and bear witness, blood began to flow from the dead king's nostrils and ceased not so long as his son remained there insomuch that the bystanders and those attending the bier were scarcely able to wipe it and cleanse the mouth and face with the cloth."

One of Richard's first acts after the death of Henry was to order the release of his mother, Queen Eleanor, from her confinement at Winchester to be regent of England until his arrival. Having secured his father's treasure, he took formal possession of Normandy and then travelled to Winchester to check the Royal Treasury, an act that had become almost traditional with new English sovereigns. Then, on September 3, 1189, Richard, walking under a silken canopy supported by lances of four noble lords, entered Westminster Abbey for his coronation.

John took a leading part in his brother's coronation, for Richard treated him with generosity, assigning him the revenues of Cornwall, Derby, Devon, Dorset, Nottingham and Somerset, as well as bestowing on him various fiefs and castles and creating him Count of Mortain with a palatine jurisdiction which almost made him independent of the crown. Added to this was the fact that four days before the ceremony John had married Isabella of Gloucester who brought him the lordship of Gloucester as her dowry. Despite this newfound power, John was soon to suffer a disappointment which was to lead to his treachery against Richard.

In 1187 news had reached France that the Saracens, under the inspired leadership of Saladin, had taken Jerusalem. Christian anger boiled over at the rumour that the True Cross had been desecrated thus inspiring a new crusade.

Although Richard may have been the idol of Robin Hood and England's most romantic king, he regarded his kingdom merely as a source of revenue for his dream of leading the greatest crusade in history. He had "taken the Cross" before he became king, and as soon as the crown was on his head he began his preparations, raising the funds by selling whatever he could, royal demesnes, positions of high office — the archbishopric of York brought in £3,000 — and exemptions from the crusade. He is credited with having declared that he would sell London itself if he could find a buyer. In December, 1189, he crossed to France and, with his friend King Philip, the Third Crusade was begun.

Though Richard had treated John generously he had shrewd doubts on the question of his loyalty, and to protect his royal interests he made it a condition that his brother should not enter England for three years, the Papal Legate William Longchamp being left in control as Justiciar. Doubtless Richard had learned from the example set by William II's relationship with his brother Robert.

What must have been particularly galling to John was the fact that the king regarded his four-years-old nephew Arthur of Brittany as his heir*, though he may have consoled himself with the thought that the laws of succession were still fluid in Europe, and should Richard succumb to Saracen steel he still might win the throne. Therefore he prevailed upon his mother Queen Eleanor, whose influence with Richard was paramount, to obtain his release from the vow to remain beyond England's shores. In 1190 he was allowed to return and, exploiting the unpopularity of Longchamp, was able to engineer a movement against him. This finally resulted in the Justiciar fleeing the country and John being recognised as the royal heir by the Council.

A note of humour now creeps into the generally depressing story of John's career. On hearing of the situation while in Sicily, Richard ordered Walter de Coutances, Archbishop of Rouen, to England to take over as Justiciar which left John in an indeterminate but powerful position. In Paris William Longchamp, still the Papal Legate, excommunicated his opponents across the Channel, and at the same time secretly offering John £700 to be allowed to return. John happily accepted the bribe – and then took £2,000 from the Council to expel him again.

When Queen Eleanor arrived in England in 1192 she was alarmed to find that John, who had control of the Tower of London and the country's major castles, was supported by the citizens of London and a number of bishops and barons. She immediately sent a message to impress Richard with the need to hurry home. On his return journey he fell into the hands of Leopold, Duke of Austria, after being shipwrecked in the Adriatic. The duke handed over his prisoner to the

*In a letter to the Pope written on November 11, 1190, Richard referred to Arthur as "carrissimum nepotem et heredem nostrum". Soon afterwards in the treaty of Messina he declared he should succeed him if he (Richard) should die without issue – a likely event as Richard was homosexual and married only for political considerations.

Emperor Henry VI, who quickly sent word of the capture to King Philip of France. Philip and Richard's friendship had not stood the stresses of the Holy Land – at one stage the English and French crusaders were practically at war with each other – and the French king lost no time in passing the news on to John, with the suggestion that they should divide Richard's French dominions between them. Part of the proposal was that John should divorce his wife, on the grounds that she was a second cousin and the Pope's approval had not been obtained for the match, and marry Philip's half-sister Alice.

In Paris John agreed to the divorce, surrendered the Vexin to Philip and in return was allowed to do homage for Anjou, Aquitaine and Normandy. On returning to England he told the Council that King Richard was dead "though no one believed it", according to the chronicle of Roger of Hoveden. He attempted to make himself king and, when he realised public feeling was against him, sent for French mercenaries. These plans were thwarted by Queen Eleanor, who at seventy was as indomitable as ever, and who rallied soldiers loyal to her eldest son and forced John to make a truce, which was also influenced by the fact that most of the magnates had remained loyal to the regency of de Coutances. At the same time Eleanor worked tirelessly for the release of her favourite son whose ransom had been set by the German emperor at £100,000, the money being collected in England, Normandy, Anjou and the queen's home country of Aquitaine. When the ransom was raised Queen Eleanor and de Coutances travelled with the bullion convoy to Germany, their main fear being that John might attempt to seize it.

When news of Richard's imminent release reached King Philip he sent a message to John "to take care of himself as the Devil was loose." This warning caused the castellan of John's fortress at St Michael's Mount to drop dead with a heart attack, and sent John hurrying to France where he and Philip offered the Emperor a large sum of money to keep Richard prisoner – a proposal which the amused Emperor lost no time in describing to Richard.

In March, 1194, Richard Coeur-de-Lion returned to England where he quickly went to Nottingham to capture John's chief castle, at the same time summoning his brother to appear before the Council within forty days to stand trial as a rebel. The next month he was recrowned at Winchester to remove the taint of imprisonment from his sovereignty. Within a few days he learned that his erstwhile companion Philip of France was invading Normandy. Leaving his mother as regent, Richard left England for the last time to defend his territory, demonstrating that his long imprisonment had in no way impaired his military ability when he easily repulsed the French forces.

At Lisieux John threw himself at his feet in submission, and the king almost carelessly pardoned him — perhaps because of his Plantagenet understanding of betrayal — only remarking that he wished he could forget his brother's crime and that his brother could remember it.

The royal brothers were soon reconciled, within a year John was given back some of his lands and an allowance of money, and for the rest of Richard's reign he decided that loyalty was the best policy. He captured Evieux for Richard and signalised the victory by decapitating 300 members of the garrison and lining the town's walls with their heads, an act that even turned Coeur-de-Lion's battle-hardened stomach.

Now once more in control of his realm, Richard proved his genius as a military engineer and made himself a lasting monument with the construction of the Chateau Gaillard which stands to this day on a 300ft cliff overlooking the River Seine at Eure. Designed to defend his continental territory against the French, it was one of the most powerful medieval fortresses ever built. When Richard saw it completed in 1198 he cried with delight, "Behold, what a beautiful daughter of one year!"

The next year a hoard of ancient gold coins was found at the Castle of Chaluz which belonged to the Viscount of Limoges. As a vassal of the English king he sent him half the treasure, but Richard deemed he had a right to the whole amount. The viscount refused to hand over another coin and the king, who had grown more cruel and embittered since his imprisonment, besieged the castle and threatened to hang its defenders from the walls.

Riding beneath these walls Richard was struck in the left shoulder by an arrow. The wound was not considered serious at first, but as the assault continued it became infected. Stubbornly the dying king continued the siege, being carried to the scene of action in a silver litter from which he fired his crossbow. While Richard was a match for his mortal enemies, he had no power over the microscopic organisms at work in his own body, and on April 6, 1199, he died in his tent. According to some accounts he named John as his successor just before he drew his last breath.

* * *

John was staying in Brittany with his nephew Prince Arthur and his mother, the Duchess Constance, when word reached him of Richard's death. Immediately he acted to safeguard his inheritance, hurrying to Chinon to seize the royal treasury there. After attending his brother's funeral at Fontevrault Abbey he rode to Le Mans only to find that a French army and a number of Arthur's supporters were about to take the town. The citizens eyed John coldly, knowing that the barons of Anjou and Touraine had declared the twelve-years-old Arthur their rightful prince. King Philip had taken over his guardianship and sent him to the safety of Paris, and his mother was travelling with her Breton troops to invade Normandy on his behalf.

Hastily John left the ill-omened town and retired to Normandy where, at Rouen, he was hailed as Duke. Soon afterwards he led a Norman army against Le Mans, exacting his revenge by razing its castle and throwing its prominent citizens in gaol. Meanwhile there remained the question of who should wear the crown of England. In Normandy at that time were two key figures, Hubert Walter, the Archbishop of Canterbury, and William Marshal, soon to become Earl of Pembroke. It was they who decided the question, in a conversation recorded by Marshal's squire.

"I think and believe that according to right we should make Arthur king," declared the archbishop.

"To my thinking that would be bad," replied William Marshal. "Arthur is counselled by traitors, he is haughty and proud, and if we set him over us he will seek to do evil against us. . . He will not come here by my advice. Look rather at Count John, my conscience and knowledge both point him out to me as the rightful heir to the land of his father and brother."

"Marshal, is that what you truly want?"

"Yes, my lord, for it is reason. Without doubt a son has a nearer claim to his father's land than a grandson."

"So be it then, but mark my words, Marshal, never have you done anything that you will repent as you will repent what you are going to do."

"I thank you. All the same, I believe that this is what should be."

Thus a few words can sometimes alter the destiny of a nation.

Back in England the two magnates declared for John with the result there was little opposition when he was crowned at Westminster on May 27, 1199. Queen Eleanor did not attend, she was too busy looking after John's interests across the Channel with the late king's mercenary forces, just as the Duchess Constance was doing her best for her son.

After the coronation King John obtained permission to divorce his wife Isabella who, though she had been married to him for ten years, had not managed to produce a child. Then, in August, 1200, he married the beautiful twelve-years-old daughter of the Count of Angouleme, who also bore the name of Isabella. Although she was a great heiress and was to have sons, it was an unfortunate match as the girl was already betrothed to Hugh de Lusignan, the son of the Count de la Marche, and he burned to revenge himself on the man who had taken his fiancee.

The following year he attacked John's Poitou possessions which forced the king to cross the Channel with an army. Meanwhile Philip of France had betrothed Arthur to his own daughter and had taken up his cause as the rightful heir to the English throne, demanding that John should compensate him by giving him his French possessions. The French king, as John's suzerain*, ordered him to Paris to hand over his French fiefs to Arthur, but John ignored the summons, remaining at Rouen where, according to one chronicler, he spent the time "eating splendid dinners with his beautiful wife and lying in bed until noon." This was to be a popular picture of John, for he had already — perhaps unfairly — been given the cognomen of "Softsword". Soon John was to achieve a remarkable victory which was to prove that he could become a man of action.

The chance for his finest hour came on July 30, 1202, with an exhausted courier carrying a message from his eighty-year-old mother, informing him that she was besieged with her small garrison at Mirebeau by Prince Arthur and Hugh de Lusignan. In her wild youth Queen Eleanor had taken part in a crusade; in her old age it was unlikely that she would meekly surrender to her young grandson; nevertheless it could only be a matter of time before the keep she was defending fell.

John received the news when he was on the march to Poitou; Mirebeau lay over a hundred miles away in Anjou. yet after forty-eight hours of hard riding he and his followers entered the town and trapped the besiegers between the castle walls and the donjon. They had been at breakfast when John's knights fell upon them, and their resistance was short-lived. In one brilliant stroke John had his principal enemies at his mercy — Prince Arthur and his sister Eleanor, Hugh de Lusignan and his uncle Geoffrey, and 200 Poictevin knights. The latter were bound hand and foot by John's elated troops and placed in a convoy of carts which wound its way triumphantly to Falaise. Some of the knights were later imprisoned in Corfe Castle in Dorset where twenty-two of them were starved to death. Arthur's sister Eleanor, "the Rose of Brittany" was kept captive in Bristol while Arthur remained for some months at Falaise in the custody of William de Braose who had actually captured him at Mirebeau.

The next step in the tragedy was described by Roger of

---

*A paramount lord with nominal sovereignty over the ruler of an internally autonomous state.

Wendover: "After a while, King John came to Falaise Castle and commanded that his nephew should be brought before him. When Arthur appeared, the king spoke to him with kindness, promising him many honours if he would break from the King of France and pledge his loyalty to his lord and uncle. But Arthur unwisely replied with indignation and threats, demanding that the king should surrender to him the kingdom of England and all the territories Richard had held at the time of his death. With an oath, Arthur asserted that all these possessions belonged to him by hereditary right, and that unless they were quickly restored to him, John would not enjoy much peace. The king was upset by these words, and ordered that Arthur should be removed to Rouen and agrieved under close guard in the new tower there. Shortly afterwards, the said Arthur disappeared."

* * *

Following his success at Mirebeau John tried to consolidate his position in France by getting on good terms with the de Lusignans (which he did by allowing Hugh de Lusignan to purchase his liberty), and by murdering his rival. There are several versions of the fate which befell the young prince. One account states that John, infuriated by the success of Breton forces against him, sent men to Falaise with orders to blind and castrate the royal prisoner, thus rendering him harmless as a rival. According to the chronicler Ralph of Coggeshall three executioners were sent to Falaise Castle to carry out their savage work, but Hubert de Burgh, the commander who had taken over from William de Braose, would not allow Arthur to be harmed — one version of the story was that his piteous cries made the garrison threaten to revolt. De Burgh told the king that Arthur had died, hoping that the loss of their duke would take the heart out of the Bretons, but it had the opposite effect, and when, in order to lessen their fury, Hubert announced that Arthur was unharmed he was not believed.

This story was used effectively by Shakespeare in his tragedy *The Life and Death of King John.* In Act IV, Scene

I, Hubert and Arthur talk, the prince not being aware that off-stage the executioners are heating the irons:

Arthur. . . . By my christendom,
So I were out of prison and kept sheep,
I should be as merry as the day is long;
And so I would be here, but that I doubt
My uncle practises more harm to me:
He is afraid of me, and I of him.
Is it my fault that I was Geoffrey's son?
No, indeed, is't not; and I would to heaven
I were your son, so you would love me, Hubert.

Hubert. (aside) If I talk with his innocent prate
He will awake my mercy which lies dead:
Therefore I will be sudden and dispatch.

Arthur. Are you sick, Hubert? you look pale to-day;
In sooth, I would you were a little sick,
That I might sit all night and watch with you:
I warrant I love you more than you do me.

Hubert. (aside) His words do take possession of my bosom.
Read here, young Arthur. (Showing him a paper).
(aside) How now, foolish rheum!
I must be brief, lest resolution drop
Out of mine eyes in tender womanish tears.
Can you not read it? is it not fair writ?

Arthur. Too fairly, Hubert, for so foul effect.
Must you with hot irons burn out both mine eyes?

Hubert. Young boy, I must.

Arthur. And will you?

Hubert. And I will.

Arthur. Have you the heart? When your head did but ache
I knit my handkercher about your brows —
The best I had, a princess wrought it me —
And never did I ask it you again. . .

In the play Hubert relents and later, in Scene III, Arthur attempts to escape disguised in "ship boy's semblance", and in leaping from a wall injures himself fatally, expiring with this couplet:—

"O me! my uncle's spirit is in these stones:
Heaven take my soul, and England keep my
bones."

The chronicler himself admitted that this version was suspect, and it does seem unlikely that King John would have inflamed his enemies' warlike determination by transforming his nephew into a living martyr.

An equally melodramatic but more widely accepted account described how the king took Arthur out in a rowing boat on the Seine one night. There were only the two of them in the small craft, and when John judged he was out of earshot of the castle, he suddenly plunged his sword into the unhappy prince. He rowed a league with the corpse huddled in the bows, then tied the anchor stone to its neck and heaved it over the side. If he thought the evidence of the crime had vanished with the concentric ripples, John was wrong — murder will out, and in this case a fisherman found the corpse in his net.

To my mind the most likely explanation is to be found in the somewhat similar description given in the *Margam Chronicle,* "After King John had captured Arthur and kept him alive in prison for some time, at length in the castle of Rouen after dinner on the Thursday before Easter when he was drunk and possessed by the Devil, he slew him with his own hand, and tying a heavy stone to the body cast it into the Seine. It was discovered by a fisherman in his net, and being dragged to the bank and recognised, was taken for secret burial."

This is much more in keeping with what we know of John and his background. It is hard to imagine him taking Arthur on the dark river to perform such a premeditated deed himself when as monarch he merely had to give the word for a secret execution. The words "possessed by the Devil" give the clue. John had his share of black Angevin temper which was considered to be a symptom of the family's satanic blood. John's father Henry II had brought about Becket's death by a sudden surge of rage; on occasions he would writhe on the ground in demonic fury and gnaw the rushes, or even bite his attendants.

It is easy to imagine King John — restless with wine and angry that his recent advantage was ebbing away — entering his nephew's cell to try yet again to persuade him to renounce his alliance with Philip of France, only to be boldly told by Arthur that, though he may be a prisoner, in the eyes of God and the people he is still the rightful heir to Richard's crown. Suddenly a combination of frustration and wrath engulfs the king — his hands reach for the prisoner's throat, or he lunges with his dagger. . .

In a letter written to his mother on April 16, 1203, John stated that God's Grace had stood him in better stead than he could possibly indicate. Some historians believe he was referring to Arthur's death thirteen days earlier.

The *Annals of Magram* were written in a Cistercian abbey of that name in Glamorgan whose patrons were the De Braose family, and therefore it was quite possible that William de Braose may have confided in the monks the true fate of Arthur. It was William who captured him at Mirebeau, and who was his first gaoler at Falaise. Not only that, William had been one of the first barons to support John's claims after King Richard's death, and as a close companion of John on his Continental campaigns he must have had knowledge of many royal secrets.

Was it this knowledge which led to his tragedy?

As a reward for his initial support King John granted him valuable lands in Wales and Ireland, but in 1207 he suddenly took back the land in Wales and seized three of his castles there. John claimed that it was because he was deeply in debt to the exchequer, but — as with so many incidents in John's reign — we do not know the real reason for De Braose's downfall.

Roger of Wendover wrote that when the king demanded the De Braose children as hostages William's wife Matilda told the emissary, "I will not deliver my sons to your lord, King John, for he foully murdered his nephew Arthur, whom he should have cared for honourably."

After such a remark she could expect little mercy. To escape the royal wrath the family (which included two sons) sought refuge in Ireland with William's son-in-law Walter de Lacy.

It must have been something much more than debt — after all the De Braose possessions had been confiscated — which, in May 1210, made King John assemble an army, supported by a company of mercenaries, at Haverford with the intention of crossing the Irish sea to punish the family and those who had supported it. William failed to appease the king by agreeing to pay a fine of 40,000 marks, and on June 20 the royal host landed at Waterford. A force was sent to take Hugh de Lacy's castle at Carrickfergus, which surrendered after Hugh and Matilda escaped by sea to Scotland, where she and her elder son were eventually captured by a Scottish lord who presented them to the English king.

The dreadful fate of Matilda and her son — which turned many feudal lords against John — was to be sealed in a dungeon in Windsor with only a sheaf of oats and a piece of raw bacon. Some weeks later the door was unlocked and it was found that the mother had gnawed at her son's flesh before starvation claimed her.

The murder of Arthur was the watershed in John's career, after it nothing seemed to go right for him. As soon as rumours of the prince's fate spread it consolidated his enemies. King Philip vainly summoned John to appear in Paris to account for his prisoner, later claiming that the supreme court of France had found the English king *in absentia* guilty of murdering his nephew. Meanwhile the Bretons, furious at the disappearance of their duke, joined with the French and Poictevins in invading Normandy. John found that many of his Norman barons were untrustworthy, some of them preferring to open their castle gates to Philip's forces rather than defend them for him. The most shattering blow fell when news reached the king in England that Chateau Gaillard, that bastion against the French which Richard had proudly dubbed his "beautiful daughter", had fallen to its besiegers on March 6, 1204. By summer King Philip had control of all Normandy; Anjou, Maine and Touraine fell one after the other so that within two years all that remained of John's Continental territories was a portion of Aquitaine.

In 1205 John began his famous quarrel with the Church over a disputed election to the archbishopric of Canterbury. Pope Innocent III consecrated the English candidate Stephen Langton against John's wishes, and when the king refused to recognise him Innocent placed an interdict on England, which meant that church services were suspended throughout the kingdom and the only offices priests were allowed to perform were to baptise babies and hear confessions of the dying. Later John was excommunicated and in 1212 the Pope went further and issued a bull deposing him, King Philip of France being instructed to carry out the sentence.

The English king realised that he had to make peace with Rome and in May, 1213, he met Pandulf, the papal legate, at Dover and agreed to Innocent's demands that he should acknowledge Langton, recall the bishops he had banished, compensate the monasteries he had oppressed. More dramatically he did homage for his kingdom, first surrendering it to the Pope and then receiving it back as a fief of Rome.

Although he was reported to have lain on the ground and sobbed when he was absolved, John had the satisfaction of knowing that the threat of French invasion was over now that he had the Pope's protection — well worth an oath of fealty.

From now on John's quarrel shifted from the Church to his own magnates. At a Great Council in London Archbishop Langton produced Henry I's charter and encouraged the barons to demand its renewal — an action that was ultimately to lead to John being forced to sign the Magna Carta at Runnymeade on June 15, 1215. The king had no intention of keeping the charter. He travelled along the south coast, loading his treasure aboard ships and, according to Matthew Paris, was "constantly raging, biting and tearing his nails, muttering and gnashing his teeth, cursing his father and mother, raving and saying that he had twenty-five kings over him" — referring to the number of barons at Runnymeade. He petitioned the Pope and his old enemy King Philip for aid, while Pandulf excommunicated the barons which polarized them into two factions, one of which invited the Dauphin of France to come to England to lead them while the other became the royalist party. In October, 1215, civil war began.

At first fortune favoured the king who secured Rochester and then marched north to Berwick. In April of the next year he reached Dover, from where he planned to send a fleet across the Channel to trap the Dauphin, Prince Louis, in Calais. A storm dispersed his ships and soon afterwards the prince arrived in Thanet.

John retreated to Winchester, after which his army prowled in the west of England until in September John decided the time was right to go on the offensive again. He took Cambridge and entered Lincolnshire to bring the east of England under his control and create a barrier between his southern enemies and those in the north. On October 12 his column was moving in the direction of Swineshead Abbey, and to reach it the army had to cross the Wellstream estuary (now known as the River Ouse) which was five miles across when the tide was out.

Behind the lines of troops straggled the king's baggage train which included wains carrying his treasure. In the autumnal mists the slow moving vehicles missed the track and their wheels sank in quicksand. The king had reached the north shore when he realised there was something amiss. He turned his horse and rode back but it was too late — tidal waters were sweeping in from the sea and swamping the train with its terrified animals and equally terrified wagonners and retainers. Roger of Wendover wrote, "The ground opened in the midst of the waters and whirlpools sucked in everything, men and horses."

Bitterly King John left the scene of the disaster and reached the abbey sick in heart and body — he had been suffering from fever and dysentery on the march. Now he made his condition worse by indulging in a supper of new cider and peaches.

According to an ancient tradition it was at Swineshead that John himself became a murder victim. Holinshed wrote: ". . . after he lost his armie, he came to the abbeie of Swineshead in Lincolnshire, a monke, being mooved with zeale for the oppression of his countries, gave the king poison in a cup

.of ale whereof he first tooke the assaie, to cause the king not suspect the matter, and so they both died in manner at one time."

This is quite possible as death was close to the king when he left the abbey and continued to Sleaford and then on to Newark. He had to be carried on a makeshift litter for the last part of the journey. He reached the Bishop of Lincoln's castle at Newark on the 16th, and here he lay dying until the night of the 18th when he expired — to the accompaniment of a shrieking wind which caused the superstitious to cross themselves — halfway through making his will in which he named his elder son Henry as his heir.

Shakespeare in his play gave the king the following death scene:

Prince Henry: How fares your majesty?

King John: Poison'd; ill-fare; dead; forsook; cast off;
And none of you will bid the winter come
To thrust his icy fingers in my maw;
Nor let my kingdom's rivers take their course
Through my burn'd bosom; nor entreat the north
To make his bleak winds kiss my parched lips
And comfort me with cold. I do not ask you much:
I beg cold comfort; and you are so strait
And so ingrateful you deny me that.

Prince Henry: O! that there were some virtue in my tears;
That might relieve you!

King John: The salt in them is hot.
Within me is a hell; and there the poison
Is a fiend confin'd to tyrannize
As unreprievable condemned blood.

Although Shakespeare is an inaccurate historian, he may have been closer to the truth than even he realised in those final lines.

CHAPTER FOUR

The Murder of Edward II

"He perishes on the rocks that loves another more than himself."

FOR THE VISITOR the mellow bulk of Lanercost Priory — especially when first glimpsed through the graceful arch of its shattered gateway — is a highly evocative monument to the Border's unruly past. Today it is partly a dramatic ruin, partly a lofty and beautiful parish church, which stands close to the line of Hadrian's Wall a few miles east of Carlisle, and, if tradition is to be believed, is the result of an ancient murder.

Founded in 1166 by Robert de Vaux, legends aver that it was an act of expiation by Robert for having killed the deposed Saxon proprietor Gilles Bueth. After various attempts to regain his inheritance the Saxon had been invited to a meeting by the Norman, and at this he was treacherously assassinated. Until 1536, when Henry VIII made his initial attack on the Church and dissolved monasteries worth less than £200 per annum, Lanercost had more than its share of vicissitudes. Several times it was ransacked and razed by raiding parties from the North. The cost of rebuilding was so high that the priory's lands had to be sold off to pay for it. But despite the depredations of William Wallace, Robert the Bruce and King David, Lanercost's highest point of historical drama came in 1307 when Edward I wintered there prior to a campaign by which he intended to fulfil his obsessive dream of permanently crushing the Scots. At the end of February that year his son Prince Edward requested that his late mother's territory of Ponthieu should be bestowed on his friend Piers Gaveston along with the title of Count of Ponthieu. This caused the old king to explode

A Victorian view of the murder of
nce Arthur by King John

Above: 15 A manuscript illustration showing an argument between Henry II and his erstwhile friend. Right: 16 Statue of Thomas Becket in Canterbury Cathedral. Below: 17 Tomb effigy of Henry II at Fontevrault Abbey

8   *Marriage of Edward II and Isabella*

19 *Edward II with his favourite Piers Gaveston*

20 *Berkeley Castle as it is today*

with wrath, and the tranquility of the cloisters was shattered as his battle-trained voice thundered: "You baseborn whoreson! Do you want to give lands away now, you who have never gained any? As the Lord lives, if it were not for fear of breaking up the kingdom you should never enjoy your inheritance!"

Then, according to William of Hemmingburgh, the furious monarch went up to his son and "seized his hair with both hands, pulled it out until he was tired, and then turned him out of the room." Following this outburst Piers Gaveston was banished from England and Prince Edward was made to swear upon the Host that he would never recall him without the consent of Parliament. Contemporary writers mention the scene in their chronicles, giving such reasons for the banishment as "the undue intimacy which the young Lord had adopted towards him (Gaveston), publically calling him brother"; that the prince "was determined to tie an unbreakable bond of affection with him above all mortals", and that King Edward realised that "his son, the Prince of Wales, had an inordinate affection for a certain Gascon knight". This friction caused by the prince's affection for his boyhood companion was the first link in a tragic chain which was to end twenty years later with the most horrific death ever suffered by an English king.

History books down the centuries have portrayed Edward II as a weak ruler fawning on his favourites; there are suggestions of perversion and charges that he despised convention. Yet in our more liberal age his character can be viewed more sympathetically than in his own day — we now applaud the "common touch" in our royalty; in the 14th Century Edward was too democratic. In his *Concordance of Histories*, Robert Fabyan wrote: "This Edward was fayre of body and great of strengthe, but unstedfast of maners and vyle in condycions; for he would refuse the company of lords and men of honour, and haunte hym with vylans and vyle persones; he also gave hym to great drynkage and lyghtly he would discour thinges of great counsayle."

And what about his relationship with Piers Gaveston? With our 20th Century psychology the reasons for it become more understandable when we examine his lonely childhood and early background. To be homosexual today is mercifully no longer a crime, so it would ill-behove us to sit in moral judgement on Edward, if indeed he was one. Thus, after six and a half centuries, we have perhaps the best chance to recognise the king for what he really was — one of history's most complex and tragic characters.

The fourth but only surviving son of Edward I and Eleanor of Castile, Edward II was born at Carnarvon Castle on April 25, 1284. His warrior father was just completing his conquest of Wales, and tradition says that he presented his baby son to the Welsh chieftains as "one who spoke neither French nor English and should be their ruler." Thus Edward became the first Prince of Wales. While still a young child he was betrothed to Margaret of Scotland who died in 1290. The boy probably found it difficult to mourn the little girl but a few months later he shared the tremendous grief of his father when his mother died. For thirty-six years Queen Eleanor had accompanied Edward I on his campaigns, sharing his dangers and triumphs, and now that death had taken her from his side the king was in despair. When he escorted her body from Grantham to Westminster, he ordered the setting up of crosses wherever the black-draped cavalcade halted to rest.

After the queen had been interred in Westminster Abbey, where William Torel's gilt bronze effigy of her is still the most beautiful in the English pantheon, King Edward resumed his harsh way of life with a vengeance, suppressing revolts in Wales, campaigning in Scotland and waging war in Flanders against England's traditional enemy the French. The lonely little prince who, with his older sisters married, might as well have been a royal orphan, was left in the guardianship of Sir Guy Ferre. This distinguished courtier and poet found that his charge had great skill as a horseman and was keenly interested in music. On the other hand the old knight frowned upon the boy's love of buffoons and theatrical performances, no doubt wishing that he would show the same enthusiasm for the chivalric exercises which were considered more befitting for his royal station. Contemporary authors complained that as the child became a youth he preferred the company of common folk, such as thatchers, blacksmiths and sailors, to that of his peers. Other complaints were that he was "given to the company of harlots" and he was over fond of gambling. What made the latter charge worse was that his favourite game was a wholly plebian one which today is known as Pitch and Toss.

In these pursuits the prince was enthusiastically abetted by Piers Gaveston, the son of a Gascon knight, Sir Arnaud de Gaveston, who was one of the king's old comrades-in-arms. This handsome, intelligent youth had been appointed a squire of the royal household during a campaign in Flanders, and had so impressed the king that in 1298 he was made an official companion of the prince who was two years his junior. A chronicler related that when Piers was presented to Prince Edward "the King's son . . . fell so much in love that he entered upon an enduring compact with him, and chose and determined to knit an indissoluble bond of affection with him, before all other mortals."

The boys immediately became inseparable companions, their time divided between London, Windsor and Langley Manor in Hertfordshire. The latter was Edward's favourite residence, which accounts for it being called King's Langley today. Here, away from disapproving courtiers and frosty barons, the prince and his "Perrot" were free to indulge in their unusual enthusiasms – training dogs, thatching cottages, digging ditches, working in the local smithy and rowing on the River Gade. When the weather confined them indoors they passed the time with minstrels and buffoons, and in drinking with the "vylans and vyle persones" which aroused the censure of the chroniclers. What escaped the pious men of letters was that briefly at Langley there was something rare for medieval times – a sense of fun. And the prince, who kept his camel in the manor stables, had a streak of humour not so far removed from today's brand of royal jocularity, as is shown in a letter he wrote at the age of twenty-one to the Count Evreaux: "We send you a big trotting palfrey which can hardly carry its own weight, and some of our bandy-legged harriers from Wales who can well catch a hare, if they find it asleep, and some of our running dogs which go at a gentle pace – for well we know that you take delight in lazy dogs. And, dear cousin, if you want anything else from our land of Wales, we can send you plenty of wild lads, if you wish, who will know how to teach breeding to the young heirs and heiresses of great lords."

Edward I, away on his campaigns, was spared the sight of his son involved in unkingly occupations, though sooner or later rumours of the prince's infatuation with Piers must have reached him. But, until 1299 when the old king married Margaret of France, the life of the friends was idyllic, and in retrospect their happiest time. And those who sneered at the Langley antics learned to do so with discretion as Piers Gaveston rapidly developed into one of the most accomplished jousters of his day, indeed he appears to have been expert in everything he put his hand to. The jig-saw portrait we can assemble from the less biased descriptions of him is that of a graceful but physically tough youth; a golden boy with a highly developed personality which could be both careless of convention and arrogant – disastrously arrogant. His great virtue seems to be that he did not exploit Edward's love for him to further grand political ambition; he was content to remain the loyal favourite, but as such he managed to earn the hatred of almost every noble in the kingdom.

Soon after his second marriage Edward I decided it was time for his son to be blooded on the field of battle, and so in the early summer of the first year of the new century the prince, naturally accompanied by Piers Gaveston, joined his father's army on a march northwards against William Wallace. On the journey the king and his son stayed at the Abbey of Bury St Edmunds, where for once the prince impressed a chronicler favourably.

"He became our brother in chapter," wrote the abbey's scribe. "The magnificence of the abbey and the frequent recreations of the brethren pleased him greatly. Every day, moreover, he asked to be served with a monk's portion such as the brethren take in refectory."

Because the Scots melted away at the sight of the English army, no great set battle was fought and therefore the prince, in command of the rearguard, had little opportunity to win glory. But he did get a taste of warfare at the siege of Caerlaverock Castle, which capitulated after five days, and in a brief skirmish in which he acquitted himself in a satisfactory manner. King Edward certainly thought so for, after the army had retired with the onset of winter, he granted his son, as Prince of Wales, all the royal lands in the principality as well as the rich palatinate earldom of Chester. It was a magnificent bequest and proved that the prince was then held in high esteem by his father.

It was not until four years later that serious discord was seen to develop between the two Edwards. This was triggered by a relatively trivial matter, yet it provoked such a stern reaction in the king as to suggest that he may have nursed a resentment against his son — a resentment which had been smouldering for some time until the sudden draught of royal anger caused it to flare. Perhaps the king had expected Edward's adolescent infatuation with Piers Gaveston to fade as he emerged into manhood, instead of which it became deeper.

As far as we know the rift was the result of a quarrel between the prince and his father's chief minister Walter Langton, Bishop of Coventry and Lichfield. This had been caused by Edward's trespassing on the bishop's property; some accounts state that Edward accompanied by Piers Gaveston had poached Langton's deer. If such was the case restitution and an apology from the heir to the throne would probably have sufficed to restore the bishop's ruffled feelings; instead, on June 14, 1305, the king had his son banished from court, and added to this public humiliation by ordering the Exchequer not to supply him with money. Edward's friends supported him with secret donations, but the harshest part of the punishment for the prince was being parted from his beloved Perrot.

Edward's exile came to an end in October and was celebrated by a feast in Westminster Hall. Meanwhile, north of the Border the Scots were again stirring dangerously. Edward I had believed that with the capture of William Wallace Scottish rebellion was at an end, and had he been wise enough to allow Wallace to fade into oblivion in some remote prison it might have been so; instead Edward made the mistake of giving the Scots a martyr. On August 28, during Prince Edward's banishment, Wallace was found guilty of treason to his lord the King of England. From Westminster he was pulled on a hurdle via the Tower to Smithfield Elms where he was hanged from a gibbet but cut down while still alive, his belly was opened and he was viscerated, after which his head was cut off to become a trophy on London Bridge. The Smithfield executioners burned his heart and entrails, and divided his body into four so that a quarter could be publicly displayed at Berwick, Newcastle, Stirling and Perth. This form of execution, which was to become traditional in England, had the opposite of the desired effect, instead of cowing the Scots it revived their nationalism and the next year Robert the Bruce — having murdered his rival John Comyn before the altar in the church of the Minorite Friars at Dumfries — declared himself King of Scotland.

The ageing Edward braced himself for yet another Scottish campaign. On May 23, he knighted the prince and 297 young nobles at Westminster in what was described as the "largest mass knighting in medieval England". At the banquet which followed the music of the eighty minstrels was halted when two royal swans in a golden net were placed before the king who vowed "by the God of Heaven and the two swans that he would go to Scotland and living or dead would avenge Comyn." The terrifying old warrior adjured his son to carry his bones into Scotland with the army should he die on the journey, but added if he was spared he would once again take the Cross when Bruce was defeated. No doubt he thought that his promise of infidel blood flowing in the Holy Land would solicit divine aid for the forthcoming campaign. Prince Edward also took the "oath of the swans", declaring that he would not sleep two nights in the same place until he had crossed into Scotland.

In the following campaign the prince played a larger part than his father who, weakened by dysentery, had to travel by litter until he was forced to remain at Lanercost

Priory. Bruce, defeated by English forces at Methven, became a fugitive while the Earl of Pembroke and Prince Edward beseiged Kildrummy Castle in which Bruce's women had taken refuge; they were his sister Mary, his wife and daughter and Isabel, Countess of Buchan, who had followed the tradition of her family by placing the crown on his head.

Kildrummy's garrison soon surrendered and by order of Edward I Mary and Isabel were each imprisoned in cages one of which was set high on the wall of Roxburgh Castle, the other at Berwick Castle, where they were exposed for three years. Although Prince Edward had not inherited such a savage streak from his father, he proved himself to be a formidable foe during the fighting and from a Scottish writer earned the description of "the starkest man of ane."

During the winter the two Edwards stayed at Lanercost Priory, and this was when the ailing king ordered Piers Gaveston to be exiled to his home country of Gascony. Yet this was in no way intended as any punishment for Gaveston who never seemed to have lost the king's approval, rather it was an attempt to break what the king rightly saw as a dangerous liaison.

The grieving prince escorted his companion to Dover, loaded him with presents and, as a gesture against his failing father, commanded his Perrot to go to Ponthieu and not Gascony.

For a short while he moped at Langley where one can imagine him looking at the thatches and ditches which he and his absent companion had worked on together in happier days, then he rode north to join his father's last campaign.

Robert the Bruce had reappeared with an army at his back and defeated the Earl of Pembroke at the Battle of Loudoun Hill. The prince had not reached his father when the sixty-eight-year-old warrior set out on July 3, 1307, from Lanercost to lead his army in person. He was so ill he had to be carried to Carlisle in a litter but here he offered it up in Carlisle cathedral and was lifted on to his destrier. He only managed to ride two miles in two days. On July 6 he reached Burgh-by-Sands, close to the ford over the Solway Firth, but now even his extraordinary will could no longer activate his worn out body for when his servants tried to lift him out of bed the next morning he fell back dead.

* * *

With the crown Edward II inherited daunting problems, not the least being the cost of his father's glory. The late king's campaigns in Scotland, Wales, Flanders and Gascony had placed a tremendous financial strain on the kingdom. There were debts over £60,000 and huge arrears of pay for for soldiers and officials, and much of the future revenue was earmarked for the Florentine bankers Frescobaldi and Bardi. On top of this there was the question of the Scottish war, with an army prepared to cross the Solway the new king must have wondered how it was to be paid — and yet his father had commanded him to carry his remains to victory against his old foes!

Edward I might have experienced antagonism from his nobles over some of his policies but as a warrior king he was revered, and he had never offended the conventions of his day. What chance did his frivolous and unconventional son have of filling his formidable shoes? But all these problems Edward managed to push to the back of his mind when he was informed he was the new king — to him the first and most important act of his reign was the recall of Gaveston, and this was done without the consent of Parliament. A chronicler wrote: "Anon he had home his love Piers of Gaveston, and did him great reverence, and worshipped him and made him great and rich. Of this doing fell villainy to the lover, evil speech and backbiting to the love, slander to the people, harm and damage to the realm."

At first many magnates must have welcomed the thought of a new young monarch, believing he would be more tractable than his father, but such hopes were to be dashed even before the body of Edward I was laid to rest in Westminster Abbey. On August 6, a royal charter made Piers Gaveston Earl of Cornwall, a tremendously rich apanage which was traditionally reserved for members of the blood royal. That an obscure Gascon should be given such an endowment rather than either of Edward's young half brothers sent a shockwave through the kingdom. Worse was to come.

On October 27 the remains of Edward I were interred in a simple tomb of Purbeck marble which today carries the famous inscription, with an incorrect date, which was cut in the Sixteenth Century: "Edvardus Primus Scotorum malleus hic est, 1308. Pactum Serva." Because of the present lack of decoration on the tomb Edward II has been criticised wrongly for not honouring his father correctly; it did in fact have an ornate wooden canopy which was destroyed as a result of a riot in the abbey in 1764. Certainly Edward failed to honour his vow to have his father's bones carried at the head of the army, for Edward I's last campaign was abandoned by the autumn, yet he did not forget the pact completely. The old king had also wanted his heart taken on a crusade after Scotland was humbled and in this regard his son issued a macabre decree that every two years the royal tomb should be unsealed and his father's shroud rewaxed to keep him in readiness for posthumous victory. This practice continued until the Plantagenet line was cut off by the usurper Henry VII in 1485.

Following the funeral Piers Gaveston was married to Margaret de Clare, niece of the king who had engineered the union. The ceremony was performed in splendour and for Edward's Perrot it was a brilliant match; for the nobles it was a cause for outrage almost as much as his elevation to the peerage. Gaveston added salt to their wounds soon afterwards at a tournament he arranged at Wallingford which he now owned as Earl of Cornwall. The young man was brilliant in the lists and revelled in unhorsing the barons whom he knew detested him. It was said that "he exulted so much that his pride damaged him more than his prowess."

Edward delivered his nobility a third slap in the face in January, 1308, when he crossed the Channel to attend to his own nuptuals and left Piers as Regent of England. "It was thought remarkable that one who had recently been in exile from the land should now be its keeper," wrote a narrator of the time.

On January 25, in the Church of Notre Dame in Boulogne, Edward II married Isabella the Fair, daughter of Philip IV of France.* It was a good political match, the youthful bride was beautiful and the ceremony was attended by an extraordinary assembly of European royalty — five kings, three queens and an archduke and various princes and dukes.

Isabella must have heard rumours of her bridegroom's infatuation with his boyhood companion, but doubtless she thought that her own charms, which were famous throughout the Continent, would soon lead him on to the heterosexual path. But a shock was waiting for her when the king's ship berthed at Dover. Edward leapt ashore before the mooring ropes were tied and embraced the waiting Piers Gaveston, almost overwhelming him with caresses and endearments. And if Isabella's French courtiers looked aghast at the scene it was merely a prelude to a greater outrage. After Edward's belated coronation on February 25 it became known that the king had bestowed upon his favourite gifts which his father-in-law had given him together with the best pieces of Isabella's jewellery.

The coronation itself was a debacle with the barons enraged that the hated Gaveston — "so decked out that he more resembled the god Mars than an ordinary mortal" — was given the high honour of carrying the crown, while the queen's uncles, who had accompanied her from France, returned in furious indignation to report to her father that at the wedding feast Edward preferred to share a couch with Gaveston rather than his bride.

Thus the scene is set for the inevitable tragedy. On the darkening stage stands the king, ignoring the portents provided he has the company of his boyhood companion; there is the haughty favourite content to bask in the glory the king has bestowed upon him; there are the barons, grizzled warlords who rode stirrup-to-stirrup with the old king and who wonder as they plot how such a son could have sprung from his loins; and finally there is the queen with disgust and resentment smouldering in her heart.

It was not long before the drama began. In the coronation

*For the story of Queen Isabella, aptly called the She Wolf of France, see The Outrageous Queens by Marc Alexander, published by Frederick Muller Ltd.

ceremony the king had sworn a new form of oath which contained an extra clause whereby he was asked to "uphold and defend the laws and the righteous customs which the community of your realm shall determine." In April the barons, who arrived at the Parliament in armour under the leadership of Thomas of Lancaster, quoted this clause to emphasise their demands for the banishment of Piers Gaveston, arguing that as they were the "community" the king was bound to his vow to "protect" them. Edward, supported only by Sir Hugh Despenser in the confrontation, was wise enough to give way and avert civil war between the baronage and the crown. He signed letters which deprived Gaveston of his titles and ordered that he should be out of England by June 25.

Edward rode with his Perrot to Bristol where he was to quit the kingdom, but here the king turned the tables on his troublesome nobility. How he and Gaveston must have laughed at the quayside for, instead of allowing his friend to leave as a humiliated exile, Edward suddenly bestowed upon him the highly desirable post of King's Lieutenant in Ireland. According to the *Lanercost Chronicle* Gaveston left with blank royal charters to use as he wished, which, if true, shows the extent of Edward's devotion to him. Then with the same determination as his father had shown in hammering the Scots, he set to work to get his favourite re-installed in England, bending his opponents "one after another to his will with gifts, promises and blandishments" so that within twelve months Piers Gaveston was back.

Edward welcomed him at Chester on his return from Ireland where he had proved himself to be a very able governor. His easy manners had won him the friendship of the Irish nobility and he had successfully quelled revolts in Munster and Thomond, so it was with the air of a hero that he greeted his king at whose side he now remained. But the delight which the pair felt at being reunited must have blinded them to the dangers which still lay ahead. Perhaps Gaveston believed that with his recall the king had proved his invincibility, certainly he did not feel constrained to be tactful to the barons who had opposed him. And having proved the effectiveness of his jousting lance against them, he now subjected them to thrusts of his wit, inventing nicknames for them. One can picture Edward and Piers laughing together as the latter referred to the Earl of Lancaster as "the Old Hog", the stout Earl of Lincoln as "Burst Belly", the Earl of Pembroke as "Joseph the Jew", and the Earl of Gloucester as "the Cuckold's Bird", an unfortunate reference to his mother's morality. The appellation Gaveston was most to regret was that of "the Black Dog of Arden" which he bestowed on the dread Earl of Warwick; strangely enough these nicknames did as much to seal his fate as his hold on the king.

It is hard for us to understand why these taunts, which seem like typical pinpricks from the gay young Gaveston, should have so deeply wounded the earls, a fact confirmed by the prominence given to them in the chronicles. One can only assume that medieval aristocratic pride had a samurai-like quality which could face changing fortune and death with equanimity, but not a joke no matter how childish.

A contemporary biographer of Edward II summed up the situation in a couple of lines which translated from the Latin read:—

> Though handsome, rich and clever you may be
> Through insolence we may your ruin see

In October, 1309, Edward and Piers travelled to York where a council of magnates had been summoned. This proved to be a failure when five of the most powerful earls, significantly including Lancaster, refused to attend because of the presence there of the favourite. The king lost Lancaster's vital support because of the overbearing treatment of one of the earl's household followers by Gaveston. Despite this setback the friends spent a happy Christmas at their favourite residence of Langley "in long wished for sessions of daily and intimate conversation." But another parliament was looming over them which was held at Westminster in February, 1310, and again the recalcitrant earls — Arundel, Hereford, Lancaster, Oxford and Warwick — refused to attend.

Again beset by the problem which had vexed him since his father had tugged out handfulls of his hair at Lanercost, Edward sent Gaveston to the north for safety, and prepared for the worst. It came in the form of a committee called the Lords Ordainers. Its twenty-one members were made up of bishops, earls and barons, and while not all were opposed to the king, its purpose was to reform the governing of the kingdom — at least from the Ordainers' point of view — and the running of the royal household which was deeply in debt largely due to the king's generosity to Gaveston and enthusiastic complicity in his extravagance.

Edward had little choice but to sign the letters patent for the transfer of power on March 16, 1310. Like his predecessor Ethelred the Redeless, who had bought off the Vikings with annual tribute of silver, he hoped to gain time, time to plan a political campaign against the Lords Ordainers and time to enjoy the society of his friend. With so much hostility from the baronage, it is easy to understand how Edward could only find relaxation with someone sympathetic to him. But even this was to be denied to him before long. The nobility may have grasped the sceptre, but their hatred for Gaveston remained as strong as ever and the next year, among the 41 Articles of the Ordainers presented to the king was one which stated that Piers Gaveston had "misled and ill-advised our lord the King, and enticed him to do evil in various deceitful ways", and continued that "as an open enemy of the King and his people, shall be altogether exiled from England, Scotland, Ireland and Wales, and from all the dominions of our lord the King. . ."

The other conditions so restrained royal freedom that the king exploded that they governed his life "as one would provide for an idiot", but as before the king's refusal would have meant civil war and for the third time Gaveston went into exile, sailing down the Thames on November 3. Although the banishment was decreed to be perpetual, Edward brought him back before the end of the year and they resided "now in the King's apartments, now at Wallingford and now at Tintagel Castle", and on January 20 all Gaveston's property and titles were restored to him.

The immediate effect of the king's defiance of the Lords Ordainers was that Piers Gaveston was excommunicated by Archbishop Winchelsey in accordance with the twentieth Ordinance, and the five leading earls took vows to protect the Ordinances. Under the pretext of holding tournaments they began to organise their private armies.

Edward, fearful for his favourite's safety, took him north with the intention of finding him refuge with his old enemy Robert the Bruce of Scotland, and like a shadow stalking the royal party, went Thomas of Lancaster with his armed retainers. Rumour sped through the country that King Robert had refused to give sanctuary to England's most hated earl, with the result that the king was stranded in Newcastle where the citizens had no heart to defend him against Lancaster's troops.

Alarmed by the approaching enemy the king and Gaveston hurriedly took a vessel from Tynemouth to Scarborough, only just avoiding capture but having to abandon their treasure, baggage and Queen Isabella who was three months pregnant. Her indignation at being forced to take the uncomfortable journey for the benefit of her husband's favourite, only to become Lancaster's prisoner, was assuaged when the earl told her that he would not rest until the king and Gaveston were permanently separated. When news reached him that they had already parted at Scarborough, he strategically positioned his forces between Scarborough and York, Edward having probably gone to the latter with the intention of raising loyal reinforcements; yet it is one of history's minor mysteries as to why he left his Perrot behind in Scarborough Castle at that time.

The ill-prepared castle was soon besieged by the Earls of Pembroke and Surrey, assisted by Henry Percy, and after three weeks Gaveston was forced to seek terms with his enemies. Pembroke offered such generous conditions that when Gaveston left the castle on May 19, 1312, he must have felt secure. It had been agreed that he would be allowed to present his case to Parliament, and that his followers would retain control of the castle, and be allowed to restock it, until August — by which time if Parliament had not reached a decision he would be free to return to it. To guarantee this Percy, Surrey and Pembroke swore an oath upon the Host, and last also pledging his "lands and tenements" to the king as an extra safeguard. He then began a leisurely journey with Gaveston south to Wallingford where he would be allowed to wait under house arrest in his own castle until he could appear before Parliament.

By June 9 the cavalcade halted ten miles south of Banbury at the village of Deddington. Here Pembroke left his prisoner with his guards in a rectory and rode a further dozen miles to his manor at Brampton to spend the night with his wife.

Early the following morning Gaveston was awakened by a gauntleted hand shaking his shoulder and a voice saying, "Get up, traitor, you are taken." As he opened his eyes the prisoner saw there were armed men in the chamber, while above him stood a man in full armour.

"I think you know me," continued the voice from the helmet, "I am the Black Dog of Arden." It was the Earl of Warwick. Without even being allowed to dress properly, the bare-footed prisoner was taken out and forced to walk towards Warwick. After some miles he was mounted on a mule and, with mock ceremony, escorted into the town to the cruel jeers of the townsfolk who lined the route to the great castle. Here he was locked in a dungeon, probably one of the cells where tourists now flock to see a collection of medieval torture instruments.

Meanwhile the unfortunate Pembroke had ridden back to Deddington to continue the journey only to find his charge had been abducted. He was furious at this betrayal for he had sworn the most sacred oath possible to protect his prisoner and now both his honour and estates were at stake. He appealed to the Earl of Gloucester to help him get Gaveston back, but he had no interest in saving the favourite, nor did the members of the Oxford University and the citizens of that town to whom Pembroke subsequently appealed. He could only watch impotently from the sidelines as the drama approached its climax.

The Earls of Lancaster, Hereford and Arundel now joined Warwick at his castle where they quickly agreed that Gaveston should be put to death. Warwick, despite earlier boasting of what he would do to him, lacked the courage to take responsibility for the act, and Thomas of Lancaster took control of the situation. Because Gaveston was still the Earl of Cornwall, and the husband of the Earl of Gloucester's sister, it was decided that he should be allowed to die "as a nobleman and a Roman citizen" – by decapitation. On June 19 Warwick remained uneasily in his castle while Lancaster, Hereford and Arundel accompanied the prisoner a couple of miles to Blacklow Hill. Here the earls watched from a distant vantage point as a Welsh soldier transfixed Piers Gaveston with a sword while another lopped off his head which he carried swiftly to Lancaster – thus publicly emphasising the earl's role of chief instigator of the murder.

The conspirators rode away and it was left to four shoemakers to carry the corpse to Warwick Castle. Here the earl sent them away from the gate and they decided to take it to Oxford, but first they used their needles and twine to sew the head back in position. The body then was received by the Oxford Dominicans who embalmed it as they were unable to bury Gaveston who had died while still excommunicated.

There was no doubt that Piers Gaveston had been treacherously murdered, for Warwick, Lancaster and Hereford were as equally bound as Pembroke by the holy oath taken at Scarborough. Later an anonymous author commented: "Gaveston was wicked, impious and criminal, and as such deserved to die, but the manner of his death was equally wicked, impious and criminal. . .And it was a death especially to be deplored because later it was the excuse for shedding of so much noble blood in the horrors of civil war." This was written fifteen years after the event, so the author could only know of the bloodshed which immediately followed the murder. Nearly six centuries later the historian William Stubbs wrote of Gaveston's death: "It was the first drop of blood which within a century and a half carried away nearly all the ancient baronage and a great proportion of the royal house of England."

* * *

Those who broke the news of Gaveston's murder to Edward were astounded by his reaction; instead of the expected tears and lamentations the king said, "By God, what a fool he was — he never got into the earl's hands at my advice." This tends to suggest there had been some disagreement. Had Gaveston stayed on at Scarborough against the wishes of his royal friend? But soon Edward's grief was almost unendurable. His contemporary biographer wrote: "I am certain the king grieved for Piers as a father grieves for his son. For the greater the love, the greater the sorrow. In the lament of David upon Jonathan love is depicted which is said to have surpassed the love of women. Our king also spoke thus, and further he planned to avenge the death of Piers."

Meanwhile the murder had certainly improved the king's position. The main cause of discontent between the king and the magnates had been removed; four earls who had broken the oaths taken by Pembroke and Surrey now found themselves in an isolated position, and perhaps best of all, the queen gave birth to the future Edward III in November to universal rejoicing. The arrival of the heir reinforced the position of the monarchy, and for a while improved relations between Edward and Isabella, especially as the king did not choose another male favourite to replace Gaveston.

In the following spring the royal couple travelled to France to attend the coronation of Isabella's cousin the King of Navarre, and on their return the guilty earls — following lengthy negotiations which had been assisted by an embassy from Pope Clement V — made a formal submission to the king. In return for this apology, and the restoration of Gaveston's jewellery which had been seized by Thomas of Lancaster, Edward granted a general pardon to the earls and 500 of their followers. The question of the Ordinances was not raised, but it was considered that they were now invalid and it seemed that Fate was favouring the king.

The apology and pardon were exchanged in Westminster Hall on October 14, 1313, and the ceremony was followed by a feast of reconciliation at which the king actually dined with Lancaster, though perhaps the earl might have shivered if he had been aware of what was in his liege lord's mind as the toasts were drunk.

The next year saw the defeat of Edward's forces by the Scots at Bannockburn where "the king fought like a lion, but he had to fly and when the royal banner was seen retreating the whole army broke up". Edward not only lost his last hold on Scotland at the battle, but also his chief supporter the Earl of Gloucester who had been one of the first to die on the wall of Scottish pikes after Edward had rashly accused him of cowardice. Bannockburn disastrously weakened Edward's position, and at the next Parliament at York Lancaster and his friends did not hesitate to take full advantage of the situation. Once again the king was forced to accept their demands, which meant the dismissal of his ministers and the control of the kingdom passing back into the hands of Lancaster and the Lords Ordainers. The expenses of the royal household were cut to £10 a day, and it was purged of Edward's supporters who were replaced by men loyal to the Lancastrian cause. Similarly the king's ministers were replaced and Hugh Despenser the elder, who alone had stood by the king in the last crisis, was forced into retirement as was Pembroke whose outrage at the summary killing of Gaveston was not forgotten nor forgiven by Lancaster.

It was a black and bitter time for Edward, a king without power whose enemy was tightening his fist upon the kingdom week by week. In his loneliness his thoughts must have turned to the golden days he had spent with Piers Gaveston. We are told that secretly the king had decided to leave his body with the black friars of Oxford until his murder might be avenged, but with the arrival of 1314 that possibility seemed remote, and Edward filled some of his empty days organising a splendid funeral in the church of the Dominican priory close to the manor at Langley. The service was performed by an archbishop assisted by four bishops, but most of the nobles stayed away, treating Gaveston in death as they had in life, and now they had the satisfaction that there was no danger of his returning from his banishment. No doubt as the king watched the ceremony he renewed his determination to be avenged on those who had robbed him of his friend, but what could he do? Only watch. Perhaps his attitude can be summed up by Charles II who, probably one of our wisest kings behind his "merrie" image, would merely say of his enemies, "Enough rope, enough rope." But at the moment all the king could do for Gaveston's memory was to provide generously for his widow and daughter.

Certainly Lancaster was having all the rope he needed; during 1315 most of the sheriffs throughout England were replaced by his nominees, while as champion of the Ordinances he received increasing support from all classes of Englishmen. But by the next year his rope started to lose its slack and he began to realise it was one thing to seize power and quite another to retain it. As an administrator he found it difficult to make decisions; he preferred to rule at long distance from his hereditary stronghold, and he had a deep dislike of attending councils, with the result that even his friends began to be disillusioned with him. Revolts became frequent, the Scots were a constant threat in the north, and the people had to endure the added burden of bad harvests and plague. For six years England suffered from chaotic government as Lancaster refused to attend Parliament and the king retired to his country houses, staying for long periods at Clarendon where he spent his time "surrounding the forest with ditches and doing other things not at all suited to his dignity."

During this troubled period Edward became more and more intimate with the son of his old supporter Sir Hugh Despenser, also named Hugh. The chronicler of Lanercost declared that this ambitious and acquisitive young man became "the King of England's right eye and, after the death of Piers de Gaveston, his chief counsellor against the earls and barons." And like Gaveston he was mistrusted by the earls and barons, to the extent that in 1321 Parliament forced Edward to banish him, and his father, just as the previous favourite had been banished ten years earlier. It seemed that the king was in the power of Lancaster and the Lords Ordainers as much as ever, but within a few months his destiny took a dramatic turn when a relatively trivial incident polarized the nobles into pro-Lancaster or royal factions and began a civil war.

Queen Isabella was making a pilgrimage to Canterbury on October 13, 1321 when she was overtaken by dusk and decided to request a night's lodging for herself at Leeds Castle near Maidstone. At that time the governor of the castle was Lord Badlesmere, who was out of favour with the king for supporting Lancaster in his campaign to have the Despensers exiled. On this evening his lordship was away and his wife, for some reason which remains a mystery, refused the gate to be opened to the queen, saying that no one could enter without her husband's authority.

Isabella retired to a nearby priory and ordered her guards to force their way into the castle. In the resulting fracas six of them were slain. At this insult the queen turned to her husband who was as furious as his wife over the slight. His indignation was infectious and by hiring merceneries and raising local levies, which were reinforced by an enthusiastic force of Londoners, he soon had an effective army marching behind him into Kent. Remarkably six earls — Arundel, Pembroke, Richmond and Surrey, and the king's half-brothers Kent and Norfolk — rallied to the royal colours at the siege, showing that the Crown was still in high regard despite Edward's follies and vicissitudes — or that Lord Badlesmere was highly unpopular. The castle surrendered after a week when thirteen of the defenders were hanged and Lady Badlesmere was packed off to Dover Castle.

Flushed with success, and with an enthusiastic army under his command, Edward knew that his moment was at hand. The Despensers were recalled and the campaign began. The first target was the Mortimers and other Marcher lords of the Welsh border who had mustered forces to support Lord Badlesmere and were therefore technically traitors. The Mortimers, Roger Mortimer of Chirk and his nephew Roger Mortimer of Wigmore, surrendered at Shrewsbury and were sent to the Tower of London. Edward swung south, taking castle after castle of those who had opposed him. The last to fall was Berkeley Castle near Bristol, and as the king watched the surrender he could have little thought what significance it was to have for him. Next Edward turned his attention to Lancaster who was isolated in the north with his private army. He must have been dismayed at the startling success of the king for it was discovered that he had signed a treaty with the Scots agreeing to mutual aid against their mutual enemy.

The royal forces regrouped at Coventry and then marched towards Lancaster's principal stronghold of Pontefract Castle. Hoping for the agreed aid from Robert the Bruce, the earl led his forces north but as they approached the narrow bridge spanning the River Ure at Boroughbridge, they found it held by an army of Cumberland and Westmoreland men loyal to the king. On March 17, 1322, Lancaster was trapped when royalists from the south caught up with him, and the Battle of Boroughbridge ended with his surrender. At Lancaster's own castle of Pontefract King Edward waited to pronounce judgement on him. In the great hall the prisoner was brought before his royal enemy who was flanked by seven earls and a large number of barons, none of whom would speak in his defence after a list of his crimes was read out. In the past these men had supported him and the Lords Ordainers, some had been his close friends, but now they knew they must condemn him for treason – his alliance with the Scots was unpardonable.

What must have been Edward's feelings as he passed sentence on Lancaster, but despite his elation he showed some mercy, ordering that Lancaster should be beheaded and thus escape more horrific forms of execution associated with treason trials. On March 22, in front of a mob who hurled snowballs at him, Lancaster had his head roughly lopped from his body on a mound close to the battlements of his castle. Other rebels, including Lord Badlesmere, were hanged and Edward's revenge was complete.

* * *

We have seen that Edward's tribulations had stemmed from his liberal devotion to an unpopular favourite, and now, with his main enemies dead and his royal authority restored, he began to repeat his folly. This time it was the Despensers, father and son, who earned the antagonism of the magnates, and the hatred of Queen Isabella. At the time the Despensers were banished in 1321 the Earl of Pembroke had written a warning to the king, "He perishes on the rocks that loves another more than himself," which suggests that Edward's affinity with the young Sir Hugh had grown in intensity. After his return to power Edward heaped riches — in the form of the lands and possessions of the defeated nobles — on his friend, just as he had lavished riches on Piers Gaveston, but there was a great difference between the first and second favourite. Gaveston may have been arrogant but his ambition went no further than to be the king's cherished companion; Sir Hugh, like his father, was thirsting for power. To be fair to the Despensers no historian has found fault with their administrative ability but their virtues in this direction were outweighed by extreme rapacity and a lack of tact which eclipsed that of Gaveston, especially in regard to Queen Isabella.

After Gaveston's death the relationship between Edward and his queen had greatly improved, as is shown by the fact that she bore him four children between 1312 and 1321. But the bitterness and jealousy she had felt as a bride when she became aware of her husband's preference for Gaveston, returned in 1322 when she saw him giving his affection to Sir Hugh. From then on she was to become the remorseless enemy of the Despensers. At first there was little she could do but suffer the insults they put upon her. In 1324 it seemed as if hostilities would break out between France and England, and the Despensers persuaded Edward to sequestrate her estates because she was a Frenchwoman, her expenditure was limited to twenty shillings a day and as a crowning indignity young Despenser's wife, Eleanor de Clare, was appointed as her "housekeeper" with the right to read all her letters.

In the same year Sir Roger Mortimer of Wigmore escaped from the Tower of London where he had been held since his surrender with his uncle at Shrewsbury. He had been imprisoned under the sentence of death, but in some mysterious way he had aroused the sympathy of the queen and then, through the efforts of an intercessor whose name has not been recorded, King Edward commuted his sentence to life imprisonment. It is an intriguing question as to whether it was Isabella to whom he owed his life. And if so was it because he was a sworn enemy of the Despensers, or was she already in love with this handsome and tough adventurer who was the antithesis of her husband?

The melodramatic escape from the Tower was effected by the drugging of the guards' wine, followed by a climb up a kitchen chimney and then a descent by rope ladder down to the Thames. Sir Roger hurried to France where Isabella's brother Charles had just become king.

The following year Queen Isabella journeyed to Paris, ostensibly to arrange a peace settlement between the two countries. Many historians have pondered why the Despensers let her go, but others have suggested that they were anxious to be rid of her, or that she played such a subtle game they were ignorant of her true motives. At the French court Roger Mortimer greeted her enthusiastically and together they planned to bring down the Despensers – and Edward who remained unaware of what was happening, to the extent that when Isabella wrote suggesting that their thirteen-years-old son, Edward Prince of Wales, should go to Paris to make the traditional homage to the French king he raised no objection. When this ceremony was completed Edward ordered the queen to return with the prince, but she declared "marriage was a bond between husband and wife, and that until the middleman who divided them was gone she would live single or in a convent" – a somewhat hypocritical statement as she entered into a passionate love affair with Mortimer.

At her refusal to return the Despensers persuaded the king to outlaw her and Prince Edward. Meanwhile she corresponded with English nobles who formed an anti-Despenser party, and proposed a marriage between her son and Phillipa, the daughter of William II, Count of Hainault, Holland and Zeeland. The delighted count gave her an advance on Phillipa's dowry to finance an invasion of England, which began on

September 24, 1326, when she landed on the Suffolk coast near Harwich with Roger Mortimer in command of her small force of English exiles and mercenaries. After she had made a theatrical pilgrimage to Bury St Edmunds in the symbolic mourning dress of a widow she was joined by a number of barons and many London citizens.

On learning the news that the queen's ever-growing army was advancing on London, Edward and the Despensers left the Tower for Gloucester where he tried to raise troops. It was in vain, the population looked upon Isabella as the saviour of the kingdom, and the king fell back to Bristol. Desperately he offered a £1000 reward for Mortimer's head − Isabella replied by offering £2000 for his.

On October 26 the queen's forces reached the city where they were given a rapturous welcome by its citizens. The elder Despenser was condemned to death by Mortimer and the earls of Kent, Leicester and Norfolk, and was hanged from a gibbet 50ft high before being disembowelled.

According to Froissart's *Chronicle* the king and Sir Hugh the younger were in Bristol Castle when the execution took place in sight of the castle walls, and it added: "Intimidated by this execution they endeavoured to escape to the Welsh shore in a boat . . . but after tossing about some days, and striving in vain against contrary winds, Sir Hugh Beaumont observing the efforts of the unfortunate bark, rowed out with a strong force in his barge. The consequence was that the royal fugitive and his hapless favourite were brought back to Bristol and delivered to the queen as prisoners."

Queen Isabella planned to take Sir Hugh to London but, aware of what must surely come, he refused to eat and became so ill that she ordered him to be tried at Hereford so that he would not escape her vengeance by dying on the journey. Sir William Trusell, who had recently passed sen-on his father, condemned him to a revolting death.

The queen watched while, crowned with nettles, he was brought before her on a hurdle. In describing the following execution, in which the prisoner was hanged, drawn and quartered, Froissart wrote that "His member and his testicles were first cut off, because he was a heretic and a sodomite, even, it was said, with the King."

Edward was taken to Kenilworth where on Janaury 16, 1327, a Parliamentary deputation told him that it had been decided at Westminster that because of his incompetence to rule the kingdom, for being controlled by wicked councillors and for losing terrritories bequeathed to him by his father, he should be deposed and his place taken by Prince Edward.

When he refused to abdicate voluntarily, the king was told that if he did not his son would be denied the crown and another sovereign be found, presumably Roger Mortimer. In order to safeguard his dynasty, Edward finally agreed.

Dressed in mourning black, he fell down in a faint in front of the deputation before the abdication ceremony began. Then, with tears rolling down his cheeks, he went through with it, declaring that although he grieved that he was rejected by his subjects, he was pleased they were accepting his son in his place. Sir William Trusell renounced all allegiance to Edward on behalf of England and the Steward of the Household snapped his staff of office to show that it was disbanded. The next month Edward III was crowned and from then on the ex-king was known as "Lord Edward, sometime King of Englande".

Queen Isabella and Roger Mortimer acted as regents to the young king, and in effect had full control of the realm. At first "Lord Edward" was reasonably treated as a prisoner at Kenilworth Castle where he is said to have written a poem on his misfortune in Anglo-Norman. Translated, the first verse reads:

> In winter woe befell me;
> By cruel Fortune thwarted,
> My life now lies a ruin.
> Full oft have I experienced,
> There's none so fair, so wise,
> So courteous nor so highly famed,
> But, if Fortune dare to favour,
> Will be a fool proclaimed.

In the spring Edward was in the charge of Thomas de

Berkeley and Sir John Maltravers. The former had been captured at Boroughbridge and his lands given to Hugh Despenser before being restored to him by Isabella; the latter had fled to France after Boroughbridge and joined Isabella's party there – neither could be said to have sympathy for their captive. He was moved from the comfort of Kenilworth to Corfe, Bristol and Berkeley Castles successively, and successively his treatment grew worse. It seems that with Isabella's increasing love for Mortimer, her loathing for her husband grew equally and she avenged herself for the neglect and slights of the past. On the journey to his final place of imprisonment he was forced to wear a crown of straw, and was given ditchwater for shaving, whereupon he said with simple dignity, "Whether you will or no, I have warm tears for my beard."

On April 5, 1327, the humiliated ex-monarch was incarcerated in Berkeley Castle and little definite information regarding him filtered out, although there was no shortage of rumours, until the official announcement of his death on September 21. But we do know that during those five months he was kept in a cell-like chamber which is pointed out to visitors to the castle today as the King's Gallery.

"The visitor will observe a deep hole like a well in one corner of the room," states the guidebook. "This is the Dungeon, and it goes down to the level of the courtyard outside, 28 feet. It was the barbarous custom to throw the rotting carcasses of cattle down the pit, when the stench of putrification would eventually asphyxiate the prisoner in the room above . . . Prisoners of lowly birth might be thrown down, still alive, on top of the carcasses, but such was not the practice with captives of gentle birth, let alone of Royal birth. The wretched Edward may thus be imagined as sitting in his small room, breathing the pestilential vapours arising form the charnel-well below."

When Edward survived this attempt to give him a fatal infection so it would appear he had died of natural causes, more direct ways were considered. It was becoming more increasingly obvious that Edward was an embarrassment to the new regime. For one thing Isabella was still Edward's wife, so that his continued existence made her relationship with Mortimer adulterous. There had been sympathy for the queen while she appeared a wronged wife, but now her own morality was open to criticism, especially by the Church.

But Edward posed a greater problem than this, while he lived he would always be a focal point of revolt for disaffected magnates, for after Edward III was crowned on January 24, 1327, it became apparent that he was king in name only. The real power remained with his mother and her paramour who had taken the title of Earl of March. The couple retained two-thirds of England's tax revenue for their own purposes, and it was obvious that once Edward had abdicated the support of the magnates began to wane. The nobility were alarmed when they realised they had exchanged a weak and foolish king for a ruthless tyrant. According to some chronicles there were several conspiracies that summer to rescue the ex-king, and one was said to have almost succeeded.

In July one Thomas Dunhead, a Dominican friar, and his brother Stephen led a band of conspirators into Berkeley Castle where they managed to release Edward and carry him off to brief safety at Corfe Castle. But soon the prisoner was retaken and the leader of the attempt was barbarously done to death at Berkeley. When a second attempt by Sir Rhys ap Griffith was betrayed to Mortimer it was no longer a question of whether they should have Edward murdered, but how. It was the custom in those days for the corpses of kings to be exposed to public view to prove that they were not the victims of foul play, and Mortimer and Isabella could not afford to be accused of the murder of the official king's father. Therefore they decided on the death in what was known as the "Italian manner". It has been suggested that Isabella saw in this form of assassination an ironic piece of revenge, and certainly the form of Edward's death strengthened the opinions of many historians as to his physical homosexuality.

There are several versions of what happened next. A fascinating story is that Bishop Orleton sent Edward's gaolers a letter in Latin which might be construed in two ways – *Edwardum occidere nolite timere bonum est,* which in translation could mean "Do not kill Edward: it is a good thing to be afraid," or "Do not fear to kill Edward: it is a good thing." Alas for popular historians, it seems that this was unlikely as the bishop was out of England at the time.

The accepted version of the following events is that Sir William Ogle (named as one of the three murderers of the king) was sent with the death sentence to Berkeley from Abergavenny where Mortimer had heard of the second conspiracy to free Edward. What happened next is thus described in *Grafton's Chronicle:* "Sir Robert sent a letter unto them (the ex-king's captors, Thomas de Gourney and John de Maltravers) signifying how and in what wise he should be put to death. And anone after the aforesaid Thomas and John had received the letter, and considered the contents thereof, they made the King in good cheer and in a good countenance at his supper, when he thought least of the proposed treason. And when bed time came, the King went to his bed and lay and slept soundly. And he being in his sound sleep, these traitors and false forsworn persons against their homage and fealty, came privily into his chamber and their company with them, and laid a great table upon his belly, and with strength of men at all four corners pressed it down upon his body wherewith the King awake at being sore afraid of death turned his body, so that he lay grovelling. Then the murderers took a horn and thrust it up into his fundament as far as they might, and then took a hot burning spit and put it through the horn into his body and in the end killed and vilely murdered him, but yet in such wise that after his death it could not be perceived how he came by his death, but being dead he was afterwards buried in Gloucester."

* * *

The chroniclers agree on the terrible method of killing the king, a way which would leave no external mark on the body and yet was so agonising that it was said that the nearby villagers were awakened by Edward's shrieks. In the *Murimuth*

Chronicle it was related that "many persons, abbots, priors, knights, burgesses of Bristol and Gloucester were summoned to view the body, and indeed superficially examined it, nevertheless it was commonly said that he was slain as a precaution by the orders of Sir John Maltravers and Sir Thomas Gurney."

After being put on view the victim's corpse was embalmed and the heart in a silver box was given as a *memento mori* to a hypocritical mourning Isabella. The following December saw a spectacular funeral for the ex-king at Gloucester Cathedral where soon afterwards the tomb became an object of pilgrimage. Edward III had a serene effigy of his father carved in alabaster placed above it — a statue which is one of the greatest pieces of sculpture to come down to us from the medieval age, and as such still attracts crowds of visitors. On the saintly features of the statue there is no hint of the triumph and disaster, the passion and the pain, which had been the dominating threads of Edward's life.

Yet as he had avenged his murdered Perrot, Edward was himself avenged. On the night of October 19, 1330, Edward III secretly entered Nottingham Castle with two dozen companions and arrested Mortimer in his mother's chamber, ignoring her agonised plea of *"Bel fitz, eiez pitie du gentil Mortimer!"* Then, for having "murdered and killed the king's father" and of usurping Edward's royal authority, he was executed in London, his body swinging for two days and two nights from a gallows at Tyburn.

Queen Isabella was confined for the remaining twenty-eight years of her life to Castle Rising in Norfolk where legend asserts that she suffered from bouts of insanity. Following her death in 1359 her wish to be buried beside Roger Mortimer was carried out; with amazing hypocrisy she had also requested that the embalmed heart of her murdered husband be placed on her breast. If ghosts are drawn back to their mortal remains, what an uneasy triangle that trio must make.

CHAPTER FIVE

The Murder of Richard II

"My God, a wonderful land this is and fickle: which has exiled, slain, destroyed and ruined so many kings, rulers and great men, and is ever tainted with strife and variance and envy."

NEVER HAVE LONDONERS shown such jubilation for a new sovereign as they did for Richard of Bordeaux when he made his magnificent entry into the capital the day after the death of his grandfather Edward III. It was a golden day as the ten-years-old boy rode under arch after triumphal arch. His procession — its noble members dressed in white to symbolise the purity of the child king — wound through streets draped with cloths of silver and gold. For the three hours it took to travel from the Tower to Westminster Abbey, conduits flowed with wine and at every turning the gorgeous cavalcade was greeted with spectacle and pageants expressing loyalty and delight at the new age which was believed to be unfolding.

"In Cheapside was erected a building in the form of a castle, out of which ran streams of wine," wrote Walsingham, "On its four turrets stood four girls dressed in white, and about the age of the king. As he approached they blew towards him small shreds of gold leaf, a favourite fancy at the time . . . They showered upon him flowers made of gilt paper, and then coming down, filling cups with wine from the fountain, and presented them to him and his attendants. Then flew down an angel from the summit of the castle and offered to the king a gold crown. Every street exhibited some pageant or device, but the merchants of Cheapside obtained the palm for their superior ingenuity."

It was an ironic twist of history that the next time such a huge concourse came to view the king at Westminster he was dethroned and lying in his coffin, his shroud carefully concealing wounds which, had someone dared to pluck it away, would have revealed the manner of his assassination and solved one of England's royal murder mysteries.

When he came to the throne in 1377 Richard II was the spoilt darling of his family and the people. Perhaps it was this early adulation which gave him his passionate belief in his divine right as a monarch, a belief which was to be a continuing controversy in British politics until the axe finally descended upon the neck of Charles I. In the pattern of Richard's life, with its tangle of plot and counterplot, its contrasts of magnificence and mystery, there is an uncanny parallel to that of his great-grandfather, Edward II. Richard himself must have become aware of this fateful similarity when, during a period of his greatest unhappiness, he endeavoured to persuade the Pope to canonise his murdered ancestor.

During his highly strung life he introduced the first breath of the Renaissance into England for, unlike many of his Plantagenet forebears, he was not a soldier king. The country was free from major wars throughout his reign, though his desire to rule alone, coupled with his love of art and personal extravagance, soured the affection of nobles and commons until it was replaced with hatred. In the bitter end he was the first victim of the Wars of the Roses.

The son of the Black Prince and his wife, Lady Joan Plantagenet, the Fair Maid of Kent, Richard was born at Bordeaux on January 6, 1367. Four years later he was brought to England where his principal tutor was Sir Simon Burley who instructed him in the code of chivalry. At the death of his famous father in 1376, the boy was presented to Parliament by his grandfather Edward III as his successor. The day after Edward died on June 21, 1377, the great seal was placed in the boy's hands and he was declared king.

The actual coronation took place on July 16 when the nobility assembled in the great hall of Westminster. The passage from it to Westminster Abbey glowed warmly in light reflected from the rich scarlet cloth with which it had been carpeted — a portent of the extravagant style which Richard was to enjoy all his life. Prelates, abbots and members of the clergy led the procession, followed by officers of state and magnates, and finally the royal child beneath a canopy of blue silk carried on silver spears by the barons of the Cinque Ports. He walked with naked feet to the altar, knelt in prayer and was then conducted to his throne.

The long ceremony which followed was an ordeal, and when Sir Simon Burley lifted him in his arms to carry him to the palace he was exhausted. After a rest he returned to the great hall where, after creating four earls and nine knights, he took his place in the royal chair. During the sumptuous feast which followed toasts were drunk to the new reign, minstrels sang and acrobats and jugglers performed in an expensive blaze of candlelight. It must have been a heady few hours for Richard who must have believed that such glory would accompany him through his career. The historian William Howitt commented: "Everything was done which could tend to inspire the boy king with an idea of that absolute greatness which had been already sufficiently instilled into his mind from very infancy by his mother, his uncles, and his courtiers. For such things kings afterwards pay a suitable compensation . . . Never before had such base laudation, such creeping protestations, been practised in this country. Both courtiers and dignitaries of the church used the same language of grovelling sycophancy towards the unsuspecting youth; and little could he dream that, while they were lauding his wisdom and royal virtues, they were preparing for him the execrations of his people and the loss of his throne and life. It has been justly said, that for much of what came afterwards to pass these vile flatterers were really answerable. While, therefore, passing judgement on the follies and the crimes of kings, we should never forget that they have been made what they are by the mercenary courtiers who perpetually throng about thrones. At this moment the youthful Richard was the idol of every class in the nation; the beauty of his person and the memory of his father surrounding him with a halo of popular favour, through which the gloom of after years could make no way."

The realm which Richard had inherited was in a state of unrest due to the result of plague, heavy taxation and the democratic ideas of the Lollards. The latter were originally

21   Manuscript illustration of King John hunting

22 *Revenge of Edward II —
    the Earl of Lancaster being condemned to death in his own*

23 *Castle Rising, once the prison of Queen Isabella*

24   *The killing of Wat Tyler*

25   *The murder of Richard II in his prison cell*

a religious community established in Antwerp in 1300 to care for the sick, but the name grew to have the same meaning as heretic, and was applied to the followers of John Wycliffe, "the morning star of the Reformation," whose ideas were distorted by wandering preachers such as the famous John Ball. Not only were the powers of the Church questioned, but the whole medieval social structure, and peasants began to gain a dim concept of the equality of men summed up in a couplet which they delighted in repeating.

> When Adam delved and Eve span
> Who was then the gentleman?

Added to this was the powerful influence of John of Gaunt and Alice Perrers during the declining years of the late king's life. John of Gaunt, Duke of Lancaster, was the fourth son of Edward III, and before his father's death he was the most influential noble in England. He was often suspected of having his eye on the crown which by right went to his nephew Richard. In collusion with him was Alice Perrers who had become the chief mistress of the tarnished old hero of Crécy and Poitiers. According to Walsingham "unmindful of her sex and frailty she used to sit by the justices on the bench and by the doctors in the ecclesiastical courts, persuading them to act against the law." And it was she who was said to have pulled the rings from the fingers of the old king when he lay dying and deserted.

Against this background the boy king was put under the care of his mother while a council of eleven was chosen to govern "until he was of age to know good and evil." For playmates of his own age he had his two half brothers, John and Richard, who were the sons of his mother by her first husband Sir Thomas Holland. His greatest friend was Robert de Vere, Earl of Oxford, who was destined to play Gaveston to his Edward II.

Despite the problems all appeared to go well at first. The Council diminished the power of John of Gaunt and Alice Perrers was exiled. But as time passed it became apparent that Richard would come into conflict with his royal uncles as he approached manhood. These men, the Dukes of Lancaster, York and Gloucester, were the sons of a king while Richard was only the son of a prince. Perhaps it was for this reason he followed the example of Edward II in choosing his favourites from lower ranks.

Five years after his coronation Richard proved his regal qualities by one of the most spectacular confrontations of his subjects ever made by a sovereign.

With the old warrior Edward III and his dreaded son, the Black Prince, safely in their graves, the French had taken advantage of the reign of a minor to continue the Hundred Years' War. In alliance with Spain, and enthusiastically assisted by the Scots, they attacked England soon after Richard's coronation, taking possession of the Isle of Wight, burning Hastings and Rye, devastating large districts of Kent and Sussex and sinking English shipping in the Channel. In the north the Scots attacked Berwick, burned Roxburgh and invaded the northern counties. The result was that the Hundred Years' War recommenced, the war which had already depleted the English treasury and thus led to increased taxation on a population already overtaxed. In December, 1380, a special shilling poll tax was introduced and next year popular resentment against this became the spark which ignited Wat Tyler's Peasants' Revolt. What added to the people's bitterness was the corrupt way in which the tax was gathered, the collection being farmed out to some members of the court who in turn sold the franchise to foreign merchants whose agents were feared for their harshness.

Trouble first occurred at Brentwood, Essex, where Thomas de Bampton summoned the people of Fobbings before him and ordered them to pay the new tax, threatening them with arrest. In reply they drove de Bampton's soldiers away. Sir Robert Bealknap, the Chief Justice of the Common Pleas, was sent to Essex to try the recalcitrants but it was too late. The locals denounced him as a traitor and he only just managed to escape with his life. The jurors and clerks of the commission were summarily decapitated and their heads stuck upon poles which were carried through neighbouring towns as a signal for an uprising led by a vagabond priest known as Jack Straw.

News of the rebellion spread like prairie fire not only through Kent but Norfolk and Suffolk. Meanwhile at Deptford, Kent, a tax collector arrived at the house of Wat Tyler who indeed was a "tiler of houses". The collector demanded the tax for Wat's daughter even though her mother protested that the girl was under fifteen and thus exempt. The tax man declared he would soon prove this and was "proceeding to the grossest outrage" when Tyler, hearing the screams of his daughter, rushed in and killed the official with a blow from his hammer.

Everywhere there was popular approval of the tiler's action for, as Froissart wrote, "the rude officers had in many places made the like trial". The news of this, coupled with the insurrection in Essex, spread from the Thames to the Humber. Natural-born leaders appeared in every district with the universal idea of marching on London where "the Commons should be of one mind, and should do so much to the king that there should not be one bond man in all England". At Maidstone, Wat Tyler was elected leader of the insurgents with John Ball as their chaplain.

As the streams of peasants converged towards the capital they plundered and pillaged. According to Froissart "they took their way thither and on their going they beat down abbeys and houses of advocates and men of the court and so came into the suburbs of London which were great and fair, and beat down divers fair houses, and especially the king's prisons, as the Marshalsea and others, and delivered out the prisoners that were therein." Wat Tyler with John Ball and Jack Straw led 20,000 men into London and at the Savoy they burned down John of Gaunt's palace after killing his servants. Howard wrote: "In destroying these noble houses the people disclaimed any idea of plunder. Their objects were, as they asserted, to punish the great traitors to the nation, and obtain their freedom from bondage. They published a proclamation forbidding anyone to secrete any booty. They hammered out the plate, and cut it into small pieces: they beat the precious stones to powder, and, one of the rioters having concealed in his bosom a silver cup, was thrown with his prize into the river."

Londoners, who at first had welcomed the insurgents, were soon terrified of them, especially as their leaders' edicts about loot did not seem to extend to the contents of wine cellars. Everywhere groups of rebels would approach citizens on the street and demand, "With whom holdest thou?" and unless the reply was "With King Richard and the Commons" death and mutilation followed automatically. The columns of smoke from aristocratic houses caused many members of the court to melt away, leaving the sixteen-years-old king to deal with his unruly subjects. This he did by sending a message to Wat Tyler that if they would retire to Mile End, which was then "open land where the people of the city did disport themselves in the summer season", he would ride out and listen to their demands.

Tyler's men moved out of the city and then Richard, with only a few unarmed followers, rode forth to meet them. At the sight of what was estimated as 60,000 peasants his two half brothers took fright and rode off leaving him to face Wat Tyler who treated him courteously and explained the peasants' demands. These were the abolition of bondage, the reduction of the rent of land at four pence an acre, the free liberty of buying and selling in all fairs and markets and a general pardon for all past offences. While the two conversed, the petitioners must have looked at the king in wonder, for he certainly showed no fear of them. At sixteen he had become an impressive figure being tall, pale-skinned and golden-haired and every inch of what they expected a king to be. He smiled as he listened to Wat make his demands and agreed that they were reasonable. He promised that if the rebels retired each to his own county he would give one of his banners to each shire to march home under, and they should leave two men from each village to bring copies of the charter he would give them. As word of this spread through the multitude most of the peasants were satisfied and they began to walk towards London to spend the night in the city. That same night thirty clerks set to work making copies of the king's charter which were to be sealed and delivered in the morning.

The king's promises failed to placate the more extreme

elements. In London they managed to enter the Tower where they rampaged through the royal apartments and insulted the king's mother, the Fair Maid of Kent. They then beheaded the Treasurer, the Archbishop of Canterbury and others they deemed to be "traitors". Encouraged by unruly London apprentices the mob was almost out of hand when Richard went forth to meet Wat Tyler for a second time at Smithfield on June 15. His courtiers advised against him appearing before the crowd of "shoeless ribalds" but, with the same cool courage he had shown at Mile End, he rode through the cattle market and faced them. What exactly followed afterwards remains confused but it was to be the king's first experience of murder.

With 60 horsemen behind him the king had reined up in front of the Abbey of St Bartholomew, where Wat Tyler was awaiting him at the head of 20,000 insurgents. The peasants' leader had refused the charter which had previously been agreed, demanding new conditions among which were the total repeal of the hated forest or game laws. Some chronicles state that Wat Tyler insulted the king, but this is doubtful as he had conducted himself with great courtesy at Mile End. We do know that, in presenting his new demands, he drew Richard aside and touched him. Perhaps it was a kindly gesture of reassurance but to Richard's attendants Tyler had committed the crime of laying hands on the monarch. A version given by Froissart was that Wat Tyler saw one of the king's squires against whom he had a grudge.

"Give me thy dagger," he demanded. The squire refused but Richard told him to hand it over. Wat Tyler then began to play with it and said to the squire: "By my faith, I will never eat meat 'til I have your head." At this moment the mayor of London, Sir William Walworth, hearing these words, said: "Ha! thou knave, darest thou speak such words in the king's presence." Then the king said to Walworth: "Set hands on him".

Whether this was true or not, the fact remains that Walworth spurred forward and struck Tyler with a baselard, a short sword which is said to have been incorporated commemoratively in London's coat of arms. This blow was followed by one from Robert Standish who may have been the squire over whom the trouble had started. Tyler wheeled his horse, riding about a dozen yards before falling to the ground and dying. In the seconds that followed a flight of peasant arrows could have altered the whole course of English history, but in the tensest moment of his life the king responded brilliantly. Walsingham related: "As they were stringing their bows, Richard spurred his horse up to them and cried: 'What is it, my men? What are you doing? Do not talk about wishing to shoot your king nor be sad about the death of a rogue and traitor. I am your king, I will be your captain and leader. Follow me to the field and you shall have all you ask for!' "

At that instant he must have appeared the ideal sovereign and Richard of Maidstone wrote rapturously: "How fresh coloured his face, crowned with yellow hair, his combed locks shining under the garland; gleaming with gold and the red robe that covers too much of his fair body." His fine ringing words and noble appearance halted the expected arrow flight. The rebels hesitated and were won over. They formed a huge procession and marched behind the king to Clerkenwell Fields where Richard signed some documents which freed them from villeinage and granted them amnesty. They then quietly left the city for their distant homes.

How they must have regretted their obedience a fortnight later when the charters were revoked and a special commission under Chief Justice Tresilian were sent forth to punish the leaders. A mere accusation was enough to get a man sentenced to death and the wholesale executions which followed spelled out to the people that Richard was not their captain but a king as jealous of his rights as any of his predecessors. Hollinshead estimated that 1500 of the rebels were executed, among them Jack Straw and Lester and Westbroom who had assumed the titles of kings of Norfolk and Suffolk.

* * *

On January 20, 1381, King Richard married "the excellent virgin" Anne of Bohemia, a daughter of the Emperor Charles

110

IV. Although the marriage had been arranged by the Council anxious for alliance against France, Richard was to fall completely in love with her. Later on he was so affected by her death that it seems to have upset the balance of his mind. But though the marriage brought him great happiness Richard was surrounded by difficulties personified by his three powerful uncles. When Parliament sat at Salisbury a Carmelite friar named John Latimer delivered into Richard's hands written details of a plot — the truth of which will never be known — to place John of Gaunt on the throne. Richard confronted his uncle with the letter and the duke swore that it was a conspiracy against him and vowed to fight anyone who doubted his innocence. He insisted that the Carmelite, who refused to deny the story, should be put in the custody of Sir John Holland, a stepbrother of the king who was one of John of Gaunt's allies. That night Sir John strangled the friar with his own hands. This act confirmed public opinion there was treason afoot but the king was in no position to take the matter further.

The following year the French sent a thousand men at arms and a vast sum in gold francs to the Scots to assist them in an invasion of England after which they ravaged Westmorland, Cumberland and Lancashire. Richard led an army north but before he had crossed the border Sir John Holland committed another murder. This time the victim was one of Richard's favourites, the son of the Earl of Stafford, who, at the time of his death, had been carrying despatches from the king to Queen Anne. Apparently an affray occurred and Sir John Holland struck him down, killing him on the spot. The motive for this killing is not clear though young Stafford was in high favour with Queen Anne and it was whispered that the deed was the result of jealousy.

Holland fled to Beverley where he took sanctuary in the church there. Naturally the Earl of Stafford demanded revenge and Richard vowed that he would hang his half brother if ever he left the sanctuary of the church of St John. Stricken with grief at her son's second murder, the Fair Maid of Kent spent four days weeping and pleading with Richard to spare Holland's life. Richard declared he would have him hanged like a common criminal and on the fifth day his mother died of a broken heart at Wallingford Castle.

Richard was so shocked by her death that he granted Sir John Holland his second pardon. He then continued into Scotland where he razed Edinburgh and several other Scottish towns. In the Parliament which followed the Scottish campaign, the king tried to allay the jealousies between his favourites and his relatives by giving the latter grants of land titles. Then by removing members of his Council who represented the old nobility and replacing them with his supporters he planned to regain control of his kingdom from the barons and Parliament. He heaped honours on his favourites especially Robert de Vere, his beloved boyhood companion, whom he created Earl of Oxford with the title of Marquis of Dublin, a title before unknown in England. Another leading favourite, a merchant's son named Michael de la Pole, was created Earl of Suffolk and, as Richard had no children, he named Roger, Earl of March, as his royal heir.

This successfully countered any of John of Gaunt's aspirations to the throne and in 1386 the duke went to Spain to press his claims on the crown of Castile through his marriage to Constance, daughter of Pedro the Cruel of Castile. The departure of his dread uncle pleased Richard so much that he gave him and his wife, the Infanta of Castile, a golden crown each as a farewell gift.

With John of Gaunt safely out of the way Richard felt free from restriction and enjoyed it by refusing to meet Parliament and increasing the number of his household to 10,000, his retainers and servants all wearing his badge of a white hart. In the royal kitchen there was a staff of 300 and this extravagance alone outraged lords and commoners alike. In October 1386 Parliament was further angered by the promotion of the hated favourite de Vere to Duke of Ireland. Demands were made that the king's Treasurer and Chancellor (his friend the Earl of Suffolk) should be dismissed to which the king replied haughtily that "he would not displace the meanest scullion in his kitchen for their pleasure."

It was a reference to the fate of Edward II that checked

the king, and the effect on him was dramatic. He went immediately to Westminster and humbly agreed to the dismissal of his Treasurer and the impeachment of his Chancellor and to the setting up of a committee of eleven lords to supervise the royal household and its income for the next twelve months. To it were elected some of the king's bitterest enemies, including the Duke of Arundel, and Richard's uncle, Thomas of Woodstock, Duke of Gloucester, who had taken over the role of John of Gaunt in Richard's life.

Gloucester now became the most powerful man in England and Richard was virtually deposed, but at least he had gained time and he immediately began scheming against the committee. He travelled through the west of England in a kind of electioneering campaign believing that if he could make himself popular with the people he could get a royalist House of Commons elected which would support him in revoking the agreement which had been forced upon him.

To help the royalist cause the king recalled de Vere and summoned his old tutor Sir Simon Burley, Chief Justice Tresilian, Archbishop Neville of York, a leading London merchant named Nicholas Brember and the Earl of Suffolk whom he managed to get released. In November, 1387, Richard returned to London and had some judges declare that the promises he had given to Parliament were not legal. This almost led to civil war as Richard's five great enemies — Gloucester, Arundel, Warwick, Nottingham and Henry Bolingbroke, the son of John of Gaunt — began mustering their soldiers.

Known as the Lords Appellant, these five nobles were obsessed with the destruction of Robert de Vere who, in all fairness, was guilty of nothing worse than being the royal favourite.

On December 12 the Lords Appellant put troops on every road leading from London to the north in the knowledge that de Vere was travelling to the capital with a company of men. It was Arundel's force which intercepted him. De Vere unfurled the royal standard and the banner of St George and prepared to fight, but Arundel shouted to his followers that if they defended him they would be defending a traitor.

At these words they melted away though de Vere managed to escape in the confusion. He fled from England in company with two other erstwhile supporters of the king, Archbishop Neville and the Earl of Suffolk, all of whom were to die in exile. Next Brember, Tresilian and Burley were captured.

Soon after Christmas the Lords Appellant rode to the Tower of London to confront the king. Despite his perilous position he received them royally, sitting in a tent in a vineyard carpeted over with cloth of gold. Though he gave them audience proudly he was soon forced to agree to their demands. Early in the New Year there was a meeting of what came to be known as the Merciless Parliament at which the Lords Appellant produced a bill of 39 charges against Richard's ministers. It sat until June 8 and at the instigation of the vindictive Gloucester it succeeded in imprisoning or driving away all the king's friends, even to his confessor and his wife's Bohemian attendants. Sir Nicholas Brember and Tresilian were executed as well as many others who had supported the king. Gloucester thirsted for the blood of his royal nephew's allies, and the fate of Sir Simon Burley excited the deepest sympathy with the public because of his long and distinguished life.

Queen Anne even was said to have gone on her knees for three hours before Gloucester imploring him in vain to spare Sir Simon. For three weeks the king resolutely refused to sign the execution warrant for his old tutor, but on May 5 he was beheaded on Tower Hill without it. All the king managed to achieve was to save him the disgrace of being hanged at Tyburn. The Merciless Parliament wound up by giving the Lords Appellant £20,000 for their "services" and granted them and their friends a full indemnity.

For a year the defeated king lived in retirement. He must have pondered frequently on the similarity of his position to that of his great grandfather following the death of Piers Gaveston, and he was equally determined to revenge himself on those who had killed and exiled his friends. By the end of that year the people were as tired of the harsh Gloucester as they had been of their extravagant king, indeed their sympathy was veering back to him. The problem of the

Lollards had grown and the Catholic population was anxious for action to be taken. Richard judged that the time had come to strike and at mid-day on May 31, 1389, he strode into the Council hall at Westminster and demanded from the astonished members to be told his age. A chorus of voices answered that he was twenty-two.

"Then I should not be of less account than any other heir in England," he declared, "since the law grants any man his full rights on his twenty-first year."

He seized the Great Seal from the Chancellor and placed it in the hands of the old Bishop Wykeham, dismissed the Lords Appellant and announced he was assuming full control of the realm in his own person. The news was greeted joyously throughout England, and Richard underlined it by persecuting the unfortunate Lollards. He ordered their excommunication, and on his tomb are still engraved the words: "He overthrew the heretics and laid their friends low".

Richard celebrated his return to power with a tournament at Smithfield which attracted knights from all Europe and lasted for three weeks. When the festivities were over, he asked John of Gaunt to return from Castile and truces were agreed with France, Scotland and Spain. A new era had unexpectedly dawned and for the next few years Richard remained popular with his subjects and had the confidence of Parliament.

This peaceful time ended in June, 1394, when Queen Anne died of the plague. The shock seemed to unhinge Richard, who had idolised her. He ordered her apartments at Shene to be demolished, and for twelve months he was unable to enter a house where they had been together. At her funeral in Westminster Abbey the Duke of Arundel gave Richard great offence by arriving late. He heightened the insult by asking for permission to leave before the ceremony was completed.

It was too much for the grief-stricken monarch. He seized a verger's staff and brought it down so hard on Arundel's head that he fell stunned and bleeding to the floor. He was dragged away and imprisoned in the Tower for a week. Meanwhile confusion reigned in the abbey. Because blood had been shed in its holy precincts, a special service of purification had to be held before the rites could continue. Night had fallen on London before all was completed. Night seemed to have fallen on Richard, too. Without the counsel of Anne, his ambition became reckless.

In his unhappiness the king had de Vere's body brought from Louvain and had it buried with great pomp, just as Edward II had with Gaveston's. He had a book prepared of the miracles which were supposed to have taken place at Edward II's tomb. This he sent to the Pope with a request that he canonise his great-grandfather. No doubt while he was doing these things he pondered deeply on the treachery of nobles to their kings. As he was without a direct heir, he now decided to marry Isabella, the pretty six-years-old daughter of Charles VI of France. This had the added attraction of infuriating Gloucester who wanted to renew the Hundred Years' War.

In October 1396, Richard went to France to meet the French king. After the centuries of hostility between the two countries, great precautions were taken to protect both monarchs from assassination. Then, on an afternoon at three o'clock at a special meeting ground, Richard stepped out of his pavilion and walked to meet Charles who was coming from his tent. Over his yellow hair Richard wore a coronet which had been sent to him by the French king, and a red gown which reached his heels. Charles was dressed in red and white hose and a gown to his knees with Richard's white hart emblem tactfully embroidered on the breast. The two kings met at a post which had been set up exactly between their tents.They smiled, grasped each other's hands in friendship and kissed. The spectators, mainly made up of unarmed French and English soldiers, dropped to their knees in thanksgiving for what seemed a final settlement between the two countries.

It was Richard's first visit abroad since his childhood, and in the following six weeks he managed to spend £200,000. A chronicler wrote: "Everyday he wore different and more gorgeous clothes, while he gave the King of France gold and crystal cups and collars of pearls." When his child bride was brought to London the citizens were so eager to see her procession that nine persons were trampled to death. Two days later, on January 7, 1397, she was crowned queen.

Meanwhile the king's love of luxury and display had been excited by what he had seen at the French court, and despite an endless financial crisis, he kept his own court as lavish as possible and thronged it with painters, musicians and craftsmen. Richard was also an enthusiastic builder, and his greatest monument is Westminster Hall as we see it today.

The historian Froissart gave the king one of his books and wrote this description of the occasion: "The King desired to see my book that I had brought him: so he saw it in his chamber, for I had laid it there ready on his bed. When the King opened it, it pleased him well, for it was fair enlumined and written, and covered with crimson velvet, with ten buttons of silver and gilt, and roses of gold in the midst, with two great clasps of gilt, richly wrought. Then the King demanded of me whereof it treated, and I showed him how it treated matters of love; whereof the King was glad and looked in it, and read it in many places, for he could speak and read French very well. . ."

* * *

What Richard had observed of the king's position in France had stimulated him in his desire for absolute rule, free from meddling Parliament and bullying nobility, and it is noted that on one occasion he was inspired to sign himself "Full Emperor of England".

He also surrounded himself with a new set of favourites. Almost unbelievably the principal of these was Sir John Holland whom the king had once sworn to hang. Following a pilgrimage to Jerusalem in penance for his crimes, he had been created the Earl of Huntingdon. As before the favourites had immense power, favours and honours passing through their hands, and thus adding to a new wave of popular dislike of the king.

Two weeks after the coronation of little Isabella, the

king summoned Parliament and announced he wanted to help his father-in-law against Lombardy. The Commons demurred, a hatred of France having been in their blood for generations. Richard flew into a rage, shouting he could "order his people to go to the support of his friends, and for that purpose to dispose of his own goods as and when he pleased." It was not "his own goods" which the Commons questioned, but the public goods he was taking. Taxes had been greatly increased, and with them the resentment of the population. Much of this money Richard was using to bribe Gloucester's supporters away from him.

On the other hand Gloucester and Arundel were making capital out of Richard's marriage. In the agreement England surrendered Cherbourg and Brest to France. It was whispered that the king had received a huge secret payment from the King of France in consideration for this. Now the two Lords Appellant added to the general discontent by spreading the rumour that the king was going to hand over Calais. This came into the open at a banquet when, according to the writer Higden, Gloucester quarrelled with Richard and cried out: "Syre, ye oughte first to putte your bodye in devoyre to gete a towne or a castell by fayte or warre upon youre enemys er ye sholde selle or delyver any townes that your predecessors Kynges of Engelonde have goten and conquered."

Richard got the excuse he needed to strike back when he was informed that Gloucester, Arundel and Warwick were plotting against him. On July 10, 1397, the king invited the three to dine with him at Westminster. Arundel wisely retired to his castle at Reigate, Gloucester excused himself as he was ill at Pleshy in Essex, but Warwick accepted the invitation.

The king ate with him and then, when the meal was over and the wine drunk, ordered him to be arrested. No doubt the thought ot how he was going to avenge his earlier humiliations and the treatment of de Vere had made him a charming host.

As soon as Warwick was under escort for the Tower, Richard and a number of his young companions galloped to Pleshy where they hammered at the door of Gloucester's lodgings. The duke came down unarmed and unattended to greet his nephew.

"Fair uncle," Richard said, "by Saint John the Baptist, what has been done will be best for you and me."

Meanwhile a strong detachment had ridden from London to arrest Arundel who, surprisingly, surrendered himself.

Soon afterwards Warwick confessed his guilt and the king exiled him to the Isle of Man. Gloucester was sent to Calais where he was imprisoned to await his trial.

Two months later Parliament was called. As Westminster Hall was partly dismantled at the time the assembly was held out of doors on a large wooden platform. Richard arrived with his private company of 600 Cheshire archers. Although it was illegal for weapons to be taken to Parliament, the archers lined up round the platform and strung their bows. In the proceedings which followed the Commons took the hint.

Arundel was brought on to the stage and charged with treason by John of Gaunt who had remained on friendly terms with Richard. Even Gaunt's son Henry Bolingbroke shouted abuse at Arundel as he spiritedly defended himself. Finally John of Gaunt sentenced the prisoner with these words: "I, seneschal of England, do adjudge you traitor, and I do by sentence and judgement condemn you to be drawn, hanged, beheaded and quartered, and your lands entailed and unentailed to be forfeited."

Richard did have enough mercy left to alter the sentence. Arundel was hurried off to Tower Hill where he met the headsman with a coolness which won him great posthumous acclaim. He tossed his gold to the spectators, tested the edge of the axe and politely asked the executioner to do his work efficiently. The man obliged with one blow.

A mandate was issued by King Richard for his prisoner, the Duke of Gloucester, to be brought from Calais to the bar of the House. Three days later the earl marshal reported that "he could not produce the said duke before the king and his council in that parliament for that, being in his custody in the king's prison at Calais, he there died."

Such a brief announcement of the death of a member of

the blood royal is still as startling today as it was in Richard's, and can only lead to one conclusion — that of murder. Obviously the king had not dared to put on trial a man so close to the crown and with a large following in the country. After Henry Bolingbroke had usurped King Richard's throne, and was anxious to defame his victim, a servant of the Earl of Nottingham, named John Hall, swore that Gloucester had been taken from prison to an inn where he had been smothered between two mattresses by Richard's agents.*

Though eight persons were accused of involvement, not one was examined. Hall, who confessed to his own part in the plot, was immediately beheaded without appearing before a judge.

Although Richard had now taken his revenge he was haunted by Arundel's death. At night it was a recurring nightmare. Then a story began to circulate that the head had miraculously joined on to the body again. This upset the king so much he had the corpse disinterred. It was found that the head had been sewn back into position.

* * *

Apart from bad dreams, Richard had now achieved all he wanted. He rewarded his friends by making them dukes, and there were so many the people called them "dukettes". At the next Parliament, held at Shrewsbury, the country was virtually handed over to the king with a series of articles including one which stated it was treason to renounce homage to the sovereign. The new statues retracted all the liberties which had been won against royal dictatorship over the years. Finally the members voted Richard a permanent income, which made it unnecessary for any further Parliaments to be called.

The powers of Parliament were then delegated to a committee of eighteen lords and six knights, all of whom were Richard's friends. Yet Richard's triumph was short-lived. Just when he was at the peak of his power it suddenly crumbled, almost as if by his own neurotic death wish.

*Froissart claimed that he was strangled in prison by four men using towels.

In Ireland Richard's cousin the Earl of March, still the royal heir, had been killed in a local skirmish. The king took an oath to avenge his death and set about raising an army. Then, in February, 1399, John of Gaunt died and on the same day Richard deprived his absent son, Henry Bolingbroke, of his inheritance and banished him from England for life. In France Henry replied by planning to invade England with Archbishop Arundel who had been exiled when his brother had been beheaded.

For some unknown reason Richard made no plans to meet the threat. Instead he held a feast at Whitsun and bade such an emotional farewell to his little wife that she was ill for two weeks. Then, on May 29, he set out for Ireland, leaving his uncle the Duke of York, one of the few men he still trusted, as regent. It seems he was in a highly nervous state, at one moment full of exaltation and deeply depressed the next. As he was departing a holy hermit gave him a warning from God to lead a better life and bring back those he had exiled. Richard had him arrested, saying: "If you are so familiar with God, go and walk on the water, so that He may know that you are His messenger."

In July the king was in Dublin where he received news Henry Bolingbroke, now Duke of Lancaster, had landed in Yorkshire and was leading his army on Bristol. The Duke of York betrayed Richard and joined Henry, while in London the council of Richard's favourites fled.

Richard called young Henry, the son of Bolingbroke and the future Henry V, who was in his retinue as a hostage.

"See, Henry my son, what your father is doing to me," said the king. "He is riding over my land like an enemy, imprisoning and destroying my subjects without mercy or reverence. Truly, my son, I am sorry for you, for because of this misfortune you may lose your inheritance." The little boy replied that he was sorry too, but that he was innocent in the matter. Richard kindly sent him off to Trim Castle and to his credit did not use him as a weapon against his father.

Richard planned to take his army back to England to fight for his throne but it was decided that the Earl of

Salisbury would go ahead to raise the men of Wales, Richard promising to join him in a week. The earl was successful as both the men of Wales and Cheshire flocked to the royal standard and Salisbury waited impatiently at Conway for the king to join him. Unaccountably Richard did not arrive while the news that the Duke of York had joined Lancaster began to thin down the ranks of royalist troops. The king arrived a fatal fortnight late at Milford Haven where, by the second day, his own army had melted away. Most of the king's companions wisely suggested that he should retire to his French provinces; John Holland urged him to hasten to Conway to join up with Salisbury. He took Holland's advice and, disguised as a Franciscan friar, he left his camp at midnight accompanied by his two half brothers and two attendants.

At Conway he found that Salisbury only had a hundred men loyal to him and they lacked provisions. According to Shakespeare when Richard asked Salisbury where his army was the earl replied:

One day too late, I fear, my noble lord,
Hath clouded all thy happy days on earth.
O, call back yesterday, bid time return,
And thou shalt have twelve thousand fighting men!
To-day, to-day, unhappy day, too late,
O'erthrows thy joys, friends, fortune, and thy state;
For all the Welshmen, hearing thou wert dead,
Are gone to Bolingbroke, dispers'd, and fled.

It seems that at this point Richard realised he had lost and he sent his half brothers to Henry Bolingbroke at Chester to ask what were his intentions. Apart from anything else this gave Bolingbroke the location of the king and he sent the Duke of Northumberland to capture him. When he arrived at Conway with only four attendants he was quickly taken to Richard who appeared to be in a state of nervous tension over the fate of his brothers and their mission. Northumberland told him that they were well at Chester, and he produced a letter written by John Holland stating that the king could put his full confidence in the offer to be made by Northumberland. This was that the king's brothers, the Earl of

Salisbury, the Bishop of Carlisle and the king's chaplain should take their trial for having advised the murder of Gloucester, that Henry Bolingbroke should be made the Justiciar of England and these terms being conceded, Bolingbroke should wait for the king at Flint "to implore his pardon" and accompany him to London.

After consultation with the few followers who remained with him — and secretly assuring those implicated that he would stand by them steadfastly at their trial — Richard agreed, though first he insisted on Northumberland swearing on behalf of Henry Bolingbroke to the strict observance of the articles.

"Like Judas," wrote an old chronicler, "he perjured himself on the body of our Lord." Which means he swore on the Host.

They then set out together and on coming to a corner of the road Richard suddenly exclaimed, "God of Paradise assist me, I am betrayed. Do you not see pens and barriers in the valley? Earl of Northumberland, if I thought you capable of betraying me it is not too late to return."

Seizing Richard's bridle Northumberland said, "You cannot return. I have promised to conduct you to the Duke of Lancaster." At that a body of lancers hastened up and Richard, seeing that any chance of escape had gone, exclaimed, "May the god on whom you laid your hands reward you and your accomplices at this last day."

The king was then taken to Flint Castle where he was left alone for the evening with his friends. Wearing a red gown with a black hood, he met Henry Bolingbroke in the courtyard of Flint Castle the next day. The duke shone in full armour as he knelt before the king and the scene would have delighted all the exponents of chivalry as the enemies con—versed politely.

"Fair cousin of Lancaster you are right welcome," greeted Richard.

Bolingbroke replied, "I am come sooner than you sent for me, the reason I will tell you. The common report of the people is that for two and 20 years you have governed them badly and most harshly, and therefore they are not well contented with you but if it please our Lord, I will help you govern them better than they have been governed in time past."

"Fair cousin," replied Richard, "if it pleases you it pleases us well."

A fortnight later Richard was escorted to the Tower through the streets of London where the citizens greeted him with jeers of "Bastard". Character assassination was already at work.* Meanwhile the little queen was sent to Leeds Castle in Kent, her French companions and servants being banished so that there could be no communication with the imprisoned king.

"And in all this the Londoners rejoiced," wrote Froissart, "only they were discontented that Richard was kept out of their sight and reach for behold the opinion of the common people when they be up against their prince or lord, and especially in England. Among them is no remedy, for they are the most dangerous people in the world, and most outrageous, if they be up, and especially Londoners."

On September 29, 1399, representatives of the Lords and Commons — prelates, barons, knights and lawyers — visited Richard in the Tower for his official abdication and to sign a document naming Henry Bolingbroke as his successor. After complying he said he hoped "his cousin would be a good lord to him."

It is recorded that Richard was quite cheerful at the ceremony and at its conclusion slipped his royal signet ring on Bolingbroke's finger, though it must be remembered that history is written by the victors.

The act of resignation was read to Parliament and accepted with shouts of delight. It has been pointed out that if Richard had thus voluntarily abdicated there would have been no necessity for what immediately followed — a series of thirty-three articles of impeachment. The chief charges were violation of his coronation oath, the murder of the Duke of Gloucester and his despotic and unconstitutional conduct.

*Froissart relates that while Richard spoke with Henry Bolingbroke at Flint his favourite greyhound Mathe, which would never take notice of anyone else, suddenly left Richard's side and fawned upon Bolingbroke and ever afterwards followed him.

Next day Henry Bolingbroke became King Henry IV of England and the Council ordered Richard to be placed in a secret prison where he was to be served by people who did not know him and where he could not receive or send letters. Dressed as a forester but stubbornly wearing the golden spurs of a knight he was taken first to Leeds Castle and then, as in the case of Edward II, to various other prisons.

When Richard was in the Tower of London Adam of Usk visited him and wrote: "I was present while he dined and I marked his mood and bearing having been taken thither for that purpose. And there and then the king discoursed sorrowfully these words: 'My God, a wonderful land is this and a fickle: which has exiled, slain, destroyed and ruined so many kings, rulers and great men, and is ever tainted with strife and variance and envy.' "

Now the mystery surrounding Richard's end deepens. While he was imprisoned Charles VI of France threatened to make war on England on behalf of the rights of his daughter Isabella. To try to avert this threat Henry IV suggested various alliances between the royal families but the French king replied that he knew no king of England but Richard. Then he received news that Richard had died and he simply demanded that his daughter should be restored to him with her jewels and dowry according to the marriage settlement. But from that moment, when news of Richard's death was made public by Charles VI, popular interest grew as to his fate.

Soon afterwards the corpse of the deposed monarch was brought, at a cost of £80, from Pontefract Castle and shown publicly in St Paul's for two days where 20,000 people filed past the coffin to see Richard's emaciated face, the rest of the body being covered by a shroud. It was then taken to Langley but thirteen years later it was buried with pomp in Westminster Abbey. The dead king's little queen went back to France where she later married Charles, the poet duke of Orleans, to die in childbirth at the age of twenty.

All we know definitely is that in January, 1400, Richard's half brothers the Hollands plotted to assassinate the new king but were caught and executed. The news of this was said to throw Richard into a state of melancholia while Henry said publicly at table "Richard's life was his death and his death his life." On January 29 the King of France spoke of him as being already dead, and a report circulated that Richard had been so grief-stricken he had starved himself to death.

There is no doubt that he was murdered and tradition states this took place on St Valentine's Day when the ex-king was seated at dinner in his cell. Sir Piers Exton with seven other men grimly entered and Richard guessed by their numbers and expression their purpose and leaping up he seized a stool to defend himself. It was said that he felled three of them but Exton got behind him, knocked him down and then slew him.

Probably the reason that we know so little about his murder is that his death caused no regret. It was written of him "that only the men of Bordeaux mourned for him for he had ever been a good lord to them."

CHAPTER SIX

The Murder of Henry VI

"Forsothe and forsothe ye do fouly to smyte a kynge anoynted so."

HENRY VI SHOULD have been pictured with a halo rather than a crown. If Henry VII, the first Tudor monarch, had lived longer it is almost certain that his efforts to get his predecessor canonised would have been rewarded, though it must be added that these endeavours were not so much to honour a holy king as to discredit Richard III, whom he had usurped, by the suggestion that he was the murderer of a saint.

One thing that the tortuous medieval mind had in common with the Roman was its untiring quest for reassuring portents and holy signs. Thus there was great satisfaction for those who managed to extract significance from the most trivial incidents when the baby Henry, already a king, made his public debut for the opening of Parliament. When he was brought out before his subjects he "schriked and cryed" so much that his mother hastened him indoors in case he "had been diseased". But the next day — a Monday — his behaviour was impeccable as he sat on the queen's lap while being borne through the tumultuous crowds. Then it was realised that the little fellow had been distressed the day before because of breaking the Sabbath.

Those responsible for his upbringing were determined that the child should not deviate from such an auspicious start, even if they had to be harsh to be kind. His nurse Alice Botillor was given an indemnity which was noted in the proceedings of the Privy Council, being permitted "to chasten us from time to time as the case shall require, so that you shall not be molested, hurt, or injured for this cause in future time."

Another guardian who required a guarantee against royal retribution was Richard Beauchamp, Earl of Warwick, who later asked the boy-king's uncle, the Duke of Gloucester, and the Council to "assure him they shall firmly and truly assist him in the exercise of the charge and occupation that he hath about the King's person, namely, in chastening him of his defaults, and support the said earl therein; and if the King at any time will conceive for that cause indignation against the said earl, my said Lord of Gloucester and lords shall do all their true diligence and power to remove the King therefrom."

The effect of chastening the youth of his "defaults" coupled with his naturally pious nature, produced a king who was to be both venerated and despised but who in his darkest hours never lost his spiritual faith, remarking once in the midst of his troubles, "For this kingdom which is transitory I do not greatly care — our kinsman of March thrusts himself into it as is his pleasure."

John Blakman, a fellow of Eton and king's confessor, left us this pen portrait: "The King was a man simple and upright, without any crook or craft of untruth. With none did he deal craftily nor ever would say an untrue word to any. With sedulous devotion he was a diligent worshipper of God, more given to prayer or the reading of scriptures or chronicles than to temporal things or vain sports. These he despised as trifling. In church he was never pleased to sit upon a seat or walk to and fro, but always with bared head kneeled before his book. When riding on a journey he would let his royal cap drop to the ground, and he preferred the Holy Cross to be set in his crown rather than flowers . . . He was chaste and pure from the beginning of his days, in word and deed. With the Queen he kept his marriage vows sincerely, even in the absences of that lady which were sometimes very long, and he made a covenant with his eyes never to look unchastely upon any woman. It happened once at Christmas time that a certain great lord brought before him a dance or show of young ladies with bared bosoms who were to dance in that guise before the King. But he angrily averted his eyes and went out to his chamber saying, 'Fy, fy for shame, forsothe ye be to blame.' At another time riding by Bath where are warm baths, the King saw in them men wholly naked with every garment cast off; at which he was displeased and went away quickly. He took great precautions to secure not only his own chastity but also that of his servants. For he kept careful watch through hidden windows of his chambers lest any woman should cause the fall of any of his household."

From this description it can be seen how untypical the king was of his Plantagenet forebears who gave their names to spectacular conquests or equally spectacular defeats, men with lusty appetites for power and the flesh who believed the blood of a devil was in their veins. Henry's father will be remembered, as long as history books are printed, for the victory of Agincourt; Henry's monument is King's College, Cambridge, and Eton College.

Against the Fifteenth Century background of intrigue, ruthless ambition and blood feud he appears as one born out of his time — a predestined victim.

* * *

The son of heroic Henry V and Catherine of Valois, Henry was born on December 6, 1421, at Windsor. Nine months later he was proclaimed King of England on the death of his father, and two months after that the death of his grandfather Charles VI of France made him sovereign of that country under the Treaty of Troyes.

Henry was crowned at Westminster — "where he beheld the people sadly and wisely with humility and devotion" — in November, 1429, the year that Joan of Arc's army forced the English to raise the siege at Orleans. The following year the young king was taken to Rouen where, it was said, he attended the trial of The Maid. In December of that year the Plantagenet dream came true when Henry was crowned at Notre Dame in Paris. By all accounts the ceremony was a disaster, the king's French grandmother stayed away, as did the nobility; the Archbishop of Paris took umbrage at the officiating English bishops and there was no public celebration — not even a Lollard was burned at the stake. Henry was hustled home to his friendlier kingdom, never to venture from its shores again.

129

Ironically the realisation of the Plantagenet ambition heralded the collapse of English influence on the Continent. Apart from Calais, Normandy and the other territories which Henry V had wrested from the French were lost by 1453.

On his sixteenth birthday Henry became king in effect though he did very little ruling; his main occupation seems to have been the giving away of charters and pardons. His Council frequently complained of his unworldly generosity, on one occasion pointing out that he had freely bestowed a stewardship on someone when the going rate for this office was a thousand marks. For a medieval monarch his indifference to money was extraordinary. When his uncle Cardinal Beaufort bequeathed him two thousand pounds he refused to accept the legacy at first, explaining to the bewildered executors that the cardinal had been so good to him when he had been alive that he felt he could take nothing more from him posthumously. It was only after it was suggested that the money could be spent on Eton and King's Colleges that Henry changed his mind. No wonder his contemporaries, regarding royal greed as part of the natural order of things, suspected insanity and darkly reminded each other that both of the king's grandfathers, Henry IV of England and Charles VI of France, had suffered mental and physical infirmities. Henry IV was subject to fits and "an itching of the flesh, a drying up of the eyes and a rupture of the intestines with such a growth of lice on his head that he could not have it uncovered" — Charles of France had been known as "The Foolish", and had died insane.

Apart from his devotions and charitable works the king had to act as a peacemaker between his uncle Humphrey, Duke of Gloucester, and Cardinal Beaufort, a descendant of John of Gaunt, in their contest to control the kingdom. The basic difference between the Gloucester and Beaufort factions was that the former was dedicated to continuing the war across the Channel while the latter wanted to end what they saw as a hopeless conflict, and planned to do so by arranging a political marriage for the king. This would have the added advantage for Beaufort's Lancastrian party in that as soon as Henry had an heir it would put his uncle Gloucester and the

Duke of York, his second cousin, out of the immediate succession.

The viciousness of this power struggle became apparent when Gloucester's wife Eleanor was accused of practising black magic, a charge which was engineered by the Beaufort family. The terrified lady sought sanctuary in Westminster Abbey but was turned away — the Church had little sympathy for witches but presumably a lot for the cardinal.

At the trial it was stated that Eleanor had carved an image of the king out of wax and had then melted it. Gloucester was too afraid to defend her, knowing that he was the real target of the Beauforts who hoped to implicate him in the most heinous of medieval crimes.

Eleanor was found guilty and condemned to life imprisonment after having been made to do a barefoot walk of penance through the streets of London carrying a lighted taper. Her two accomplices did not receive such merciful sentences; the man was hanged, drawn and quartered and the woman burnt alive.

Following this attack on Gloucester, the Lancastrians were able to proceed with the plan to get a suitable bride for the king. Henry was certainly eager to marry. Although prudish, he saw nothing wrong with sex provided it was lawful, and he went to great pains to ensure that the appearance of his future wife would be up to his requirements. When it was thought that one of the Count of Armagnac's three daughters might be appropriate, he asked for a portrait of each of the sisters and ordered the artist to "portray the three daughters in their kirtles simple, and their visages, like as ye see, their stature and their beauty and colour of skin and their countenances, with all manner of features; and that one be delivered in all haste with the said portrait to bring it unto the King, and he to appoint and assign which him liketh." Perhaps the painter was too honest, for nothing came of this.

In 1443 William de la Pole, Earl of Suffolk — and a prominent member of the Lancastrian "peace" party — went to France to negotiate the marriage of Henry and Margaret, the daughter of the cultured but impecunious Duke Rene of

Anjou, titular King of Sicily. Cardinal Beaufort believed that the political connotation of this alliance would halt the Hundred Years' War and at the same time preserve English territory in Calais, Normandy and Guyenne. Inevitably Gloucester, who led the Yorkist party, opposed the match with Margaret of Anjou and it was only natural that when the new queen arrived in England she should favour the Lancastrians, and influence her royal husband to do likewise. Rumours were soon to spread — enthusiastically encouraged by the Yorkists and later perpetuated by Shakespeare — that before she crossed the Channel this spirited princess had fallen in love with Suffolk who, despite the fact he was three times her age, was a paragon of chivalry with all its virtues and vices.

Whatever the truth of the gossip, which seems to have been heard by everyone in England except Henry, a powerful political bond was to remain between the two until it was severed by a rusty sword.

It was told that Henry fell in love with Margaret's portrait before he saw her, and the artist must have presented an accurate likeness because the king was in no way disappointed when they met and remained in love with her until his murder twenty-six years later. Nor did her lack of a dowry worry him despite his never-ending financial difficulties which were largely attributable to his altruistic attitude to money. Margaret of Anjou was so poor that after the vessel carrying her was beached in a gale at Porchester she had to pawn "divers vessels of mock silver" to pay the crew. The marriage took place at Titchfield Abbey on April 23, 1445, and when she arrived in London her new subjects, anxious for the stability of a direct heir and captivated by her beauty, enthusiastically greeted her with marguerite daisies in their caps. Had they known that Suffolk had secretly agreed to return the hard won territories of Anjou and Maine to Duke Rene as the brideprice they would have been crying for blood.

After the queen was crowned in Westminster Abbey on May 30, the sixteen-years-old girl was soon aware of the court intrigue which surrounded her saintly and unsuspecting husband. The Duke of Gloucester discovered Suffolk's secret pact with Margaret's father, and because of this and the threat he posed to Cardinal Beaufort and the Lancastrian faction, the queen regarded him as her arch-enemy. She set to work to impress Henry that his new-found happiness was endangered by the machinations of his uncle Gloucester. This frightening thought made him take an uncharacteristic action which led to the first death in the dynastic struggle first known as the Cousins' War. This name reflected the fact that Edward III had left eleven children to dispute the succession; later the conflict was referred to as the Wars of the Roses.

Aware that Gloucester's greatest support lay in London, the king arranged for a Parliament to be held in February, 1447, at Bury St Edmunds which was loyal to Suffolk and the Lancastrian party. On the second day a messenger arrived at Gloucester's quarters with a request that he present himself before the king. It appeared to be such a routine summons that the duke immediately set off without bothering to buckle on his sword belt, but as he entered the royal chamber he must have immediately sensed the ominous atmosphere.

One can easily imagine the scene: the king grim-faced and silent; beside him Queen Margaret, her lips giving a hint of her satisfaction, while Suffolk, standing close to his royal master and mistress, does nothing to hide his expression of triumph.

Even before Gloucester made his formal greeting Suffolk's voice rang out, accusing him of slandering the queen and plotting against his liege lord. Realising the danger of his position, Gloucester immediately began to declare his innocence. Having refuted the charges, he approached the king's dais and asked Henry if he did not remember how he had looked after him when he was a child.

Henry remained silent and Margaret answered for him, "The king knows your merits, my lord."

At a pre-arranged signal guards stepped forward, surrounded the duke and escorted him to his quarters where he was kept under strict house arrest. Three days later he was dead.

We do not know how he died, and if it was murder who

was responsible. It seems unlikely that pious Henry VI would have been involved in an assassination plot, and some modern historians believe it possible that the duke might have died of a stroke brought on by indignation at his treatment. Holinshed wrote: "Some judged him (the Duke of Gloucester) to be strangled, some affirmed that a hot spit was put in at his fundament, others wrote that he was smouldered (smothered) between two feather beds, and some have affirmed that he died of very grief."

The body was displayed publicly to demonstrate that no violence had been done to it, but this did nothing to allay the suspicion that Queen Margaret and Suffolk had plotted the duke's murder — there were any number of ways a prisoner could be killed without his corpse being marked. To the people Gloucester became a posthumous hero and King Henry must have been dismayed at the dislike so many of his subjects felt for his beloved young wife, a feeling which intensified when the embarrassing terms of the marriage settlement became known.

To add to Henry's problems Cardinal Beaufort died two months after Gloucester. This gave Suffolk full control of the Lancastrian party but such was the resentment against him that he demanded an opportunity to defend himself before the Council. Though officially vindicated after he had presented his case, the move did nothing to appease popular indignation. And although the Lancastrians no longer needed to fear Gloucester, there was still the Duke of York, who was now heir to the crown should the king die without issue. To remove him from the sphere of influence Suffolk arranged for him to be made Lieutenant of Ireland, a strategem which kindled "a torch of rage" in the duke's breast. Even so, Suffolk could not halt the tide which was running against himself and the queen.

In March, 1449, Charles VII of France renewed his campaign against the English by invading Normandy with new and devastating artillery trains. It meant the collapse of Suffolk's peace policy and to add insult to injury Duke Rene, father of the queen on whom the policy had been based, rode beside the French king. One by one the cities held by his son-in-law fell . . . Evereux, Lisieux, Mantes, Louviers, Gourney and finally Rouen.

As the news reaching King Henry from across the Channel became gloomier and gloomier, the Yorkists seized the opportunity to attack Queen Margaret in a statement which claimed that "the king was fitter for a cloister than a throne, and had, in a manner, deposed himself by leaving the affairs of his kingdom in the hands of a woman, who merely used her name to conceal her usurption since, according to the laws of England, a queen consort hath no power but title only."

The hostility against Margaret was dramatically demonstrated in January, 1450, when the Lord Privy Seal, Bishop Moleyns of Chichester, was murdered in Portsmouth by the very soldiers and sailors he had gone to pay. His "crime" was that he had assisted in arranging the royal match. But it was Suffolk who received the most universal opprobrium; men declared that his policies had lost English territory which had been so hardly won by the king's glorious father, and this "lover of the French" must atone for his scheming. On January 26, 1450, Parliament impeached him and he was imprisoned in the Tower of London.

The king managed to get the hearing postponed until March but then Parliament introduced a Bill of Attainder in which Suffolk was accused of giving aid to France, misappropriating funds from the royal treasury and plotting to put his son on the throne. Henry saved him from execution by summarily banishing him for five years, but the citizens of London were so outraged by the king's lenient treatment of the duke, whom they dubbed "Jackanapes", that they tried to take the law into their own hands. Suffolk managed to escape being lynched by leaving his house in St Giles through a rear exit; minutes later the mob broke in and ill-treated his servants.

On April 30 he left Ipswich for Flanders, but in the Channel his ship was overhauled by a Yorkist vessel, the *Nicholas of the Tower,* and the duke was taken aboard as a captive. After a mock trial he was placed in an open boat in which a block had already been set. An Irish sailor, "the lewdest of the ship, bade him lay down his head . . . and took a rusty sword and smote off his head within half-a-dozen strokes, and took away his gown of russet and his doublet of velvet mailed."

The boat then landed on the shore of Dover where the body was unceremoniously thrown on the sand while the head was fixed upon a stake.

When the news of the murder reached Queen Margaret she locked herself in her apartments and, refusing food and solace from her ladies-in-waiting, abandoned herself to her grief. When she emerged three days later all could see that she was a changed woman. There was a new air of determination about her, determination to avenge the man who had played such an important role in her life and determination that her husband should be preserved from his enemies.

Five months later she and Henry discovered that it was not just the Yorkists, who had engineered the death of the favourite, that they had to fear; following the Feast of Pentecost for 1450 the followers of the enigmatic rebel Jack Cade began their march on London. The identity of Cade, who was also known as John Amend-all, still remains a mystery, but he was certainly a gentleman and one of great organising ability. The men of Kent who followed him were not peasants such as had swarmed after Wat Tyler but were squires, farmers and artisans who passionately believed in Cade's succinct demands. These centred round the belief that King Henry should take back the crown lands which he had so freely bestowed on his friends so that their revenues would lighten the tax burden. Cade's manifesto *The Requests of the Captain of the Great Assembly in Kent* also complained that the people of Kent had been extortioned by tax-gatherers and that justice was not impartial. There were demands that those responsible for the loss of English possessions abroad and for mis-government at home should be punished, and that the Duke of York should be recalled from Ireland which suggested that there had been a Yorkist hand in the penning of *The Requests of the Captain.*

Troops under the command of Sir Humphrey Stafford were sent against the insurgents when they assembled at

*Choosing the emblems
~~ch~~ gave the name to the
~~s~~ of the Roses*

*Henry VI as a youth,
~~c~~opy of an illustration in
~~L~~dgate's 'Life of St Ed-
~~m~~nd'*

28 A manuscript illustration of the tradition that King John unwittingly accepted a poisoned drink from a monk

29   Henry VI, drawn from
an Eton College portrait

30 Margaret of A
jou from an engra
ing by Henry Co
burn

31 Queen Margar
mocks the severe
head of the Duke
York.

Blackheath, and when they retreated to Sevenoaks Sir Humphrey followed too swiftly with the result that he only had part of his force when the rebels suddenly turned and attacked him. He was slain in the rout and Jack Cade buckled on his armour before returning to Blackheath in triumph. One effect of the victory was to make the royal troops, who were loyal to the person of the king but not necessarily to the Lancastrian party, question why their comrades had fallen to fellow Englishmen, and soon it seemed that they were becoming dangerously sympathetic to John Amend-all and his demands for reform. Henry hastily disbanded them and retired to Kenilworth while a more reliable army could be assembled.

Cade now took possession of Southwark and on July 2 he led his men over London bridge into the city which, fearful of the rebels' threats to burn it down, offered no resistance. At first Cade managed to maintain strict discipline among his followers, leading them back to Southwark at nightfall. The next day he returned and Lord Say, the Lord Treasurer, and his son-in-law Cromer, the sheriff of Kent, were executed and their decapitated bodies dragged through the streets while their heads were paraded on poles. Many Londoners had been sympathetic to Cade's cause, but this changed on the third day when Cade robbed the house of an alderman — an act which was to ruin his cause.

It seemed an uncharacteristic action — though it appears he only took some jewels belonging to the Duke of York which the alderman held in pawn — but he needed money to buy supplies for his men in order to prevent them foraging for themselves. The robbery made the citizens nervous; and when it was followed by some pillaging, they decided to seize London Bridge on the night of July 4. At ten o'clock they marched on to it and, backed up by soldiers from the Tower, stood their ground when Cade attacked it from Southwark.

A savage battle was fought in the narrow space between the houses and shops which lined either side of the bridge; fire began to sweep through these wooden structures but the conflict continued amidst the smoke and flame until, according to one chronicler, "some desiring to eschew the fire leaped on his enemy's weapon, and so died; fearful women with children in their arms, amazed and appalled, leaped for fear into the river."

By morning the rebels drew off, painfully aware that the Londoners had done the king's work for him. When the Chancellor, Cardinal Kemp, offered Cade and his men a general pardon at St Margaret's church in Southwark, they accepted it with relief and dispersed. Soon Cade, no doubt uncomfortably remembering the fate of Wat Tyler's followers, repented his credulity. With his hardcore companions he unsuccessfully attacked Queensborough Castle; as a result he was attainted and his pardon declared invalid on a technicality. His hopes of raising a fresh army at Rochester came to nothing and he fled on horseback. He was finally discovered hiding in a garden in Kent and after a brave fight was slain by a country gentleman named Alexander Iden, after which his head was parboiled and placed over the Drawbridge Tower of London Bridge.

With the rebellion over Henry and Margaret sought a champion to replace the murdered Suffolk, and they found one in Edmund, the second Duke of Somerset and a nephew of the late Lancastrian leader Cardinal Beaufort. He had been the ineffectual commander of the English forces in France and the public were stunned when this man, who was held responsible for England's defeats across the Channel, was made Constable of England, commander-in-chief of the army in the absence of the king and Supreme Judge in the Court of Chivalry. Popular feeling was expressed by giving a hero's welcome to York who crossed the Irish Sea and hurried to London to confront Henry.

"The great rumour that is universally in this your realm is that justice is not duly ministered," he declared and added that he would assist the king to reform the kingdom. Henry's reply was to promise him a larger share in the government, after which York went to Fotheringay Castle to await the forthcoming assembling of Parliament.

According to tradition it was at this stage that the contesting factions took roses as their symbols. Somerset met the Earl of Warwick in the Temple Gardens by the Thames, and soon angry words were exchanged during which the duke plucked a red rose, whereupon Warwick picked a white one. Their companions followed the example so that the flowers became party badges, the red rose for the House of Lancaster and the white for York.

By the end of the year political tension electrified the atmosphere of the capital; armed men emboldened by the party emblems they wore swaggered in the taverns loyal to their factions, the Dukes of York and Norfolk paraded through the city with three thousand followers at their backs, a mob pillaged the houses of Somerset and his supporters, and the Lord Mayor ordered the narrow thoroughfares to be fenced across with chains to deter running crowds of rioters.

When Parliament convened in January, 1451, the powerful Yorkist party had a bill passed to attaint the memory of Suffolk — how this posthumous insult must have enraged Queen Margaret. Another bill called for the removal from about the person of the king of the Duke of Somerset, the widowed Duchess of Suffolk and thirty members of the Lancastrian court party. King Henry agreed only to the exile of some of the minor people named, and was adamant that Somerset should remain.

In May, in one of his moments of misjudgement, York persuaded a Bristol representative named Young to move that as the king was childless the duke should be officially declared heir apparent. The Yorkist majority in the Commons cheered the proposal, but the Lords rejected it as they had no wish to see York as their master. Following this Henry dissolved Parliament and Young was imprisoned in the Tower.

For the remainder of the year the situation appeared to be one of stalemate; Somerset remained in power while York brooded in the country, yet throughout the kingdom there was a sense of impending conflict which was made more bitter by the news from the Continent of more English fortresses falling to the French. In the following February York yielded to the ever increasing pressure for positive action and issued this manifesto: "I, after long sufferance and delays, though it is not my will or intent to displease my sovereign lord, seeing that the said Duke (Somerset) ever prevaileth and ruleth about the King's person, and that by this means the land is likely to be destroyed, am fully concluded to proceed in all haste against him with the help of my kinsman and friends . . . to promote ease, peace, tranquillity and the safeguard of all this land, keeping me within the bounds of my liegance."

When Henry heard that York was advancing on London with an army of over ten thousand men, he acted with unusual determination — probably inspired by his beloved queen — and marched to meet him. This positive response unnerved the duke who was not yet psychologically prepared to make war on his anointed sovereign; to him the enemy was Somerset. Therefore he bypassed the royal army by crossing the Thames at Kingston and made for Kent where he hoped to be reinforced by the old followers of Jack Cade. In this he was disappointed, and when he learned that Henry's army was approaching his camp at Dartford he agreed to meet the Bishops of Ely and Winchester who acted as envoys for the king.

Having explained that he had not taken up arms out of disloyalty to the crown but to protect himself from his enemies, York went on to demand that all persons "noised or indicted of treason" should be brought to trial. This was promised, and as Somerset was the chief person on the treason list, the duke was told that the king had given the order for his committal, and that a new Council would be summoned in which the duke would be included.

Forgetful of even recent history, York declared that he was well satisfied and would comply with the request to dismiss his forces. When this was done he arrived bareheaded at the king's pavilion. What happened next was out of keeping with Henry's honourable character; it savoured more of Queen Margaret.

No sooner had he bowed to the king and launched into a tirade against his enemies than a curtain behind the king was pulled aside and Somerset stepped forward, challenging the duke to mortal combat. Furious at allowing himself to be betrayed so easily, York turned to leave but was told that he was now a prisoner. Somerset urged the king to have him tried and executed immediately, but Henry had a pious horror of bloodshed and allowed him to be freed after he had taken an oath at St Paul's that he would not raise a force without the king's permission. The defeated duke then retired to his castle at Wigmore.

The threat of civil war had turned into a triumph for the Lancastrians and the king, who underlined it by making a progress to the West Country and through the Welsh Marches. In each town the citizens who had supported York begged for mercy with symbolic nooses round their necks, and true to form Henry bestowed pardons upon them. Once the royal procession moved on Somerset saw to it that their halters were put to practical use.

* * *

In 1453 the Hundred Years' War came to an end when the French slew Lord Shrewsbury, England's last military hope, in Gascony; now all that remained of Henry V's conquests was Calais. Then, in August, the king mysteriously lost his reason; according to one chronicle "by a sudden and terrible fear he fell into such infirmity that he had neither natural feeling, nor sense of reason nor understanding, nor could any physician or medicine cure him." When Queen Margaret gave birth to a child on October 13, the poor king merely stared at his son vacantly.

The birth of Prince Edward may have ended York's chances of ever succeeding to the throne but it increased his chances of gaining power in another direction.

As the king's oldest adult relation York now could see himself in control of the kingdom as regent for the next sixteen years but, as he was mistrusted by the House of Lords, he had to be content with the title of Protector and Defender of the Realm. Nevertheless the White Rose was in the ascent.

At a Council meeting held in November York's ally the Duke of Norfolk demanded that Somerset be impeached for "the loss of two so noble duchies as Normandy and Guienne" and for corruption, with the result that he was sent to the Tower.

141

At Christmas, 1415, the game of power took a dramatic and unexpected turn — King Henry regained his senses. According to the Paston Letters, "On Monday afternoon the Queen came to see him and brought my Lord Prince with her. And then he asked what the Prince's name was, and the Queen told him Edward; and then he held up his hands and thanked God therefor. And then he said he never knew til that tyme nor wist not what was said to him, nor wist not where he had be while he hath be seke til now. And my Lord of Winchester was with him on the morrow after Tweltheday and he spake as well as ever he did. And he saith he is in charitee with all the world, and so he would all the Lords were."

Although he was still weak from his illness, Queen Margaret hurried Henry to Westminster where he dissolved Parliament and ordered the release of Somerset. Having lost the protectorship the Duke of York, bitterly aware that he was now further from power than before, retired to his castle at Sandal. Here the Duke of Norfolk, the Earl of Salisbury and his son the Earl of Warwick, soon to be known as the King-Maker, hurried to join him. It was soon agreed that the only hope for the Yorkist cause lay in open war. The nobles dispersed to recruit their forces, meanwhile the piously optimistic Henry planned a Council meeting at Leicester to debate ways of promoting conciliation between Somerset and York. Alas for Henry's good intentions — before the meeting could take place news reached him that Warwick had joined up with York and Salisbury on their march from the north, and by May 20 they were at Royston with three thousand troops.

Next day the king led a force of less than two thousand to Watford where the men slept briefly before marching through the dawn to St Albans. Here they took up positions in St Peter's Street while the Yorkist army stood within bow shot to the south-east. The Duke of Buckingham was sent to York to ask "the cause for which he had come there with so many men."

He replied that they had come as true subjects wanting their king to deliver to them "such as we will accuse."

This reply enraged the usually mild Henry.

"I, King Henry, charge and command that no manner of person, of what degree, or state, or condition that ever he be, abide not but void the field and be not so hard as to make any resistance against me in mine own realm, for I shall know what traitor dare be so bold to raise a people in mine own land . . . And by the faith I owe to St Edward and to the crown of England, I shall destroy them every mother's son; and they shall be hanged and drawn and quartered that may be taken afterward, of them to have example to all such traitors to beware to make any such rising of people within my land, and so traitorly to abide their King and governor. And for a conclusion, rather than they shall have any lord here with me at this time, I shall this day for their sake and in this quarrel myself live and die!"

Queen Margaret must have felt a brief moment of pride in him.

Soon afterwards the royal standard was unfurled, signifying that the king was now at war and any Englishmen who opposed him were guilty of treason. Yorkist banners fluttered a vivid reply and the first battle in the Wars of the Roses began.

* * *

The royal army had a good defensive position but the Yorkists attacked with inspired desperation — now that they were officially traitors they knew that if they lost all they could expect would be the horrors of disembowelling and castration, their estates would be seized by their rivals and their families disinherited. The Duke of York attacked the barricades at the town entrance while Warwick led his men through some gardens and made a surprise attack on the royal troops. As the cry "A Warwick! A Warwick!" echoed through the narrow streets York redoubled his efforts and forced an entrance creating confusion among the defenders.

Abbot Whethamstede, who gazed down on the battle from the top of the abbey tower, wrote: "Here you saw one fall with his brains dashed out, here another with a broken arm, a third with a cut throat, and a fourth with a pierced chest, and the whole street was full of dead corpses. Four of those who were the King's bodyguard were killed by arrows, and the King himself was struck by an arrow in the shoulder."

As the royal troops faltered and then began to flee between the houses and through the gardens Henry's remaining bodyguard hustled him into a tanner's house while Somerset and some of his retainers sheltered in the Castle Inn. When Yorkist men-at-arms began to hammer on its doors the duke rushed into the street at the head of his men. As he gazed wildly round the scene of defeat his heart must have faltered when he saw the inn sign above his head, for a soothsayer had predicted that he would die beneath a castle. And die he did, though he slew four of his enemies before being struck down by a battleaxe.

Soon afterwards Henry was found by York, Salisbury and Warwick.

"God be praised, Sire, the traitor Somerset is dead!" said York as he went on his knees. He then asked pardon for having imperilled the king's person and declared that he had taken up arms only against the false ministers who had surrounded him.

Despite the agony of the defeat, Henry was mindful of his subjects and as the Yorkist troops began to sack St Albans he asked his fawning captors "to cease their people and that there should be no more harm done."

* * *

Henry was taken to London where he had no option but to summon a Yorkist Parliament, but the shock of his defeat and the arrow wound brought the return of his malady and in July, 1455, he was once more shut away from public sight, this time at Hertford Castle where Queen Margaret had custody of him and little Prince Edward.

The Duke of York was declared Constable of England, and Parliament censured the queen, declaring "that the government, as it was managed by the queen, the duke of Somerset, and their friends, had been of late a great oppression and injustice to the people."

Just when it seemed that York had achieved all that

he had schemed for, his triumph was snatched away from him. Once again King Henry recovered his sanity and on February 24, 1456, he made a surprise visit to Westminster where he told Parliament "that being now recovered by the blessing of God, he did not think his kingdom was in any need of a protector, and requested permission to resume the reins of empire." York was not there to rally his party and the members could think of nothing to do other than meekly acquiesce to the royal request.

In the moves which followed Henry was a pawn rather than a king, while Margaret assumed the role of the queen on a chessboard. The saintly Henry did not seek revenge on those who had fought against him, rather he worked for the reconciliation of the factions whose hatred of each other had been tempered by the blood-letting at St Albans. To avert further violence the king summoned the Council to meet in London at the beginning of 1458 to try and find a solution to the "variancies as be betwixt divers lords of this our realm."

The "divers lords" came each with a private army and such was the tension between the Red Rose and the White that the Lord Mayor had four thousand armed citizens on patrol at night, and a thousand more than that during the day, to ensure that London did not become a battleground. Despite the inauspicious start Henry persevered, and a token peace was reached when it was agreed that the Duke of York and the Earls of Salisbury and Warwick should found a chantry at St Albans where masses would be sung for the repose of the slain, that York would pay five thousand marks to the widowed Duchess of Somerset and the Earl of Warwick would pay a thousand to Lord Clifford as compensation for the death of his father in the battle.

This agreement was celebrated on March 25 when the king led a procession of Lancastrians and Yorkists to St Paul's, the lords of the opposing parties walking side by side, and followed by Queen Margaret on the arm of York. To see such bitter foes thus united made the spectators marvel at the king's victory as a peacemaker, but it was a hollow victory. After the nobles returned to their estates the spirit of detente evaporated and the old intriguing was resumed. Deep in the tangle of plot and counterplot was the queen, determined as ever to destroy the Yorkist party, to avenge past injuries and to ensure that the throne of England would be secure for her son. And she knew that the only way to eradicate the White Rose was by the sword.

By spring of 1459 the queen had a warrant issued for Warwick's arrest and once more the country was heading for civil war. Both sides mustered troops, and on October 13 the Yorkist forces faced a royal army of superior numbers across the River Teme at Ludford, near Ludlow. Queen Margaret had assembled an army of over thirty thousand, and it was written that some of her troops had been enlisted "for the love they bore to the King, but more for the fear they had to the Queen, whose countenance was so fearful and whose look was so terrible that to all men against whom she took small displeasure her frowning was their undoing and her indignation was their death."

The main strength of the Yorkists, who were commanded by York, Salisbury and Warwick, was several batteries of cannon. In order to encourage his men, who were dispirited by the size of the Lancastrian army, the duke announced that King Henry had died and had an outdoor mass sung for him. But across the river King Henry was far from dead and behaving in a typical way by offering pardons to his enemies if they would lay down their arms. And it was such a promise that brought him an almost bloodless victory.

The new Duke of Somerset managed to get a letter to Sir Andrew Trollop, marshal of the Yorkist army, in which he reproached him for waging war against his soverign lord and added that if he and his followers "wished to return to serve the King, he would pardon everything and give them great rewards." Sir Andrew democratically discussed the offer with the six hundred men he had brought from Calais with the result that when night fell they crossed over to the royal lines. This defection demoralised the rest of the troops, and they too melted away.

When the sun rose all that remained of the Yorkists was their banners fluttering over a deserted field.

The Duke of York fled to Ireland, his eldest son Edward, Earl of March, escaped to Calais in company with Salisbury and Warwick. But fortune was to be as fickle with the Red Rose as the White. On July 10 the next year a Yorkist army was once more arrayed against the king outside Northampton, and ironically it was a defector which brought defeat to the royal forces. The half-hour battle began at two o'clock in the afternoon. Rain had been falling with the result that the king's cannon would not fire, and as the Yorkists reached a flooded trench Lord Grey de Ruthyn, the commander of the royal vanguard, suddenly displayed the Ragged Staff emblem of Warwick and ordered his men to assist the Yorkists, after which the combined force smashed the centre of the Lancastrian line. In the rout which followed Warwick ordered the Yorkist troops to spare the common soldiers but to slay the leaders and the gentry. Things had reached such a bitter point that gentlemen were no longer ransomed. It was now a fight to the death — what was the point of ransom when the victors attainted the vanquished so that their estates were subject to forfeiture whether they lived or died? Among the Lancastrian dead were three hundred knights and gentlemen, including the Duke of Buckingham and the Earl of Shrewsbury.

On the steaming field Warwick and the Earl of March hurried to the pavilion over which hung the sodden standard of the king. They found Henry was seated alone. As at St Albans his captors dropped to their knees and declared that they were his true liegemen, after which he was escorted to London where he remained a captive figurehead.

York arrived in the capital from Ireland to attend the Parliament "with great pomp and no small exaltation of spirit," and it was rumoured that he was going to dispute Henry's right to the crown, claiming direct descent from Henry III while the king was descended from the usurper Henry IV. In the Hall of Westminster he strode up to the empty royal throne and ran his hands over the cushions as though he was about to sit there. It was a dramatic moment, and according to a chronicler, "he turned his face to the people. Standing beneath the canopy of state, he looked eagerly for their acclaim."

But there was no acclaim, only a silence which told York that he had misjudged the moment. Now that the king's unpopular advisers were dead or fled there was no wish for mild Henry to lose the throne, or to see the ambitious York gain it. At last the Archbishop of Canterbury broke the hush by asking York if he would go with him for an audience with the king.

"I know of no one in the realm who would not more fitly come to me than I to him," snapped the duke and when he entered the palace he broke open the doors of the king's apartments where he was to lodge "more like a king than a duke," while Henry "gave him place" and retired to the queen's apartments. York emphasised the king's position by putting a guard outside them.

On October 16, he formally laid claim to the crown to the embarrassment of the Chancellor, the Lords, the King's Justices and all concerned. No one wanted to be held responsible for deposing Henry, on the other hand there was no desire to thwart the Duke of York who was now the most powerful man in England.

When Henry heard of the claim from the lords, he said simply, "My father was king, his father was also king. I have worn the crown forty years from my cradle; you have all sworn fealty to me as your sovereign . . . How then can my right be disputed?"

The main legal objections to the duke's claim were that by swearing fealty to King Henry in the past he had renounced any right of descent, that Parliament had confirmed the right of Henry IV and his heirs to the throne, and that this right had been accepted for three reigns. In the end a compromise was reached in which it was decided that Henry would "keep the crown, and his estate and dignity royal, during his life, and the duke and his heirs to succeed him in the same." And to endorse this York was created Prince of Wales, though it was little consolation to York who, at the age of fifty, was ten years older than the king.

The news that her son Edward had been deprived of the right to inherit his father's throne stung Queen Margaret into action. She had not been with Henry at the Northampton defeat, and when news of it had reached her at Eccleshall Castle she had fled to Wales with the young prince. On the way she was robbed by one of her own servants "who despoiled her and robbed her and put her in doubt of her life," but once she crossed the border she found sanctuary until York was declared Prince of Wales (a title already borne by her son) upon which she travelled secretly to Scotland to raise an army. Though she was not successful there, her old supporters began to rally to her cause until she had fifteen thousand men under arms.

Early in December, 1460, York marched north from London to confront the queen who was with her army at Pontefract. He made his base at Sandal Castle, close to Wakefield, and a truce was agreed to avoid fighting during the twelve days of Christmas. On December 30 a Lancastrian force approached the castle, and the duke, infuriated at this breach of the truce — or, according to some chroniclers, the taunts from Queen Margaret that it ill-behoved a potential king of England to skulk before a woman — had his gates flung open to sally forth with his army. He attacked the Lancastrians near Wakefield, only to find that he had fallen into the queen's trap. The first Lancastrian force had been a decoy to draw him from the safety of his castle to where a much larger one was hidden in ambush. No sooner had the fighting started than the Yorkists were surrounded by two wings of the queen's army which had been lying concealed.

The Yorkists were taken by surprise and numbers and, in the swift slaughter which followed, the Duke of York was among the two thousand slain. When his corpse was found the head was struck off and decorated with a paper crown.

"Hail, king without a kingdom," mocked the jubilant Lancastrians. Later the trophy was spiked above the Micklegate Bar at York, along with the heads of other White Rose nobles.

After Wakefield the victorious army marched south as it was the queen's intention to save King Henry from the clutches of Warwick. On February 17, 1461, she defeated him at the second battle of St Albans. At the end of the day, after three thousand men, most of them Yorkists, had been killed King Henry was found beneath an oak tree from which he had watched the battle, laughing and singing and "smiling to see the discomfort of the army." He was soon joyously reunited with his queen and his eight-years-old son whom he knighted. The next day the little fellow, dressed in purple velvet, was allowed to sit in judgement on two prisoners who had been Henry's escorts and who had stayed with him through the battle on his assurance that they would come to no harm if the Lancastrians won.

"Let them have their heads taken off," piped the boy.

"May God destroy those who taught you that manner of speech," said one of the condemned men in horror.

* * *

For some obscure reason the Lancastrians turned north again, giving Warwick the chance he needed to earn his nickname of King-Maker. With Henry in the care of the triumphant queen he knew that he could never be used as a political figurehead again, therefore he must give the country a new sovereign. On March 4 he had Edward Earl of March, the son of the slain Duke of York, proclaimed king at St Paul's in London, after which the sceptre was bestowed upon him in Westminster Abbey. Both Warwick and the new Edward IV knew that this was merely a gesture – the crown still had to be won by force of arms. And this took place in the frozen fields between the villages of Towton and Saxton, ten miles south of York, on Palm Sunday, March 29, 1462.

Warwick slew his horse with his sword in front of his troops as a dramatic pledge that he would fight on foot beside them, and Edward ordered that no quarter should be given. Then, at nine o'clock in the morning, the bloodiest battle of the war began.

The Lancastrians were arrayed on the slope of Towton Hill and they felt they had the advantage as they saw the Yorkists advancing towards them, heads down in the chilling wind. The archers waited patiently to send waves of arrows to add to their discomfort when suddenly the wind changed its direction and began to drive snowflakes into the faces of

Lancastrians. The swirling curtains became so thick the armies could no longer see each other.

The Yorkist bowmen had a newly designed arrow which, thanks to extra feathers, had an increased range of forty yards. They began firing in the direction of the enemy lines with the result the Lancastrian bowmen believed they were within bowshot of the unseen Yorkists. They replied with flight after flight of arrows, unaware that their conventional shafts were falling far short. Thus such trivial things as feathers can affect the course of history.

With their firepower exhausted the Lancastrians had to leave their high ground and trudge through the blinding snowstorm to engage the enemy hand to hand. All morning they fought until, according to the Bishop of Exeter, bodies were littered over an area six miles long and three wide. Finally the Lancastrian line broke and so many armoured men were drowned retreating across a swollen stream that their corpses formed a bridge for the fugitives who followed, pursued by vengeful Yorkists who butchered them as far as the walls of York. Over thirty thousand men died that bitter day, the majority being Lancastrians.

Because it was a holy day King Henry had not wanted to commit sacrilege by being present at the scene of the slaughter, so when news of the defeat reached him at York he was able to escape with the queen and Prince Edward. Meanwhile the victorious Edward took down the head of his father, his brother and his uncle from the Micklegate Bar and replaced them with the heads of his fallen foemen. In June he returned to London for his coronation.

Leaving Henry hiding in Harlech, Queen Margaret journeyed to Brittany to solicit help from Louis XI. At Chinon he offered her twenty thousand livres and an authorisation to raise an army among French knights eager for profitable adventure. In return he demanded the last piece of English territory on the Continent — Calais. Margaret agreed to this on behalf of Henry, should he win back his crown. In October, 1462, she landed her small army near Bamborough Castle which she took along with the castles of Alnwick and Dunstanburgh. But the tide was still running hard against the Lancastrians and the following year, on May 15, the queen's army was routed at the battle of Hexham.

Again King Henry and Queen Margaret escaped; he fled north into Scotland where for a period his movements remain a mystery, she crossed to France with her son and lived in Anjou for the next seven years.

* * *

For a year Henry was a hunted fugitive, travelling secretly between the homes of old Lancastrian supporters in Westmorland, Lancashire and Yorkshire. To this day traditions of his clandestine visits remain in various castles. Finally he was betrayed at Cantlow, and in June, 1465, he was taken to London astride a miserable hack, his legs bound to his stirrups and with a mocking placard on his back. Warwick met the fallen king at Islington and encouraged the mob to jeer him by personally leading him three times round the pillory as though he was a criminal, shouting, "Behold the traitor!"

Henry did not respond to the insults until he received a blow on the face whereupon he rebuked the man who had done it with the expression "Forsooth and forsooth, ye do foully to smite a king anointed so."

For the next five years he remained a prisoner in the Tower, "dirty, sickly, ill-dressed and neglected," but he bore his misfortune with almost superhuman patience. It would seem that he did survive because it was in the new king's interest to keep him as long as Prince Edward lived so the youth could not lay claim to the throne as Henry's successor. And before his mysterious death Henry was destined to be once more hailed as a king.

This came about as the result of a bitter quarrel between Warwick and King Edward in 1470. Warwick fled to France and sought his old enemy Queen Margaret. After apologising for his past offences against her he astounded her by announcing that he wished to espouse the Lancastrian cause. Their combined armies would invade England and in his role of King-Maker he would restore Henry to the throne. This alliance would be sealed by his daughter Anne Neville marrying Margaret's son Edward. After some hesitation the thought of a return to power conquered the queen's aversion to Warwick and she agreed.

In September King Edward was in the south suppressing a revolt when Warwick's army, which had been backed by Louis XI, landed unopposed at Portsmouth and Dartmouth. In London excitement grew when a Franciscan, Dr William Goddard, preached at St Paul's in favour of King Henry, the men of Kent rose against the Yorkists who had usurped him and so many men flocked to Warwick's standard that he had an army of sixty thousand when he reached the capital. Now it was Edward's turn to fly across the Channel.

In London two bishops sought Henry in the Tower, finding him "not so clenely kepte as schuld seme suche a Prynce." They dressed him in a blue velvet gown and took him to Westminster where he was described as "a sack of wool, a shadow on a wall, the blind man in a game of blind man's bluff, a crowned calf." But as Warwick's puppet he wore the crown of England for six months.

Edward returned to England in March, 1471, and after raising an army he arrived in London where the mob, having cheered Henry a short while before, welcomed him back as their king. Henry greeted him with the sad words, "Cousin you are welcome, my life will be safe in your hands."

Warwick was defeated at Barnet on Easter day, and Henry was returned to the Tower. Some weeks later Queen Margaret — still the She Wolf of France — landed with French troops in Dorset for her final attempt to win back her son's birthright, but Edward defeated her at Tewkesbury and Prince Edward was among those killed. King Edward then returned to the capital and Henry was murdered.

Twelve years after the event John Warkworth, master of St Peter's College, Cambridge, wrote: "And the same night that King Edward came to London, King Henry, being in ward in prison in the Tower of London, was put to death,*

*According to Wright's Suppression of the Monasteries, among the relics preserved at Reading Abbey at the time of its dissolution in 1539 was the dagger that was said to have slain Henry VI.

the 21st day of May, on a Tuesday night betwixt eleven and twelve of the clock, being then at the Tower the Duke of Gloucester, brother to King Edward, and many other, and on the morrow he was chested and brought to Paul's, and his face was open that every man might see him. And in his lying he bled on the pavement there; and afterwards at the Black Friars was brought, and there he bled new and fresh; and from thence he was carried to Chertsey Abbey in a boat, and buried there in Our Lady's Chapel."

The hint is there that Richard Duke of Gloucester, brother of King Edward, had a hand in the murder. De Commines wrote that the duke "killed poor King Henry with his own hand, or else caused him to be killed in his presence." Yet there is no proof of this other than the statement that he was in the Tower that night, but the Tower was a royal residence as well as a prison so there is no great significance in this, most of the court were probably there as well.

On the other hand household accounts suggest that Henry was alive until the 24th of the month, and if this were so Richard is exonerated from being involved in the actual killing as he was then in Sandwich.

A writer in the Croyland Chronicle declared: "I pass over in silence how at this period the body of King Henry was found in the Tower of London lifeless. May God spare and grant time and repentance to him, whoever thus dared to lay such sacrilegious hands on the Lord's Anointed; whereof the doer deserves the title of a tyrant, and the sufferer that of a glorious martyr."

On this the historian James Gairdner commented: "When we consider that the writer of this was a member of Edward IV's Council, we must own that the language is remarkably strong, and at the same time intentionally vague, so as not to implicate anyone expressly. The deed was so clearly abetted by authority, that it was not expedient then to speak the whole truth about it."

The official version of Henry's death given out at the time was that he had "died disconsolate and of pure melancholy" on hearing of the death of his son, but we do know for certain that there was another cause. In 1911 Henry's bones were disinterred and to one of the pieces of the cranium there was still some hair attached which was brown in colour except in one place where it was much darker and seemed to be matted with blood, while the back of the skull appeared to have been crushed by a blow.

Some time after Henry was interred at Chertsey his body was translated to Windsor where the tomb became a shrine for pilgrims who remembered the saintly character of the king. Soon there were stories of miracles occurring there, and over the centuries more than a hundred and seventy-four* have been attributed to the royal martyr, making him one of history's great miracle workers.

*Twenty-two of Henry's miracles have been confirmed by the Vatican, and in England today the King Henry VI Society still endeavours to promote his canonisation.

CHAPTER SEVEN

The Murder of the Duke of Clarence

". . . growing daily in more and more malice."

THE EXPEDIENT CHANGING of allegiances was a common-place aspect of politics during the Wars of the Roses; cynical magnates weighed the benefits of the White Rose against the Red, commanders joined the enemy in the midst of battle, citizens hailed a leader one year and howled for his death the next — yet no one achieved the turncoat fame of Edward IV's brother George who became known to history as "false fleeting Clarence."

Edward of York could have had no inkling of this when he was declared king in place of Henry VI in March, 1461. One of his first acts was to recall his brothers George and Richard, aged eleven and eight respectively, from Utrecht where they had been sent when their father had been killed at the battle of Wakefield the year before. Soon George was made Duke of Clarence, a title emphasising the hereditary claims of the House of York, and Richard became Duke of Gloucester.

In 1466 there was an attempt to arrange a match between Clarence and Mary, the daughter of the Count of Burgundy, but this came to nothing as Warwick the King-Maker had other plans for the young duke. This was due to an increasing rift between Edward and the grim earl who had played such an important role in winning him the crown. At first there was no doubt that Warwick, as the power behind the throne, was more influential than the golden young man who sat upon it. The situation was put pithily in a letter to the King of France from the Governor of Abbeville who collected the gossip of English-held Calais for his master. "They tell me they have but two rulers in England," he wrote, "Monsieur de Warwick and another whose name I have forgotten."

The situation irked Edward who was determined to be a proper sovereign and not a puppet like the poor pious king he had deposed, but he held his peace until he judged the time was ripe for him to prove his independence. Warwick, meanwhile, was endeavouring to arrange a politically advantageous marriage for the king with a lady of the royal household of France. King Louis was eager to sign the agreement but as time passed he began to sense that something was wrong, and this was confirmed in October, 1464, when he learned Warwick would never be coming to seal the settlement, King Edward had created a sensation at a Council assembly by announcing that he had been secretly married for the past four months.

One can imagine the mortification of the haughty Warwick. That his protege had thrown away a great political opportunity for the sake of a highly unsuitable woman was bad enough, but worse was the fact that Edward had made him appear a fool before the English nobility and the French king. In his letter of explanation to the latter he was unable to hide his chagrin and Louis believed that he was ready to make war on his old comrade-in-arms. But Warwick was too old a campaigner to allow himself to fall into such a trap. He bit back his resentment and on Michaelmas Day actually led the new queen into Reading Abbey for presentation to the Council; her other escort was the Duke of Clarence.

Dame Elizabeth Grey, the daughter of Sir Richard Woodville, was the widow of a Lancastrian knight who had been fatally wounded at the second battle of St Albans. She already had two sons and was five years older than the king when he met her at her mother's house at Grafton. It is said that she waited by the road along which Edward was riding in order to appeal to him to restore her children's inheritance. He was greatly attracted to her and, used to easy conquests, was surprised when she refused to fall into his arms and bed. Instead she told him that "she knew herself to be unworthy to be a queen, but valued her honour more than to be a concubine."

Then, according to the *Chronicle of the White Rose,* "Edward being a lusty prince who attempted the stability and modesty of divers ladies and gentlewomen, when he could not perceive none of such womanhood, wisdom and beauty, he then with a little company came unto the manor of Grafton and after resisting at divers times, seeing the constant mind of the said Dame Elizabeth early in a morning he wedded her."

Although the marriage was seen as unsuitable because the bride was "not the daughter of a duke or earl", it is likely that Edward, who certainly loved her, also saw the value of a Lancastrian connection and envisaged the Woodville family as a counter-balance to the domineering Neville clan of whom Warwick was the leading member. This certainly became his policy for within little more than a year of Elizabeth Grey becoming queen her five sisters were married to the Duke of Buckingham and the eldest sons of the Earls of Arundel, Essex, Kent and Pembroke, her brother, aged twenty, was wedded to the immensely rich Duchess of Norfolk, then eighty, and her son was betrothed to the Duke of Exeter's heiress whom Warwick had intended for his own nephew. The queen's father was created Earl Rivers, made a knight of the Garter and appointed Treasurer.

Warwick must have brooded on the ever-increasing power of these upstarts, but the blow came when Edward yet again humiliated him before the French. Warwick's foreign policy had always been to ally with France against Burgundy and in 1467 he went to Paris for this purpose. On his return he learned that behind his back Edward had arranged for his sister Margaret to marry the Duke of Burgundy, a scheme which was guaranteed to alienate the French. To add insult to injury Warwick's brother, Archbishop George Neville, who had been chancellor, had been deprived of the Great Seal by the king in person.

Warwick's indignation was monumental. Was this his reward for all the years he had fought for the White Rose? His father and brother had died for the cause, and now he was being rejected in favour of the Lancastrian Woodvilles!

In retaliation the earl proposed to the Duke of Clarence,

who was still heir presumptive, that he should marry his elder daughter Isabel — Richard, Duke of Gloucester, was already in love with Anne, the younger girl. To Clarence this meant that he would stand to inherit vast estates, and feeling resentment at the meteoric rise of the queen's family he was eager to fall in with Warwick's intrigues — perhaps the King-Maker had already hinted that if he could make one king he could make another. The obstacle to the marriage was the fact that Clarence and Isabel were related which meant a papal dispensation would be required. This must have given some comfort to Edward when rumours of the proposed match reached him — he had a highly organised network of spies — for he knew that if his brothers married Warwick's two children the earl would come dangerously close to the throne.

He summoned Clarence and Gloucester and demanded the truth from them. Clarence immediately denied the suggestion but added that "it would not be a bad match". At this the king ordered them from him in a fit of rage worthy of his Plantagenet blood.

When Warwick attempted to buy a dispensation the king prevailed upon the Pope not to grant it, but he knew that this would not be the end of the matter. He sensed danger and enrolled "two hundred strong varlets of the best archers in England to be about his person", and once again the kingdom became tense with impending conflict. In June, 1469, Edward had to march to Yorkshire to quell an uprising which had been engineered by the Nevilles. His absence allowed Clarence to cross the Channel to Calais where Warwick, as Keeper of the Sea, was preparing a fleet which he claimed was to sail against the French. He had obtained a secret dispensation from Paul II and on July 11, 1469, his brother the archbishop married Anne Neville to the Duke of Clarence in the Church of Notre Dame.

The next day the three conspirators signed and issued a manifesto calling upon all "true subjects" to assemble at Canterbury on July 16 to assist them in an armed demonstration to call King Edward's attention to the "deceivable covetous rule and guiding of certain seditious persons."

The conspirators landed at Kent and marched north to join forces with a rebel army under the command of a mysterious gentleman known simply as Robin of Redesdale. It is thought that Robin was in fact Sir John Conyers who, like his lieutenants, was related to Warwick. There was no opposition to the earl and Clarence when they passed London as King Edward was based at Nottingham awaiting reinforcements.

On July 26 Robin of Redesdale attacked the royalist position at Edgecote. Edward's Welsh troops gave a good account of themselves until a contingent of Warwick's men bore down on them from the rear; the King-Maker and Robin were now joined and the royal troops fled the field. At news of the defeat Edward left Nottingham, hoping to link up with an army led by the earls of Devonshire and Pembroke. The morale of his soldiers was shattered by Edgecote and they began to desert on the march. Few remained when the king halted for the night at Honiley, three miles from Kenilworth. At midnight he was awakened by the clatter of weapons and looking out he saw the house was surrounded by armed men loyal to his brother Clarence and Warwick. He ran into the next room to be greeted by Archbishop George Neville who ordered him to dress. Typically Edward retorted that he would finish his rest first.

"Sire, you must rise and come to see my brother of Warwick," said the archbishop, "nor do I think you can refuse."

Edward was escorted by his "rescuers" to Middleham Castle which was Warwick's main stronghold. The earl was savouring his greatest triumph, he held King Edward a captive while in London King Henry was locked in the Tower, and it seemed that he was in a position to bestow the crown on his eager son-in-law. But first he had his revenge; the queen's father Lord Rivers and her brother Sir John knelt before his headsman, as did other supporters of Edward and the Woodvilles. These summary executions, rushed through without the pretence of legal hearings, lost Warwick the support of the people. They had been ready to side with him when he declared that he was going to reform the realm, now they saw him behaving with a brutal arrogance which contrasted ill with Edward's good-humoured, larger-than-life character or even poor Henry's Christian piety.

In London the citizens rioted in protest and the Duke of Burgundy offered to come to their aid if they would support King Edward; on the Scottish border the Lancastrians seized the opportunity to raise a Red Rose rebellion. When Warwick called for men to suppress it there was no response. It was clear that now if was only King Edward whom men would follow and Warwick realised that he had overplayed his hand. Without popular support even the King-Maker was power-less to control the kingdom.

Always a realist, Warwick knew that if he continued to hold Edward it would only increase the feeling which was running against him, therefore he freed the king in what a chronicler described as "a manner almost miraculous and beyond all expectation." Almost immediately Warwick's popularity began to return; men hurried to follow his banner against the Lancastrian rebels. He soon put down the insurrec-tion for Edward and underlined his success by bringing back the leaders for execution at York. By the end of the year Warwick and Clarence had regained enough confidence to return to the court in London where it appeared that the events of the summer had been conveniently forgotten. With the kingdom still restless the king and the earl needed each other, Warwick had learned that his power still depended on royal authority while Edward still required the support of the most powerful noble in England. Their reconciliation was cemented by Warwick's nephew and heir being created Duke of Bedford and betrothed to Edward's infant daughter. Sir John Paston wrote to his mother: "The King hath good language of the Lords of Clarence and Warwick, and of my Lords of York (Archbishop Neville) and Oxford saying they be his best friends, but his household men have other lan-guage, so that what shall hastily fall I cannot say."

Clarence may have gained Isabel as a result of the past intrigue but having been so tantalisingly close to the crown left him in a fever of discontent. His only consolation must have been that secretly proud Warwick felt the same — he desperately needed to prove that he was the real master of the realm. So the conspiracies continued. According to the

Chronicle of the White Rose, when Archbishop Neville invited Edward to Moor Park, "a little before supper, when they should have washed, John Ratcliffe warned the King privily and bade him beware for there were ordained privily an hundred of arms the which should take him and carry him out of the way. Whereupon the King, faining to make his water, caused a good horse to be saddled, and so with a small company rode to Windsor."

Early in 1470 a rebellion broke out in Lincolnshire and before the king set out with his army Clarence joined him in St Paul's to pray for the success of the expedition. Clarence seemed so concerned for his elder brother that on March 8 a letter reached Edward offering to bring Warwick to his aid. In reply Clarence and Warwick were authorised to raise troops on the king's behalf. It was only when Edward attacked the insurgents at the village of Empingham, five miles from Stamford, that he became aware of his brother's renewed treachery.

In the heat of the fight some of the rebels forgot political caution and automatically gave voice to their usual battle cries, "A Clarence! A Warwick!" When they had been defeated by the royal troops documents were found which proved that Clarence and Warwick had planned the rising "to destroy the King and to have made the said duke King."

Edward dispatched the Garter King of Arms to Coventry, where Clarence and Warwick were waiting with the demand that they dismiss their troops and come to him. They agreed, but having done so led their armies north. Again Edward called upon them to disband and present themselves before him; they demanded safe conduct and full pardons for their men. At this the king decided to attack, whereupon they retreated to Dartmouth from which they escaped to Honfleur.

The king's hardening attitude to the traitors can be judged by the revolting fate meted out to those supporters who had the misfortune to be captured. The Earl of Worcester earned the epithet of the Butcher of England when he ordered them to be impaled — a lingering form of execution which he introduced to the country.

* * *

King Louis of France gave the fugitives a warm welcome; enemies of Edward were friends of his, and he hoped their arrival heralded trouble for England. He was not disappointed when Warwick confided in him his latest scheme, though he was probably amazed at his guest's audacity. If anyone was going to be disappointed it would be Clarence.

Through Louis Warwick arranged to visit Queen Margaret at Angers in July 1470 and what an extraordinary meeting it must have been — she had ordered the execution of Warwick's father, he had deprived her husband of his throne and twice had driven her out of England. Remembering the harm the earl had done to her and her friends she was loath to listen at first, but persistently he explained that now he wished to restore Henry to the throne. The new alliance would be cemented by the marriage of her son Prince Edward to his daughter Anne — the girl with whom Richard of Gloucester was in love.

Gradually Margaret allowed herself to be persuaded; much as she detested Warwick he represented her only chance of ever obtaining power again. Finally when he went on his knees before her, swearing fidelity, she kept him in this uncomfortable and humiliating position for nearly twenty minutes before she consented to his pleas. On July 25 Prince Edward was betrothed to Anne Neville and five days later Warwick swore on a fragment of the True Cross to be faithful to King Henry.

Although Warwick tried to placate Clarence by promising him the Duchy of York, and the succession should Prince Edward have no issue, it was the crown that the duke had wanted. His dream evaporated as he watched Warwick planning to get control of England through a Lancastrian rather than a Yorkist king. He burned with hidden resentment when he and the King-Maker set sail on September 9 with an army and fleet provided by King Louis.

In England the Lancastrians proved to be as pragmatic as Queen Margaret; they flocked to the standard of their old enemy. There were also many other Englishmen who, becoming disillusioned with Yorkist rule after the atrocities committed under the Earl of Worcester, had no objection to seeing Henry back on the throne.

King Edward had yet again been lured from the capital to deal with a northern insurrection organised by Lord Fitzburgh, Warwick's brother-in-law.

"He had left the Queen, great with child, in the Tower of London," recorded the *Chronicle of the White Rose.* "But in the north country as he lay in his bed the sergeant of his minstrels came to him in haste and bade arise for he had enemies coming to take him, the which were within six or seven miles."

With his brother Richard of Gloucester he rode to Lynn where he hired three ships to carry his men to Flanders. The escape had been so sudden that the king was without money and he gave the captain his gown lined with marten fur as payment.

In London the bewildered Henry VI suddenly found his old enemy Warwick kneeling before him, then cheers rang in his ears as he was escorted to the Palace of Westminster and soon afterwards he felt the weight of the crown in a second coronation ceremony.

The mob cheered louder when Worcester, the Butcher of England, was sentenced to walk from Westminster to the execution ground on Tower Hill. Such was their hatred of him that they tried to lynch him on the way and he had to be sheltered in the Fleet Prison. He is one of the minor enigmas of history, for it is hard to equate the impaling of prisoners with this polished gentleman who had graduated from Oxford and Padua, had been Caxton's patron and was a Greek scholar and author. When on the scaffold he was upbraided for his cruelty he retorted that he had only been harsh in the service of the state; then he turned to the headsman and coolly asked him to use three blows, one for each member of the Trinity.

With Henry on the throne, Warwick back in power and Worcester punished it seemed that all concerned in the coup were satisfied — except the Duke of Clarence.

* * *

On November 1 in the sanctuary of Westminster Queen

Elizabeth gave birth to a son whom she named after his father. This meant that both rival kings now had heirs. Soon afterwards Queen Margaret, seeing that Warwick had fulfilled his promise to restore King Henry, kept hers and on December 13 Prince Edward was married to Anne Neville at Amboise. The queen put off returning to England until the spring as, like most travellers, she feared the winter weather in the Channel.

Also waiting for a safe crossing was Edward. As Louis of France had supported Clarence and Warwick, so the Duke of Burgundy assisted the fugitive king. On March 11 he set sail from Flushing with fifteen hundred men in a small fleet of ships which had been hired for him by the duke. It seemed a forlorn hope, yet Edward knew he had one secret ally, his mother and sisters had arranged a reconciliation between him and his brother Clarence.

After landing at Ravenspur Edward declared that he had merely come to claim his duchy of York, and he entered the city hurrahing for King Henry. This ruse satisfied the citizens as it demonstrated that they were not traitors to Henry when they opened the gates to Edward's troops. From York he marched towards Coventry where Warwick waited confidently within the city walls. Such was Edward's magnetism that more and more began to follow his sun-in-splendour standard.

Warwick was confident because he had a superior force and the Duke of Clarence had promised to bring him four thousand reinforcements which he had levied in the name of King Henry. Clarence had urged his father-in-law not to attack Edward until he arrived to help him, and this delay became a vital factor in Warwick's defeat as it prevented him attacking Edward while he still had the advantage of numbers. When Clarence finally approached from the southwest Warwick's plan to crush Edward between the two Lancastrian armies failed — for the simple reason that Clarence marched the men, their Lancastrian emblems hastily covered by those of the White Rose, into his brother's camp.

Edward and Clarence met on the Banbury road on April

3 when Clarence fell on his knees to his brother who raised him to a fanfare of trumpets while Richard of Gloucester looked on approvingly at the reunion. Thanks to Clarence's betrayal of Warwick, Edward was now confident to march on London. Leaving the earl fuming in Coventry, he entered the capital to an enthusiastic welcome on April 14.

"Three causes led to his welcome," wrote De Commines. "He owed many debts there, he had many mistresses among the citizens' wives and the Queen had just borne him a son."

News came that Warwick had left Coventry and was marching to join up with Lancastrian forces in the south, and Edward knew that it was essential to defeat him before this happened. He led an army of ten thousand to Barnet where, on a foggy Easter Sunday, he confronted the man who had done so much to win him the throne.

Richard of Gloucester, then aged eighteen, was given command of the Yorkist's right wing and although Clarence was present at the battle Edward placed the duke's troops in the centre under his own command to make sure that his brother did not switch sides again.

At first success seemed to favour Warwick; the Earl of Oxford attacked the Yorkist left wing so effectively that he pursued the fleeing White Rose troops all the way to Barnet town. But when he marched back to the battlefield veils of mist caused the Lancastrians to mistake his star emblem for Edward's sun-in-splendour and immediately the fatal cry of "Treachery!" was raised. Panic spread and the Lancastrians fled. The Earl of Warwick, hampered by heavy armour, tried to reach his horse but, having been wounded, he stumbled and fell. Despite Edward's order that he was not to be harmed, his vizor was prised open and he was stabbed to death.

All that remained was for Queen Margaret's army to be defeated, and Clarence played his part in this at Tewkesbury. Polydor Vergil described him joining with Gloucester and Hastings in the cold-blooded murder of Queen Margaret's son Edward after the battle. Holinshed elaborated on this, writing that Edward was taken before the king after the battle and asked why he had come to England. The youth replied that he had come to recover his father's heritage "at which words King Edward said nothing but with his hand thrust him from him, or (as some saie) struke him with his gantlet, whome incontinentlie George, Duke of Clarence, Richard, Duke of Glocester, Thomas Graie, marques of Dorset and William, Lord Hastings, that stood by, suddenlie murthered." The only contemporary reference to Edward's death is Warkworth's statement that he "cried for succour" to Clarence.

* * *

Following the murder of Henry VI England began to settle down under the rule of Edward, and Clarence had to resign himself to the fact that he would never feel the weight of a crown, yet ambition and intrigue were second nature to him and it was not long before he was at odds with his younger brother. In appreciation for his military services Edward bestowed the late Warwick's Yorkshire and Cumbrian estates upon Richard and agreed to his request to marry Warwick's daughter Anne Neville, the widow of Prince Edward and co-heiress to her mother's vast domains. Clarence, being married to her elder sister, had no intention of sharing these lands with his younger brother. Claiming Anne as his ward he carried her off and when King Edward commanded him to surrender her to Richard he hid her in a house in London "disguised in the habit of a workmaid".

After some time Richard managed to locate her and, after a romantic scene, placed her in sanctuary at St Martin le Grand. Then the two brothers argued their cases in person before the king in council "with a skill and pertinacity which astounded the lawyers."

In February 1472 Clarence reluctantly agreed to the match in return for Richard's office of Great Chamberlain, together with the title of Earl of Warwick and Salisbury, but he could not forgive Richard for having won the girl he loved. Sir John Paston wrote: "It is said for certain that the Duke of Clarence maketh him big in that he can, showing as he would deal with the Duke of Gloucester; but the King intendeth in eschewing all inconvenience, to be as big as they both, and to be a stiffler between them."

Discord between Clarence and the king became evident again after the death of his wife Isabel in December 1476. A fortnight later Charles the Bold of Burgundy died, leaving his daughter mistress of his vast dominion.

His territorial ambitions reawakened at the thought of gaining Europe's greatest duchy, Clarence sought to renew his old suit with Mary until Edward forbade it, explaining that politically it would cause difficulties — but this did not stop Queen Elizabeth pressing the claims of her brother Anthony. Clarence suspected that the queen had been responsible for getting the king to veto the match, a suspicion which appeared to be confirmed when Edward presented Anthony as the official suitor for the Burgundian heiress.

Clarence sought to revenge himself against the queen and her upstart family by discrediting them with the people. To this end he went to ruthless and bizarre lengths. He ordered the arrest without warrant of one of his late wife's attendants named Ankarette, widow of Roger Twynho, for having brought about her mistress' death by "a venymous drynke of ale myxt with poyson" — the implication being that the murder had been committed at the instigation of the queen. The unfortunate woman was hurried to Warwick where she was condemned by the justices in Petty Sessions and hanged in the presence of Clarence. A writ of *certiorani** was issued but it came too late to save her from this judicial murder. Executed with her was a man whom Warwick had accused of poisoning his infant son.

The Woodvilles were not slow to repay Clarence in his own coin by arranging the arrest of an Oxford clerk named John Stacy, who was reputed to be a wizard. Under torture he denounced one Thomas Burdet, a member of Clarence's household, for practising witchcraft.

On May 17 1477, the men were examined by a special commission at Westminster. Burdet was charged with having "composed the death of the king" in April 1474; with encouraging Stacy and another necromancer to "calculate and

A writ from a higher court for records of a case tried in a lower.

168

Coronation of Edward II

33   *The drowning of Clarence in Malmsey wine*

34 The Bloody Tower, the traditional scene of the murder of the Princes in the Tower

35 Elizabeth Woodville bidding farewell to Edward V

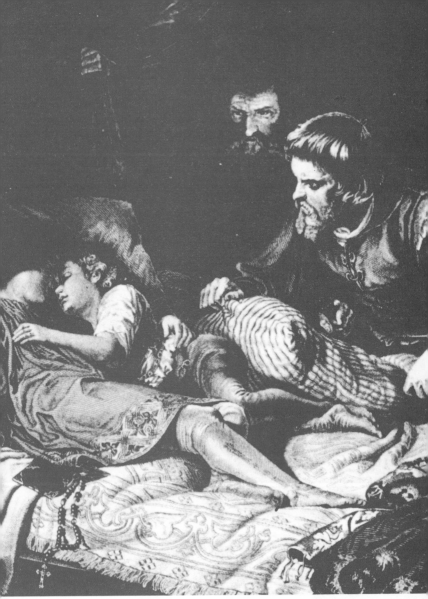

36 *The traditional view of the fate of Edward V and his younger brother in the Tower of London*

work out the Nativities of the King and the Prince of Wales", with predicting Edward's death and circulating treasonable rhymes.* Found guilty, Burdet and Stacy were hanged at Tyburn on May 10.

It would seem that Clarence's anger deprived him of his last remaining shreds of caution. After the execution he burst into a meeting of the Council with Dr William Goddard to testify that Burdet and Stacy had protested their innocence right up to the moment of death. This was an unfortunate move as it was the same Dr Goddard who had preached at St Paul's on King Henry's right to the crown. Then, as though overcome by madness, Clarence followed this by declaring that the king was a bastard and a sorcerer. Edward responded by having him imprisoned until January 1478, when he was charged before Parliament with slandering the sovereign, making preparations for a new rebellion and sending his son secretly to Ireland after replacing him with a substitute at Warwick Castle.

Every member was afraid to read a bill of attainer on the king's brother so it was left to Edward to read it himself.

"Wherein it is to be remembered that the King's highness of tender youth, unto now of late hath ever loved and cherished him, as tenderly, as kingly as any creature might his natural brother. . ." Edward intoned. "He gave him so large portion of possessions, that no memorial is of, or seldom hath been seen, that any King of England heretofore within his realm gave so largely to any of his brothers. . ."

This was followed by a list of the king's kindnesses to Clarence. No one stirred as he continued: "The said duke nevertheless, for all this no love increasing, but growing daily in more and more malice, hath not left to·consider and conspire new treasons, more heinous and loathly than ever afore, how that the said duke falsely and traitorously intended and proposed firmly, the extreme destruction and disheriting of the King and his issue. . ."

At last Edward finished, and it was written that "in that sad strife not a single person uttered a word against the duke

*Sir James Ramsey thought this refers to a prophecy that King Edward would be succeeded by someone whose Christian name began with G.

except the King; not one individual made answer to the King except the duke." Clarence declared his innocence and challenged Edward to a "wager of battle", which meant that the two of them should fight a dual before the Constable of England. The king refused and on February 7 the Court of Chivalry sentenced Clarence to death.

Even though Richard of Gloucester asked Edward to forgive their brother, and their old mother the Duchess of York mourned that one of her sons should bring about the death of another, the king remained adamant. Yet, in the days when an execution was usually carried out immediately after a verdict of guilty, Clarence remained locked away under sentence of death.

Did Edward fear to bring him to the block in case he should avenge himself by revealing a dreadful secret at the last moment? Did Clarence possess some piece of information which he hoped would save him? In the next chapter we shall see that if Robert Stillington, Bishop of Bath, was telling the truth after Edward's death, the king did indeed have a secret which could have jeopardised his position, abrogated the succession and discredited the Woodvilles.*

If Clarence did have a secret he never got the chance to make it public. Although he had been found guilty of treason and Edward could have had him legally executed whenever he wished, it was found necessary to murder him. He was put to death by unknown assassins on February 18, 1478.

Three contemporary writers — two English and one French — stated that he was killed by being thrust head down into a butt of Malmsey, "the much-prized vintage of Malvasia in the east of the Morea". Jean Molinot added a curious anecdote to the murder by saying that Clarence was allowed to choose the manner of his death and he asked to be drowned in his favourite wine.

The Duke of Clarence was the last of "the idols to whom the people had been accustomed to look for revolution", yet when he was rid of him King Edward was said to suffer

It may be of some significance that eighteen days after the murder of Clarence Bishop Stillington found himself imprisoned.

remorse over his fate. When asked to show royal clemency to malefactors, he sometimes exclaimed, "O unfortunate brother, for whose life not one creature would make interception!"

CHAPTER EIGHT

The Murder of Edward V

". . . let me kisse you ere you go, for God knoweth when we shall kisse together againe."

THE FATE OF Edward V, the eldest son of Edward IV and his queen, Elizabeth Woodville, remains the classic mystery of English history. On November 2, 1470, his mother gave birth to him while in sanctuary of the abbot's house at Westminster, his father having just escaped to Flanders when Warwick the King-Maker restored the crown to the bemused Henry VI. The baby was christened "with small pomp, like a poor man's child", but six months later he and his mother were taken to live at Baynard's Castle in London when his father returned to wrest back the throne. Following the battles of Barnet and Tewkesbury the tragic child was created Prince of Wales.

At the age of three little Edward had a tutor and governor appointed for him, the former being the Bishop of Rochester, the latter Earl Rivers who was the least unpopular member of the queen's now powerful relatives. The rules Edward IV drew up for the training of his son are preserved in the *Chronicle of the White Rose.*

Every morning the prince had to rise early and "till he be ready" no one but Earl Rivers, or a chaplain to say matins, was permitted to enter the royal chamber. When he was dressed he went to chapel to hear mass, while on holidays and feast days he had to attend divine service when special sermons were preached to him. After mass he was allowed to breakfast, then came a period of study "before he go to meet". One rule stated: "That no man sit at his board but as Earl Rivers shall allow, and that there be read before him noble stories as behoveth a prince to understand: and that the communications in his presence be of virtues, honour, cunning, wisdom and deeds of worship, and of nothing that shall move him to vice.''

His meal was followed by a further two hours of study, after which he was shown "all such convenient disports and exercises as belong to his estate to have experience in". Before supper he attended evensong and then it seems the little prince was allowed to play until his bedtime which was "nine of the clock". He lived with his brother Richard at the Westminster palace or in a Woodville stronghold in the west of England.

In January 1478, Richard, then aged four and with the title of Duke of York, was married to the six-years-old heiress of the rich Mowbray family. The princes' uncle, Richard of Gloucester, travelled from his domains in the North to attend the ceremony, and as he spoke pleasantly to the children none dreamed that he was destined to be remembered down the centuries as the world's wickedest uncle.

Little has been recorded of Edward's character or appearance, but a panel portrait in St George's Chapel at Windsor shows a rather full-faced child with shoulder-length hair gazing upwards with little expression other than conventional piety while a crown floats symbolically above his head.

On April 9, 1483, while staying at Ludlow, the twelve-years-old boy began what was to be the shortest reign of any English monarch. At this time Richard of Gloucester, who had been appointed Protector of the Kingdom and guardian of the new king during his minority, was fighting the Scots and ten days were to elapse before he learned of his brother's death. During this period there was feverish activity in London for the Woodvilles knew they had to act fast if they were to retain the power they had enjoyed under the indulgent Edward IV. Plans were made to bring Edward to London, with a guard of 2,000 armed men, to be crowned before his uncle Richard could arrive to challenge the authority of Elizabeth Woodville as Queen Regent.

The Marquess of Dorset, a son of Elizabeth Woodville by her first marriage, held the post of Constable of the Tower which contained the mint and the huge personal treasure of the late king. He used this money to man a fleet under Sir Edward Woodville ostensibly to protect England against the French, the gold that remained he divided between him-

173

self and his mother. With control of the treasury, the fleet and the person of the king, the Woodvilles felt secure against any meddling by Richard of Gloucester or the old aristocracy resentful of their extraordinary rise to power through Edward IV's impetuous marriage.

While a message was dispatched to Earl Rivers at Ludlow urging him to bring Edward to London by May 1 so he could be crowned three days later, no official letter was sent to Richard of Gloucester and his name was pointedly omitted from an official prayer which did, however, refer to "our dread lord King Edward V, the lady Queen Elizabeth, all the royal children. . ." Patents were issued to tax officials authorising them to make their collections in the names of Dorset and Rivers, and again the name of Richard was omitted despite the fact the late king had named him Lord Protector.

According to Dominic Mancini, an Italian priest who was in London at the time and wrote an account of the events, the Marquess of Dorset boasted: "We are so important that even without the king's uncle we can make and enforce our decisions." But the citizens of London became alarmed as tension between the Woodvilles and their opponents, led by Lord Hastings, increased. Memories of past power struggles became frighteningly vivid again.

Richard of Gloucester learned of his brother Edward's death and his appointment as Lord Protector through a letter sent by Hastings. He replied by writing to the Council agreeing to fulfil the late king's wishes, and also sent a letter of sympathy to Elizabeth Woodville. He then began a slow journey south with 600 gentlemen dressed in black. The mourning cavalcade halted at York where Richard had a requiem mass said for the repose of the dead king's soul.

At this point a second message from Hastings, telling of the anxiety in London, caused Richard and his retinue to resume their journey. On April 29 they reached Northampton where Earl Rivers admitted that young Edward had travelled on to Stony Stratford.

As Richard entertained the earl at an inn, the Duke of Buckingham arrived and after Rivers had retired the two dukes conferred. What Buckingham told his cousin Richard is not known, but doubtless he emphasised the warning in Hastings' letter about the machinations of the Woodvilles. Early next morning Richard had Earl Rivers arrested before spurring off towards Stony Stratford.

Edward V was about to start on the final stage of his journey to the capital when his uncle and the Duke of Buckingham reined up at the head of a column of funereal horsemen. Richard of Gloucester took control of the situation with such determined authority that although he was greatly outnumbered not a weapon was drawn, even when he commanded the arrest of Lord Richard Grey, another of Elizabeth Woodville's sons, and two members of the new king's household. Buckingham then told Edward that his mother's relations had been plotting against him. According to Holinshed the boy replied, "What my brother marquess hath done I cannot saie, but in good faith I doe well answer for mine uncle Rivers and my brother here that he be innocent on anie such matter." He was then escorted towards London by his uncle who throughout showed him the respect befitting a sovereign.

On learning of what had transpired at Stony Stratford, Elizabeth Woodville desperately tried to raise a force to seize her son from her brother-in-law, and when this plan failed she once again sought sanctuary in Westminster Abbey. With her went her younger son Richard, her five daughters and all her household goods. Stones were even knocked from the wall of the abbey to allow the entrance of the larger pieces of furniture.

Dressed in blue velvet, Edward arrived in London on May 4, and Richard of Gloucester presented him to the crowds lining the streets as their new sovereign. Doubtless many felt relief that the Lord Protector, whose reputation for valour, loyalty and administration were second to none in the kingdom had come from the North to take the boy into his charge and thus prevent conflict between the two court parties. Edward was taken to stay at the Bishop of London's house while his uncle went to Baynard's Castle. The Council then ratified Richard's position as Lord Protector, and Edward's coronation was fixed for June 22.

It was said that Edward's uncle was present when the boy was fitted for his ceremonial robes, and there was such certainty the crowning would take place that proclamations were issued in Edward's name. Following the usual procedure, he quit the bishop's house on May 19 and took up residence in the Tower of London, which, it must be remembered, was a royal palace as well as being a fortress and a prison.

Preparations for the enthronement continued but on June 13 an extraordinary scene took place at a Council meeting held at the Tower to discuss the forthcoming ceremonies. Richard of Gloucester suddenly accused his old friend Lord Hastings of conspiring with the widowed queen, the dead king's mistress Jane Shore and some nobles in a plot against his life. Hastings was executed almost immediately, and Jane Shore was handed over to the Church who confiscated her possessions and made her do penance for being a harlot. Despite this drama, Elizabeth Woodville three days later allowed her younger son Richard to leave the Westminster sanctuary to join Edward in the Tower. To this day it seems unbelievable that such a shrewd, politically-minded mother should allow her son to leave the safety of the abbey if she thought the boys had anything to fear from their uncle, especially when he had demonstrated by the execution of Hastings his streak of Plantagenet ruthlessness.

Holinshed, building up a dramatic situation without any traceable evidence, reported the queen as saying: "Fare well mine owne sweete sonne. God send you good keeping: let me kisse you once ere you go, for God knoweth when we shall kisse together againe. And therewith she kissed him and blessed him and went her waie, leaving the child weeping as fast."

This was soon followed by an announcement stating that Edward's coronation would be postponed until November. Then on June 22 — the day the boy king should have felt the weight of England's crown upon his head — a certain Friar Ralph Shaa preaching at Saint Paul's on the text "Bastard slips shall not take root", revealed a secret which had

176

been made known to the Council a few days earlier, namely that at the time Edward IV married Elizabeth Woodville he already had a precontract with Lady Eleanor Butler, the daughter of the first Earl of Shrewsbury, and consummation had taken place. As a result the children of Edward and Elizabeth Woodville were illegitimate.

It is thought that the Council learned of this when Robert Stillington, the Bishop of Bath and Wells, announced that, knowing of the contract between the late king and Lady Eleanor, his conscience would not permit him to see a bastard ascend the throne. Although the proofs Stillington had that he had actually married the couple have not survived, they did seem to convince the Council at the time and were written into an Act of Parliament later on.

The bishop had been a favourite of Edward IV until the murder of Clarence when he was suddenly imprisoned in the Tower and was released only after making a solemn vow not to speak to the demerit of the king. It has been suggested that Stillington had been indiscreet enough to tell Clarence of the secret marriage. Clarence would know that the illegitimacy of his royal nephews would give his own son the right to the throne: and it was this dangerous knowledge which prompted Edward to have him finally killed, after having forgiven so much past treachery.

Detractors of Richard of Gloucester suggest that Bishop Stillington was playing a key role in a plot to get the Lord Protector on to the throne, but an intriguing point emerges in the writings of Sir Thomas More who refers to a letter written by Edward IV's mother, the Duchess of York, in which she implores her son not to commit bigamy. It was written at the time of his infatuation with Elizabeth Woodville.

Logically if the children of Edward were declared bastards, the next heir would be the son of the Duke of Clarence, but he was barred by an attainder which dated back to his father's death. Therefore the heir was the late king's brother, Richard of Gloucester. On June 24 an important meeting took place at Westminster made up of peers and commons who had assembled for what had been planned as Edward V's first Parliament. Here the proofs of Edward's contract with Lady Eleanor were debated after which a petition was drawn up requesting Richard to take the place of his nephew on the throne. With some show of reluctance Richard agreed, and was crowned with his wife on July 6.

But what of Edward V and his brother Richard in the Tower of London? Holinshed wrote the accepted Tudor version with these words which have inspired compassion for the little Princes in the Tower to this day: "When he had shewed it unto him that he should not reigne but his uncle should have the crowne he was sore abashed and began to sigh and said 'Alas I would that my uncle would let me have my life yet though I lose my kingdom'. Both the young princes were now shut up and all others removed from them, onelie one called Blacke Will set to serve them and see them sure. After which time the prince never tied his points nor ought wrought of himself but with that young babe his brother lingered with thought and heavinesse."

According to the *Croyland Chronicle* a rumour spread that the two children had been done to death in the Tower that autumn when there was a sudden rebellion led by Richard's old friend Buckingham, but it seems to have been originated by the rebels to discredit the new king. After the revolt had been crushed the story of what in fact could have been regicide died down. The next rumour came in April, 1484, following the death of Richard's only son, when the deaths of the two princes were mentioned by the French Chancellor. Apart from these two rumours, nothing more was known of the fate of the two boys for nearly twenty years.

One cannot help wondering why Richard had not shown them to the people to refute the rumours — if they were still alive. It is equally puzzling that Henry Tudor, who had every reason to discredit the king he had supplanted, did not produce evidence of the murders if he had any cause to believe the boys had been assassinated by their uncle. Yet when he had an act of attainder passed on the dead Richard he accused him of all manner of crimes — except the murder of the princes.

During seven years of his reign Henry was plagued by Perkin Warbeck who convinced several foreign monarchs he was the younger of Edward IV's sons. Again it seems logical that if Henry had any real knowledge of the princes' fate, or even merely suspected it, he would have literally left no stone unturned to find their bodies and thus prove the troublesome Warbeck an imposter. Could it be possible that Edward V and his brother were alive when Henry Tudor seized the throne, though not necessarily in the Tower at the time?

Nineteen years had to pass before Henry VII gave a verbal explanation for the boy king's disappearance, and his spoken words, without any documentary evidence to endorse them, are the only answer we have to the riddle of Edward's disappearance.

In May, 1502, a certain Sir James Tyrell was executed at the Tower for "matters of treason". This knight had been a trusted friend of both Edward IV and Richard III, receiving his accolade after the Battle of Tewkesbury. At the time of King Richard's death at Bosworth he was across the Channel as Governor of Guisnes. Henry Tudor pardoned him for his old loyalties and allowed him to continue at his post. Then, in 1502, his arrest was ordered for having been in correspondence with the Earl of Suffolk, a nephew of Richard III. Tyrell prepared to stand seige in his castle, whereupon Henry guaranteed him safe conduct if he would attend a reconciliatory conference aboard a ship in Calais harbour, a promise backed by the Lord Privy Seal. Tyrell accepted the word of the king, boarded the vessel and was immediately abducted to England. He was held for a short while in the Tower and then died beneath the headsman's axe.

Following this Henry Tudor announced that Tyrell had confessed to a part in the murder of the princes although no document of confession was ever produced. Henry's account of this confession which was quoted by various Tudor historians and has been taken as fact ever since, stated that when Richard III was on a royal progress following his coronation in August, 1483, he sent a message to Sir Robert Brackenbury, the Constable of the Tower, ordering the deaths of the princes. Horrified, Brackenbury refused, whereupon Tyrell travelled to London with a letter authorising him to take complete command of the Tower for one night.

On arriving at the Tower with his groom, John Dighton, he presented his credentials to Brackenbury who handed over the keys. Tyrell then set about the arrangements for the assassination — the victims were to be smothered in their beds by the groom Dighton, a known murderer by the name of Miles Forest and the jailer Black Will Slaughter Then, according to Sir Thomas More: ". . . this Miles Forest and John Dighton about midnight (the seelie children lieing in their beds) came into the chamber and suddenlie lapping them up amongst the clothes, so bewrapped them and entangled them, keeping downe by force the feather-bed and pillowes hard unto their mouths, that within a while, smothered and stifled, their breathe failing, they gave up to God their innocente soules."

As soon as Edward and his brother were dead, Tyrell was called to view their naked corpses after which he ordered them to be buried under a great pile of stones at the foot of the stairs in the White Tower. He then returned to the king to report his terrible task was accomplished. More wrote that Richard "gave him great thanks and some say made him a knight", but he did have one objection, declaring that as the princes were of royal blood they should have been buried on consecrated ground. This was rectified by having them secretly disinterred and reburied by a priest.

When King Henry gave this account the main characters in the plot were dead (including the priest who reburied the bodies), except for John Dighton. This man, said to be guilty of regicide, was not punished but, if we are to believe Francis Bacon, was given a pension provided he resided in Calais. While it was known that Henry had little love for the Plantagenets, it is curious that he allowed the murder of his own wife's brothers to go unavenged.

Other questions arise. For example, Brackenbury was appalled at the thought of the murders, and if he handed over the Tower to Tyrell he must have known of the monstrous crime committed at Richard III's command, yet he still died fighting for his cause on Bosworth Field. The reaction of Elizabeth Woodville adds to the mystery. Polydore Vergil, an author commissioned by Henry VII to write a history in 1506, described her hearing of her sons' death in these words: ". . . forthwith she fell into a swoon and lay lifeless a good while; after coming to herself she weepeth, she cryeth out loud, and with lamentable shrieks maketh the house ring; she struck her breast, tore and cut her hair, and overcome in fine with dolour prayed also her own death."

Yet six months after this harrowing scene was supposed to have taken place, the dowager queen ended her feud with Richard and remained on friendly terms with him until Bosworth, her daughters often being guests at his palace for court festivities.

Then there is the question of motive: why should Richard wish to murder Edward V when he had already achieved his ambition of taking over the throne? What was there to be gained by secret murder which, should the truth become known, would only bring great discredit to him? If he wished to set the seal on his position by murder he could not have stopped at Edward, there were his five sisters whose claim to the throne as daughters of the late king were as valid as Edward's, while the Duke of Clarence's son was only barred from the throne by an attainder which Richard, who himself had been under the ban of an attainder earlier on, knew only too well could be revoked.

Richard III has been described as a "deep dissimular", yet if he chose to kill his nephews in the manner described by Henry VII he showed very little cunning. If he believed Edward remained a threat to his position, the whole point of killing him would be for it to be known he was dead and therefore no longer a potential focal point for revolt. With so much power at his disposal, Richard could easily have arranged for the deaths of the princes to appear as the result of natural causes (perhaps by incarcerating them with plague victims) so their bodies could be traditionally displayed at St Paul's.

Since Tudor times the enigmatic Richard has been regarded as our greatest royal villain. Tudor writers, including Shakespeare,* vied with each other in portraying the last Plantagenet monarch as a despicable monster. Yet the only evidence against Richard was given by Henry Tudor nearly two decades after he had usurped Richard's throne.

To some the pendulum has made a full swing and Richard is seen as a wronged Sir Galahad. We do know that he was a man of his times and when necessary could be ruthless, yet it does seem to me that there is considerable doubt as to his guilt over the murder of his nephews.

In 1674, when excavations were being carried out at the Tower, workmen found two skeletons ten feet beneath the foundations of a staircase in the White Tower, a point which does throw doubt on the part of Tyrell's confession about a priest managing to re-inter them secretly. The bones were left on a pile of rubbish until Charles II heard of them and, despite their being the third set of bones found in the precincts of the Tower which were thought to have been those of the princes, he commissioned Sir Christopher Wren to design a tomb for them in Westminster Abbey.

The marble sarcophagus was opened in 1933 by a Professor Wright who examined the bones. All he could conclude was that they were the skeletons of two children aged twelve-and-a-half and ten years, and no further light was shed on what really happened to Edward V.

* *Shakespeare's history was so faulty that he described Richard as fully adult and revelling in the slaughter of the Battle of Towton when in fact he was only eight years old. He also portrayed him as a hump-backed cripple, for which there is no evidence. Indeed, Richard must have been of good physique to have been able to make his gallant last charge at the Battle of Bosworth wearing his white German armour.*

CHAPTER NINE

The Murder of Count Philip Koningsmark

"Adorable one, I will love thee to the tomb!"

SOPHIA DOROTHEA OF Zell would have been crowned Queen of England when her husband became George I had it not been for a secret murder. "The story of the romantic life of the uncrowned queen has been shrouded in mystery," wrote the historian W.H. Wilkins. "She has been even more misrepresented than Mary Queen of Scots, her imprisonment in the lonely castle of Ahlden was longer and more rigorous than Mary's captivity in England, and the assassination of Koningsmark was as dramatic as the murder of Rizzio."

The proof of this royal murder only came to light after the actors in the tragedy had quit the stage. At first that stage resembled a setting for a Ruritanian masquerade in which extravagant ladies flirted with handsome men whose only concession to the background of war was their resplendent uniforms.

The master of the masque was Ernest Augustus, Elector of Hanover, who was famous throughout Europe for his devotion to excessive drinking, hunting and sex, and whose more esoteric interests included astrology and alchemy. No doubt his ambition to find the Philosopher's Stone was fired by the heavy financial demands of his sumptuous court and his stables which held six hundred horses. A glimpse of the elector's style is given by W.M. Thackeray in this description of a royal carriage ride, " . . . the stout coachman driving the ponderous gilt waggon, with eight cream-coloured horses in housings of scarlet velvet and morocco leather; a postilion on the leaders and a pair or half a dozen of running footmen scudding along by the side of the vehicle, with conical caps, long silver-headed maces which they poised aloft as they ran, and splendid jackets laced all over with silver and gold. I fancy the citizens' wives and their daughters looking out from the balconies; and the burghers over their beer, raising up, cup in hand , as the cavalcade passes through town with torch-bearers, trumpeters blowing their lusty cheeks out, and squadrons of jack-booted lifeguardsmen, girt with shining cuirasses, and bestriding thundering chargers, escorting his Highness's coach from Hanover to Herrenhausen; or halting, mayhap, at Madame Platen's country house of Monplaisir, which lies half-way between the summer-palace and the Residenz . . . "

One of the elector's most profitable ways of raising money was through the hiring out of his well-drilled troops. He once supplied 6,700 of them to the Seignority of Venice, of which only fourteen hundred eventually returned to Hanover.

"The ducats Duke Ernest got for his soldiers he spent in a series of the most brilliant entertainments," wrote Thackeray. "Nevertheless, the jovial Prince was economical, and kept a steady eye on his own interests. He achieved the electoral dignity for himself: he married his eldest son George to his beautiful cousin of Zell, and sending his sons out in command of armies — now on this side, now on that — he lived on, taking his pleasures and scheming his schemes, a merry, wise prince enough, not, I fear, a moral prince . . . "

Towards the end of the Sixteenth Century it was not uncommon for adventurers of both sexes to drift from court to court until their charm, sex appeal or martial prowess gained them a position of influence. Two such adventurers — one a female, one male — were to shape the destiny of Hanover under Ernest Augustus. The first was Clara Elizabeth von Meysenbuch, then aged twenty-three, who, with her sister Maria Catherine, was determined to win a place close to a crown.

The sisters first attempt to captivate a royal lover had been aided by their father, Count Charles Philip von Meysenbuch, who escorted them to Paris in the hope that one of them might succeed in becoming a mistress of the French king. It was an ambitious plot but the trio had not reckoned on the tenacity with which the established concubines were determined to keep their position. So frightening were their threats that the sisters quit France and, inspired by stories of the licentiousness of Ernest Augustus, arrived hopefully in his city.

In Hanover the girls discovered the conquest of the elector was not to be accomplished overnight, and in order to entrench themselves in his circle they married two courtiers. Maria Catherine allowed Major General John von dem Bussche to lead her to the alter while Clara Elizabeth was wed by Baron Ernest von Platen and from then on was known — and feared — as "La Platen".

This necessary matrimony did not dampen her ambition, and she began a series of intrigues which promoted her husband to the position of prime minister while she finally succeeded in becoming the elector's chief mistress. As such she was to reign supreme for the remainder of his lifetime, being shrewd enough not to object to him quenching his sexual appetites in other directions, sometimes with ladies of the court and sometimes with the maids who served them. His wife Sophia had been long accustomed to his blatant infidelities and focussed her energies upon her children.

In 1682 the elector saw it was in his financial interest for his eldest son George Lewis (later George I of England) to marry Sophia Dorothea, the daughter of the Duke of Zell. It was said that the bridegroom was "purchased in hard cash" by the duke who saw many political advantages in the match. An agreement was reached for him to give Ernest Augustus the equivalent of £30,000 in contemporary English money plus a £10,000 annual payment for the next ten years. George Lewis was reluctant to follow his father's plan, and only agreed to it on condition that he could keep Sophia Dorothea's handsome dowry, which was separate from the duke's payments, for himself.

"He did not like it, but the money tempted him as it would anyone else," his mother wrote.

The court of Zell, in which Sophia Dorothea spent the first sixteen years of her life, had a strong French influence which made it one of the most polished in Europe, and though the Hanoverian court was lavish the princess was to yearn for the wit and gaiety which characterised her home. Historical writers agree that she was as intelligent as she was attractive, and she had been engaged to a prince of Wolfenbuttel before family ambition cast her as the link between Zell and Hanover.

The wedding took place quietly in her apartment on November 21, and a few days later George Lewis took her on the state journey of thirty miles to Hanover with a cavalry regiment as an escort. A column of coaches full of courtiers, ministers and members of the elector's family rolled out to greet them and doubtless Dorothea was especially interested in the magnificent equipage in which her new father-in-law's mistress always travelled alone and in great splendour.

The only person to be completely satisfied with the marriage was the elector who, with the injection of money from Zell in his exchequer, ordered his architects to work on a new hunting lodge, magnificent new stables and a system of reservoirs for his country palace of Herrenhausen to provide it with fountains similar to those at Versailles.

The elector was more enthusiastic over his fountains than his son was over his bride who was equally indifferent to her dull and unpleasant husband. Already George Lewis had proved that he had inherited his father's sensual appetites, and Lord Chesterfield wrote of him after he had become King of England: "The King loved pleasure, and was not delicate in his choice of it. No woman came amiss to him, if they were very willing and very fat . . . the standard of His Majesty's taste made all those ladies who aspired to his favour, and who were near the staturable size, strain and swell themselves like the frogs in the fable to rival the bulk and dignity of the ox. Some succeeded, others burst."

George Lewis of Brunswick-Luneburg was born in Hanover on March 28, 1660, the first son of Ernest Augustus and his wife Sophia. She was the youngest daughter of Frederick of Wittelbach and Elizabeth Stuart, a daughter of King James I of England. It was through this thin blood line that George Lewis was to become the founder of the Hanoverian dynasty in England. He received the usual thorough education of a German prince, but his great interest was in stag hunting which was only equalled by his enthusiasm for the army when, at the age of fifteen, he went on his first campaign "bearing himself bravely at the battle of Conz on the Imperial side".

From the beginning of his marriage George Lewis did not disguise the fact that he preferred the military camp to the company of his high-spirited wife. He was at the siege of Vienna when she bore him his only son, the future George II of England; after which he went away on various campaigns, being at Buda when it was captured from the Turks and then soldiering in Greece, Germany and Flanders.

Though the birth of the royal heir seemed to have no emotional effect on George Lewis, it did cause the old elector to take an affectionate interest in Sophia Dorothea. While on a prolonged holiday in Italy in the winter of 1685 he sent word back to Hanover inviting her to join his party along with the von Platen and von Bussche families. Soon afterwards George Lewis arrived in Hanover from commanding the Emperor's troops in the east. It was a year since he had seen his wife, and he journeyed to Venice to join his father's entourage. On his arrival he found that the royal party had progressed to Rome, and rather than bother to follow it he remained in Venice to pursue his predictable pleasures before returning to the war.

When he returned to Hanover the following year he openly took a mistress. This was the result of intrigue by La Platen who, it was said, had encouraged the match between the Hanoverian heir and Sophia Dorothea in return for a bribe by William of Orange who feared the possibility of the elector's son marrying Princess Anne of England. Having helped to bring Sophia Dorothea to Hanover, La Platen soon found that the princess made no secret of her disdain for the official mistress. When the elector showed a growing affection for his beautiful daughter-in-law La Platen began to feel her position threatened. She therefore planned to isolate the princess as much as possible, and her first move in this direction was to find "a woman to control George Lewis" who was now spending more time at court.

She remembered that her now widowed sister Maria Catherine had entered into a brief affair with the prince before his marriage, and she endeavoured to reawaken his interest in her. If this had succeeded it would have given the sisters immense power as the favourites of the elector and his heir, but when George Lewis showed he had no desire to revive the old passion La Platen put forward another candidate for the royal favour.

Wilkes wrote: "The lady whom she chose as a decoy was Ermengrada Melusina von der Schulenberg,* the daughter of an illustrious and noble house. The young lady had only recently arrived in Hanover and was staying at Monplaisir. The countess introduced her to George Lewis on his return from Hungary with the result that he openly showed his preference for the company of the new arrival to that of his wife and it was this public humiliation which removed the last vestiges of any loyalty Sophia Dorothea might have felt towards her boorish husband."

Mademoiselle Schulenberg was certainly no beauty and as dull as her lover, which is perhaps what he found attractive about her.

"Look at them walking," the electress once said in disgust to an English lady visiting the court, "and think of her being my son's passion!"

There was no pretence of secrecy over the prince's relationship with La Platen's protegee, indeed it was regarded as something of an honour to be a regular bedfellow of one of the royal males of Hanover and special apartments were allocated for mademoiselle. Proud Sophia Dorothea could not accept the situation with the same equanimity as her mother-in-law accepted the promiscuity of the elector, and the birth of her daughter did nothing to reconcile her. Instead she ridiculed her husband's mistress to his face and made a fatal enemy of Countess von Platen whom she regarded as the author of her humiliation.

* * *

At last the stage is set, ready for the entry of the last actor in the tragedy. The year of 1688 was one of special splendour

In England she was to become the Duchess of Kendal, remaining a royal mistress until the death of George I.

in Hanover; the elector still had a huge income from Sophia Dorothea's father and his palace was completed, as was his new Italian opera house with its triple set of seats for court, nobility and citizens. The festivities of his court had become so famous that wealthy and noble personages made a habit of visiting it to take part in them.

In the March of that year the second adventurer in the story arrived upon the scene like a meteor flashing into the Hanoverian firmament. He was Count Philip Christopher von Konigsmark, a handsome soldier of fortune and scion of a distinguished Brandenberg family which had settled in Sweden where his father was a minister general.

The count was a member of an elite breed, which Thackeray described thus: "In the good old times of which I am treating, whilst common men were driven off by herds, and sold to fight the Emperor's enemies on the Danube, or to bayonet King Louis's troops of common men on the Rhine, noblemen passed from court to court, seeking service with one prince or the other, and naturally taking command of the ignoble vulgar soldiery which battled and died almost without hope of promotion. Noble adventurers travelled from court to court in search of employment; not merely noble males, but noble females too; and if these latter were beauties, and obtained favourable notice of princes, they stopped in the courts, became the favourites of their Serene or Royal Highnesses . . . "

As a boy Count Philip had spent some time at the court of Zell where he was frequently in the company of the pretty little princess; later he was to claim that even then her beauty and charm had captured his youthful heart. Now he was in Hanover to enjoy the final masquerade of the annual carnival, and Sophia Dorothea, arrayed in the crimson robes of a cardinal, was delighted when he was placed at her table. How the talk of her old playmate must have revived her carefree days before her odious marriage.

Since his days at Zell the count had built up a distinguished military career, and has been described as "a veteran amongst the most brilliant men of his time, a time when high rank, profuse expenditure and dashing manners gave entrance to society everywhere".

The following year Konigsmark returned to Hanover, accompanied by his beautiful sister Aurora and a splendid retinue which he was able to afford thanks to a welcome inheritance. The charm and obvious wealth of this noble couple greatly added to the lustre of the court, and in order to make it permanent the elector offered Konigsmark the highly prized post of Colonel of the Hanoverian Guards, which the Swede accepted gladly.

In the following months it was quite natural that Sophia Dorothea should enjoy the company of the glamorous brother and sister; in Aurora she found her first congenial friend in Hanover. At the balls and entertainments, which were so frequent at the court, it was protocol that she should be paired with the count as he was the most distinguished nobleman present after the elector and his sons.

Konigsmark and Prince Charles, a son of the elector, set out for the war against the Turks in distant Morea in the autumn of 1689. During the carnival of 1690 word came that the detachment commanded by the prince had been cut off and that he and Konigsmark were missing. The carnival was cancelled and the court changed into mourning when news came from Istanbul that the prince had been killed; the news of Konigsmark was that he had escaped. It is believed that the shock of the first message, followed by relief of the second, made Sophia Dorothea aware of the depth of her feelings for the count.

When he returned to Hanover in April he must have been surprised at the warmth of the welcome given him by the young woman who had been the target of his flirtatious flattery. And perhaps he saw for the first time the possibility of a relationship much more intimate than the superficial friendship permitted at court masques and royal picnics, especially as he would now be staying in Hanover. The elector gave him command of the royal guard and Konigsmark occupied a house close to the palace.

Despite his growing passion for Sophia Dorothea, Konigsmark was not the man to ignore the chance of another conquest. According to the author of the *Histoire de la Duchesse d'Hanover* when the Countess von Platen sought him out at a ball, "he replied to her overtures that he was overcome by her kindness, and would eagerly avail himself of her permission to visit her that evening. Konigsmark repaired to her house and found her *en deshabille* lying on a couch. She rose, and, having long since abandoned any sense of modesty, embraced him and declared the attraction his person had for her, to which avowal the count made a suitable response. At daybreak he retired, and on his return threw himself on his bed; but could not sleep, being overcome by self reproach arising out of the fact that he had succumbed to the charms of an open enemy of the princess."

When a rumour of the count's brief affair with La Platen reached the princess she was so distressed that Konigsmark contritely rejected the favourite with the inevitable result that she became an implacable enemy. At first this did little to reconcile Sophia Dorothea, and it is possible that had the count remained in Hanover she would have dismissed him as an untrustworthy philanderer, but the elector sent Konigsmark on a diplomatic mission and his absence did more for his cause with the princess than his presence.

It was on this journey that he began his correspondence with Sophia Dorothea, the letters being addressed in care of of her faithful lady-in-waiting from Zell, Elenora von dem Knesebeck whom the lovers were to refer to as La Sentinelle.

The following excerpt from his first letter gives an indication of the style of the scores which were to follow it: "I am now at an extremity and there is no means of saving myself excepting by a few lines from your incomparable hand; if I was so happy as to receive some I should at least be somewhat consoled: I hope you will not be so uncharitable as to refuse me this favour, since it is you who are the cause of my affliction it is just that you should be the one to comfort it . . . If I were not writing to a person for whom my respect is as great as my love I should find better terms to express my passion, but fearing to offend I must stop short, only entreating you not entirely to forget me, and to believe me to be your slave."

* * *

191

Some of the letters which passed between the couple were printed in *The Love of an Uncrowned Queen* by W.H. Wilkins, MA, of Clare College Cambridge, Fellow of the Royal Historical Society, which was published in 1903.

"My researches were made from love of the work," he wrote. "In my quest I followed as closely as possible the footsteps of Sophia Dorothea during her life. I visited Zell where she was born, Hanover where she lived during her unhappy marriage and Ahlden where for more than thirty years she was imprisoned. To Hanover I went again and again, and I also visited Berlin and Dresden, but it was not until 1897 that I lighted by chance, while turning over old volumes in a secondhand bookshop at Leipzig, upon the fact that an unpublished correspondence between Sophia Dorothea and Konigsmark existed. For a long time I could not find where these letters were deposited and went in vain search to Upsala, but at least I learned they were reposing in the library of the little university of Lunde in Sweden. To Lunde accordingly I went and with permission of the university authorities carefully examined the manuscripts."

These letters had found their way into Sweden through Konigsmark's sister Amalie, Countess Lowenhaupt, who married a Swedish nobleman.

Other letters were found in Berlin. After the death of Konigsmark Hanoverian agents seized many of the letters which had passed between the lovers and these were used to convince Sophia Dorothea's parents of their daughter's guilt. Her father asked for them to be sent to Zell so he could destroy them but the elector refused. Later they were found among the papers of Frederick the Great. Sophia Dorothea's daughter was his mother, and it is thought that George Lewis, when he had become George I of England, sent them to her to undermine the sympathy she felt for her mother. Wilkins wrote that the letters in Berlin were similar to those he saw at Lunde, the handwriting, style and ciphers being identical. Some of the Berlin letters were replies to some held at Lunde and vice versa. The Lunde collection was made up of six hundred and seventy-nine sheets, one hundred and twenty-nine of them being written by Sophia Dorothea and the remainder by the grandiloquent count. They were written mostly in French, with a few pages in German, and unfortunately shed little light on the events which led up to the tragedy, rather they were full of jealous reproaches and passionate avowels.

When Konigsmark returned to Hanover he continued to write to the princess, the following example giving an indication that at this stage the count was still pursuing a lady who on the surface at least showed reluctance to become his lover: "For God's sake, do not show me any coldness! I fancied that when you left the room you would not deign to look at me. How that seeming affront stung me! I am not the cause of what happened yesterday, you must blame the stars that rule our lives — you must blame them and not me, for I love and adore you, and think only, day and night, of how to please you. Behold my face, my conduct, my steps, my looks — do you think I fail in the least trifle? Do you notice any signs of weariness? Alas! Far from that, I love you more than ever. My passion upsets my reason, and that is why I cannot conceal what I feel. Adorable one, I will love thee to the tomb! Tonight thou shalt be mine — yea, though I perish."

At last Sophia Dorothea admitted her feelings to the count and underlined them by finally committing herself to paper. The significance of this caused Konigsmark to write while on a journey to the frontier: "Were you to see me you would say to yourself: Is it possible for a man to be so sad? This is merely the result of this absence. My noble travelling companion could tell you the state in which he sees me daily. I hide the cause from him, as you may well believe. You will not perhaps believe it, but, on the word of a gentleman, I have been many times so beside myself that I thought I should faint."

Though the count's letters followed the extravagant and flowery style of his day, he sometimes included a playful or amusing touch. In one he wrote to Sophia Dorothea while she was visiting Zell that he had not given up feminine companionship in her absence, indeed there was one lady so like herself that he spent as much time as possible in her company. He added to the confession that he had an inkling that his feelings were reciprocated but he would not mention her name in case it should arouse feelings of jealousy.

If the princess was puzzled by this frank admission, she soon saw it as a piece of teasing when a letter from one of her ladies-in-waiting mentioned that Count Konigsmark must indeed be bored to spend so much of his time playing with children; he would spend hours building houses out of playing cards to amuse Prince George and little Princess Sophia Dorothea, the lady who was so like her mother.

The couple became lovers early in 1692, the princess allowing her heart to rule her head when Konigsmark gave her the choice of sharing his passion or seeing him volunteer for active service in Morea. After this they enjoyed secret assignations in Hanover through the connivance of Elenore von dem Knesebeck whose official duty it was to act as chaperone whenever her mistress received a visitor.

Sometimes separation heightened the intense love they felt for each other. In June Konigsmark had to spend some time with his regiment under George Lewis in Flanders, on another occasion the princess visited Zell. Here her mother discovered the cause of her daughter's new found lightness of heart, and fearful of the consequences implored her to break off the dangerous relationship. Sophia Dorothea was so impressed by her mother's concern and her portrayal of the ruin it could lead to that she wrote a panic-stricken letter to the count begging him to marry — marry anyone suitable for his situation in life! — so that they would be both placed beyond temptation and peril.

Marriage to an unloved spouse had not removed temptation from Sophia Dorothea so why she thought it would have such an effect on someone like Konigsmark we do not know, but such dramatic pleas and ultimatums give the impression of two children playing an exciting make-believe game, unaware or careless of menacing forces in the background.

To the suggestion that he should marry the count replied: "At last the tragic day which I have so much feared has arrived! I must marry, since you wish it done. I must follow your wishes; you will it so — that is enough, my death warrant is signed by the hand I adore. I should never have expected so fatal a sentence signed by you. But of what can I complain? I must remember that I have loved you a year. I ought to have known the sex better than to believe all you have said to me, but alas! as I was weak enough to believe it, I must now be firm enough to bear all the consequencies."

The tone of this letter ended the princess' plan and the relationship continued with dozens more letters passing between the couple. These letters were to be their bane, mainly because of Konigsmark's carelessness. When he was away he would number them so that his royal mistress would know if a letter had gone astray, but as he often forgot the number of the previous letter the system only added to the confusion. Intervals between the arrival of letters were often inexplicably erratic; sometimes Sophia Dorothea would realise by the content of one letter that the one before it had never arrived and, most sinister of all, there were signs of tampering.

Once Konigsmark wrote to Prince Ernest, the youngest of the elector's sons and the count's special friend, and the letter was delivered to and partly read by George Lewis. This postal error alarmed Konigsmark because he had written some coarse jokes at the expense of the von Platens, yet the incident did not make him realise the perils of his correspondence with Sophia Dorothea.

Soon friends were warning the count of his danger. A court flirtation was acceptable provided it went no further, than whispered words at a ball or languishing glances at receptions, but to take the princess as a lover was a deadly insult to the royal house, even though her husband had no use for her. Aurora Konigsmark repeatedly warned her rash brother, as did one of his best military friends, as this letter to the princess in the autumn of 1693 shows: "What will you say, Madam, when you learn that they did not let me go through the day without the misfortune I dreaded? Marshal Podevils was the first to tell me to beware of my conduct because he knew on good authority I was watched . . . Prince Ernest has told me the same thing; he is not quite so guarded as the other, for he admitted that the conversation I had from time to time with you might draw upon me very serious and unpleasant consequences."

At this time Konigsmark was suffering an economic set-back as the result of continuing in the service of the elector in order to be close to the princess. Sweden had come into conflict with Hanover, and Konigsmark was warned by the King of Sweden that if he continued his loyalty to the elector his estates at home would be confiscated. When this happened a large portion of his income dried up which meant he could no longer afford to gamble like a gentleman or keep up his extravagant retinue. Yet he must have found compensation in Sophia Dorothea's promise that she would devote herself to him for the rest of her life if she could escape from Hanover to some safe refuge. Sweden would have been an ideal haven had not Konigsmark fallen out with the king. The only other possible place they could elope to was Brunswick-Wolfenbuttel whose duke, Anthony Ulrich, had a grudge against Hanover and would have been delighted to shelter its runaway princess — or so he claimed years later when he said that he had expected the fugitives to seek sanctuary with him.

Konigsmark realised the difficulties of trying to escape without money for bribes and livelihood, and now that he was relatively poor it would have to come from the princess. She appealed to her mother for an allowance and the Duchess of Zell, aware that despite the immense marriage settlement and dowry her daughter was not allowed money of her own, told her that she would do what she could.

In the spring of 1694 the duchess consulted James Cresset, the English envoy to the duchy, about investing money for Sophia Dorothea in the newly-established English Funds. But there was delay over this because the Duke of Zell's finances had long been embarrassed by the large sums he had paid to the elector.

Though nothing definite had been arranged for the elope-ment by the beginning of 1694, it seemed that Fortune was going to unexpectedly remember her favourite soldier. Konigsmark's old friend Duke Frederick Augustus unexpec-tedly inherited the electoral throne of Saxony through the death of his brother. He owed the count a huge "debt of honour" and Konigsmark hurried to Dresden to claim it.

Frederick Augustus had to admit that he was not yet in a position to pay, but meanwhile he would do everything in his power to help and offered him the post of major general in his army. Not only would this help financially, but the transfer of his services from Hanover would be the first step to a reconciliation with the King of Sweden.

At last the count had something to celebrate, but in doing so he committed the biggest blunder in his indiscreet career. The riotous court at Dresden was a byword even in those days of aristocratic debauchery and Konigsmark plunged into its revels with the new elector. While drunk he boasted too freely about his amorous conquests and let two forbidden names past his lips — the Electoral Princess Sophia Dorothea and Countess von Platen. After such an affront to Ernest Augustus and George Lewis the count's companions wondered if he would dare to set foot in Hanover again, for without doubt spies would have hastened there with news of his indiscretion.

Yet in June Konigsmark did return. On his arrival he drew a month's pay to which he was entitled and made plans to sell his house. He ordered his steward to collect a train of fifty-two horses and mules, a fine carriage and a number of extra servants to convey his household and furniture to Dresden. This was done, and the wagons were ready to set out when, on the night on Sunday July 1, Count Konigsmark left his house at ten o'clock in the evening and disappeared.

* * *

There has been much speculation as to how he met his fate, but first let us look at the known facts. Because of his irregular habits his servants felt no anxiety for two days, but when he did not come home on the third his secretary, Hildebrande, became uneasy and visited Marshal Podevils who advised him to wait a couple more days before taking action. After twelve hours the faithful secretary could wait no more and he sent a message to the authorities in Dresden informing them of their new major general's disappearance. On the following day, Friday, he wrote to Aurora in Hamburg stating that he did not now think he would ever find his master alive and that he was in "the liveliest anxiety that a mortal can be in", being convinced of the death of "him whom all my life I shall mourn with hot tears".

Rudiger, the count's chamberlain, also wrote to Aurora, describing how he had seen Konigsmark leave his house in some sort of disguise, being dressed in poor grey clothes with a brown coat over his shoulders.

On Friday, July 7, an adjutant visited the Konigsmark household with a rumour that the count was still alive but was being held prisoner in La Platen's house. The same rumour reached Konigsmark's brother-in-law General Lowenhaupt who was stationed on the Rhine, but this was followed by other tidings that the count had been assassinated.

From Zell James Cresset wrote: "Konigsmark's commerce with our electoral princess is all come out and the count is murdered . . . Konigsmark's papers have all been seized and the princess and her letters discovered. She is undone and her mother and father will hardly outlive the disgrace. I am in their confidence and comfort them all I can you may be sure, for better princes or people there cannot be on earth."

Aurora did the most to try and establish the fate of her brother. First she travelled with her sister Amalie, Countess Lowenhaupt, to Zell, and gaining no information there she set out to Hanover to demand her brother. When she was met with outright discourtesy and negative statements she hurried on to Saxony to enlist the help of Konigsmark's old friend the Elector Frederick Augustus. She remained there "beseeching for her brother as if he was still alive", while the elector called for an explanation from Hanover as to the disappearance of his officer. A brief reply came that Konigsmark was technically in the Hanoverian service since he had not resigned his commission or presented his accounts, therefore if he was found the Elector of Hanover would be at liberty to deal with him as a deserter.

It was not only the Elector of Saxony who was interested in the fate of Konigsmark. Hanover was bombarded with letters of inquiry and indignation from courts all over the Continent and it was feared the affair would endanger the

Grand Alliance. Threats from Saxony became so extreme that Ernest Augustus prepared for hostilities, and it took the intervention of the Emperor and William III of England to allay the fury of "that madman at Dresden". One result of Frederick Augustus' interest in the case was that Aurora became his mistress and bore him a son who became the celebrated Marshal Saxe.

Meanwhile in Hanover the name of Sophia Dorothea was deleted from the state prayers, and in the palace every token of her presence removed after she was sent to the Castle of Ahlden where she was to remain a prisoner for thirty-two years until her death there. Her children were never allowed to visit her, but her son did manage to secrete a portrait of her which he kept hidden during his father's lifetime. As a young man he tried to plan her escape: this came to nothing but his resentment of his father's treatment of his mother never abated.

Ernest Augustus instituted proceedings on behalf of his heir, the case going before an ecclesiastical court which, on December 28, 1694, granted the divorce and gave the innocent party permission to marry again if he wished. It was granted on the grounds of desertion by the princess; throughout the case no mention of Konigsmark or adultery was raised as this would have reflected on the honour of the House of Hanvover.

At the time of the scandal the Viscomte de Beaucaire wrote of the princess: "Whether she was guilty or not mattered little. They wanted no more of her. They had to be bribed to take her; she had given children to assure a succession; they had got her money and they had made certain of her inheritance, and that was enough."

Elenora von dem Knesebeck was imprisoned without a trial in the ancient fortress of Scharzfels perched on a crag in the Harz Mountains. For three years she remained shut up in one room until she was dramatically rescued by a loyal servant of the family she had served who, disguised as a tiler, lowered her on a rope down the eighty-foot castle wall. She managed to reach Vienna where she lived quietly until her beloved mistress' daughter Sophia married the Crown Prince

199

of Prussia and Brandenburg whereupon she entered her services in Berlin.

In 1698 Geoege Lewis became the new elector and Sophia Dorothea wrote to him that she hoped that the "depth and sincerity" of her repentance might soften his heart so that he might "permit me to see and embrace our beloved children. My gratitude for this . . . will be infinite since I desire nothing else to enable me to die content."

He made no reply, nor did he relent in 1714 when prior to his departure to claim the English crown his family tried to induce him to relax the harshness of his ex-wife's imprisonment. It is thought that had he done so it might have lessened his unpopularity in Britain where his treatment of Sophia Dorothea, contrasted with his fondness for his two German mistresses known descriptively as the Elephant and Castle by the irreverent English public, were the subject of endless pamphlets, lampoons and ballads.

When Sophia Dorothea died in November 1726, there was no recognition of the event in Hanover, but in England the *London Gazette* did announce the demise of "the Duchess-Dowager of Hanover."

* * *

There have been several accounts of what actually happened to Konigsmark, at least one of which is said to be based on a confession by one of the guards involved in the assassination. Apart from minor details, the main difference between the versions is the amount of guilt apportioned to the Elector Ernest Augustus, his mistress Countess von Platen and his son George Lewis.

A representative description of the crime was given by Wilkins who wrote: "On Sunday, July 1 1694, Konigsmark received a note from the princess written in a feigned hand asking him to come to her that night without fail and appointing the hour and mentioning the signal. In obedience to this summons long expected the same night between ten and eleven he stole out of his house . . . Arriving at the Liene Schloss Konigsmark went round to the wing where the prin-

Count Philip Konigsmark (By courtesy of the Radio
nes Hulton Picture Library).

38 *A manuscript illustration of Henry VI's court
with the Earl of Shrews-
bury presenting a book to
Margaret of Anjou*

9 *Sophia Dorothea of
ell, wife of George I (By
ourtesy of the Radio Times
ulton Picture Library)*

40   *Albert Victor, Duke of Clarence, son of Edward VII and Ripper suspect. Photograph taken in 1891 (By courtesy of the Radio Times Hulton Picture Library).*

cess's apartments were situated and gave the signal, whistling a few bars of a well known air. The signal was probably answered by a light at the window and a minute later he was admitted through the postern by Knesebeck and conducted to the princess's chamber. Here she withdrew and the lovers were left alone. They had not seen one another for more than three months and now met under the shadow of great peril.

"Both were ready to take the fatal plunge and brave the consequences. There could hardly be a more favourable time than the present, so it seemed to them: the electoral prince was in Berlin, the electress at Herrenhausen; there was no one of all the royal Hanoverian family in Hanover but the old elector, weak and ailing, in a far off wing of the palace; time and circumstances alike were favourable for flight."

Wilkins claimed that through one of her spies the Countess von Platen, still enraged by Konigsmark's drunken gossip about her in Dresden, learned of the meeting and hurried to the elector's apartment where she told him with much agitation and many gestures that Konigsmark was even now in the chamber of the electoral princess and besought him to take immediate steps to punish the offenders . . . If His Highness would leave the matter to her she would find a way to arrest Konigsmark quickly and then the elector might punish the delinquents at his leisure.

On obtaining his agreement La Platen hurried to the guard-room where she swore four halberdiers to secrecy and then posted them close to Sophia Dorothea's apartments. When the count left the outer door of these he stole down a long corridor leading to a magnificent hall known as the Rittersaal.

Wilkins continued: "A door had purposely been left unbarred for his exit and it was now locked . . . he turned to retrace his step. At that moment the four desperados sprang from their hiding place and rushed upon him with their weapons. The unfortunate man realised he was caught in a trap but though taken by surprise he defended himself. For a few minutes there was fierce conflict during which two of his adversaries were wounded and although Konigsmark was fighting in the dark against four armed men the results seemed uncertain until his sword broke. This placed him at the mercy of his assailants and he fell severely wounded in the hip by a cut from a battleaxe and run through the body by a sword. As he fell his cry was 'Spare the princess. Spare the innocent princess.'"

Other authors lay the blame squarely on the elector and his son George Lewis, declaring that the motive had not been inspired by La Platen's desire for revenge but because proof had come to light that the couple intended to elope. Certainly it would seem that the removal of a noble as famous as Konigsmark, who was an excellent swordsman, in the midst of the royal palace could only have been done with the knowledge and discretion of the elector and his son. They must have certainly watched the progress of the affair, allowing the couple every chance to incriminate themselves, until a point was reached where, for the honour of the royal family, it was decided to remove the count.

In her book *The Life and Times of George I* Joyce Marlow wrote: "One set of the proliferating rumours stated that Ernest Augustus had ordered the assassination with the agreement of his son. Another set had Ernest Augustus actually present in Sophia Dorothea's apartment during the gruesome murder, though it was agreed that George Lewis was not in Hanover when it took place ... The saddest set of rumours said that Sophia Dorothea and Konigsmark had finally realised that their love was star-crossed and could not continue. He had come to the palace to bid the final 'adieu' to his beloved mistress, only to be cruelly butchered, either at the instigation of Ernest Augustus with the connivance of George Lewis, or by the hirelings of the Countess von Platen."

Though nothing definite about the count's murder came to light during the lifetime of George I, his body was discovered beneath the floor of Sophia Dorothea's apartment when alterations were being made to the palace during the reign of George II.

"The discovery was hushed up," wrote Horace Walpole. "George II entrusted the secret to his wife, Queen Caroline, who told it to my father; but the king was too tender of the honour of his mother to utter it to his mistress ..."

CHAPTER TEN

Royalty and the Ripper by Colin Wilson

"AT A QUARTER to four on Friday morning, Police Constable Neil was on his beat in Bucks Row, Thomas Street, Whitechapel, when his attention was attracted to the body of a woman lying on the pavement close to the door of the stable yard in connection with Essex Wharf. Bucks Row, like many other minor thoroughfares in this and similar neighbourhoods, is not overburdened with gas lamps, and in the dim light the constable at first thought that the woman had fallen down in a drunken stupor and was sleeping off the effects of a night's debauch. With the aid of the light from his bull's-eye lantern Neil at once perceived that the woman had been the victim of some horrible outrage. Her livid face was stained with blood and her throat cut from ear to ear. . ."

Thus the *Illustrated Police News* for September 8, 1888, introduced the British public to the handiwork of the killer who would become known as Jack the Ripper. In fact, the woman in Bucks Row may not have been the Ripper's first victim; two other women — Emma Smith and Martha Tabram — had been stabbed by unknown assassins in the Whitechapel area earlier that year; but their deaths had attracted little attention. What caused the sensation in the Bucks Row case was that when the body was stripped in the morgue, it was found to have been disembowelled.

Moreover, by the time the *Illustrated Police News* was on sale with its account of the Bucks Row murder — the victim had been identified as a forty-two-year-old prostitute named Polly Nichols — the Whitechapel murderer had already killed another woman. She was Annie Chapman, another prostitute, and she was found in the backyard of a lodging house at 29 Hanbury Street; she was lying on her back, with her throat cut, and her stomach slashed open — some of the intestines had been pulled out. The doctor who examined the body gave his opinion that she had been killed with a thin bladed and very sharp knife. A woman who had passed the entry to 29 Hanbury Street at five thirty that morning saw a woman — probably the victim — talking to a dark haired man who wore a deerstalker hat. "He looked like a foreigner".

This second mutilation murder caused a sensation — particularly when it became known that her kidney and ovaries were missing. At the inquests on both victims, the murderer's swiftness and silence had been emphasised; in both cases, people were sleeping with open windows within yards of the murder. It looked as if a madman of exceptional savagery and cunning was responsible. The newspapers clamoured for action. The police made several arrests, and had to release their suspects almost immediately. A woman in Blackfriars Road collapsed and died as she read about the murder. There had been no comparable sensation since the Ratcliffe Highway murders of 1811, when the butchery of two families in East London had caused panic from end to end of the British Isles.

The killer seems to have had a highly developed sense of drama; three weeks later, on the morning of September 30, he killed two women. The first was a Swedish prostitute called Elizabeth Stride, who was killed in the backyard of a workers educational club in Berner Street; the Ripper seems to have been interrupted when a cart drove into the yard, and escaped as the driver — seeing the woman's body — ran inside for help. He walked a mile in the direction of the City, picked up a prostitute who had just been released from Bishopsgate Police Station, and killed and disembowelled her in a corner of Mitre Square. A policeman patrolled the square regularly, and had probably passed the Ripper and his victim without seeing them when he came back a quarter of an hour later, the mutilated woman lay on the pavement; her face had been slashed, and her left kidney and entrails removed and taken away. The murderer had paused to wash his hands at a public sink within yards of the body, then paused again in nearby Goulston Street to discard a piece of the dead woman's apron and to chalk on a wall: "The Juwes are The men That Will not be Blamed for nothing." The following morning, the Central News Agency received a post-card smeared with blood, and signed 'Jack the Ripper'. The writer informed the 'boss' of the agency that they would hear of a 'double event' the next day, and noted that the first victim 'squealed a bit'. In fact, a woman near the Berner Street yard *had* heard a muffled scream at about the time of the murder.

The card was written in a neat, legible handwriting, and was not the first of 'the Ripper's' communications. A letter-card had been received two days before the double murder, explaining that the writer had 'a real down on whores and I shan't quit ripping them till I do get buckled.' He also promised to clip the lady's ears off next time and send them to the police. The handwriting and signature were the same as on the letter card; here the writer apologised for being unable to get the ears for the police. The card had been written and posted on Sunday, September 30 — the day of the murder, before the newspaper had time to print news or details of the crime — a point that has led most writers on the case to conclude that these two letters are probably genuine.

The final murder, the most gruesome and spectacular of all, occurred in the early hours of November 8, 1888. At 10.45 that day, a man knocked on the door of 13 Miller's Court, Dorset Street, to try to persuade the tenant to pay her rent. The woman — another prostitute named Mary Jeanette Kelly — was thirty-five shillings in debt. Unable to obtain a reply, the man peered through the window — and saw a naked bloodstained corpse on the bed. When police entered the room through a window — the door was locked — they saw a scene like a butcher's shop. The heart had been placed beside the head; the breasts were on the table; some of the entrails hung on a nail on the picture rail. The killer must have spent hours cutting up the body.

It was the greatest sensation so far. But it was also the Ripper's last bow. He was never heard of again, although two women who were stabbed to death in the following year are sometimes described as Ripper victims.

Understandably, the case has continued to excite morbid curiosity ever since. For many years after the crimes, the most widespread theory was that the killer was an insane doctor, perhaps suffering from 'religious mania.' This story was given its definitive form in 1929 in *The Mystery of Jack the Ripper* by a Member of Parliament, Leonard Matters. The Ripper, he said, was a certain Dr Stanley, whose only son had contracted venereal disease from a prostitute. Mad with grief, Dr Stanley set out to track her down. Every woman he questioned about her he murdered – in case they warned his intended victim. The latter was, of course, Mary Kelly. Years later, Matters claims, Dr Stanley died in Buenos Aires where he confessed his crimes to a former student, who was present at his deathbed.

But then, the medical report on Mary Kelly says nothing about venereal disease. What it *does* say is that she was three months pregnant. And it was this that led another 'Ripperologist' William Stewart, to the odd conclusion that Jack the Ripper was actually a woman – a sadistic midwife, who had gone to Miller's Court to perform an abortion.

Another story that is almost certainly pure fiction and is recounted by the novelist William LeQueux; in a book called *Things I Know* (1923), he claims that after the murder of Rasputin in St Petersburg, the Kerensky government handed him a manuscript written in French; it had been found in the basement of Rasputin's house, and was called *Great Russian Criminals*. This, says LeQueux, revealed that Jack the Ripper was a mad Russian doctor named Alexander Pedachinko, who had been sent to London by the Russian secret police to embarrass their British colleagues; he committed his murders with the aid of two accomplices. In an appendix to my own biography of Rasputin, I have disposed of LeQueux's story by pointing out that Rasputin spoke no French, and that his house had no basement – he lived in a flat on the fourth floor. In 1959, the Pedachenko theory was revived by a journalist named Donald McCormick, buttressed by 'new evidence' – the manuscript of a book called *Chronicles of Crime* by a Dr Thomas Dutton. McCormick had seen this book, and taken extensive notes, in 1932, while the doctor was still alive; Dutton believed that Pedachenko was also called Konovalov, and that he made a living as a barber surgeon — like another Ripper suspect, George Chapman, the sadistic poisoner. But then, anyone who has read LeQueux's two books on Rasputin will have no difficulty in concluding that the man was an unscrupulous inventor of 'facts', and that therefore, the 'French manuscript' story is probably invention. And since Dutton's manuscript *Chronicles of Crime* has also vanished, there is no way of knowing how he came to be convinced that the Pedachenko story has some basis in fact.

I have mentioned these various theories because it is as well to dispose of them before we turn to the real subject of this chapter — the scandalous suggestion that Jack the Ripper was a member of the royal family. There are, in fact, now no less than three theories, all involving the same man, Edward, the Duke of Clarence, grandson of Queen Victoria, and heir to the throne of England. The simplest way of introducing these theories is to speak of my own involvement.

In 1960, I wrote a series of articles for the London *Evening Standard* under the title 'My Search for Jack the Ripper.' I had been interested in the case ever since, as a child, I had heard my grandmother describe how she had been a child in East London at the time of the murders, and how the children were always made to come home before dark for fear of the Ripper. In the early 1950s, I began to write a novel based loosely on the murders — it was called *Ritual in the Dark*. When I married and came to live in London, I began to study the case, wandering around the murder sites in Whitechapel — most of them looking exactly as they had in 1888 — and reading accounts of the murders in *The Times* for 1888. (This is available in the Reading Room of the British Museum).

As a result of these articles, I received many letters. One of them came from a doctor named T.E.A. Stowell, who told me that it was clear that I know the identity of the Ripper, even if I had been careful to conceal it. I replied that I had no idea of his identity, and saying that I would be glad to hear Doctor Stowell's own theory. The result was that he invited me to lunch at the Athenaeum.

Stowell proved to be a charming old gentleman who was obviously close on retirement. From something he said, I vaguely gathered that he was a brain surgeon — an idea I later found to be erroneous — and remember observing with a certain fascination the shaking of his hand as he cut his steak.

Stowell had a strange story to tell me, and one that, I must confess, I found hard to follow. (My knowledge of the royal family was minimal, and I was too embarrassed to admit that the only Duke of Clarence I'd heard about was the one who was drowned in a butt of Malmsey.) In essence, it was as follows:

In the 1930s, Stowell was acquainted with Caroline Acland, the daughter of Sir William Gull, Physician in Ordinary to Queen Victoria. At some point, she asked Stowell's advice about certain of her father's papers, which contained some curious matters pertaining to the Duke of Clarence. Their most interesting revelation, he said, was that the Duke (who was known as Eddie) did not die in the 'flu epidemic of 1892 — as stated in the history books — but in a mental home near Sandringham, of a softening of the brain due to syphilis. There was also some mysterious hint about Jack the Ripper, and about a scandal in Cleveland Street, Soho (concerning a homosexual brothel) in which the Duke had been concerned.

At all events, Stowell had apparently advised Caroline Ackland to destroy the papers — or perhaps this was a decision she had taken anyway. Then Stowell began brooding on the strange documents and on the secrets they concealed. And he soon came upon some interesting clues. There was, for example, the odd story of the medium R.J. Lees, who is often mentioned in spiritualist circles as the man who caught Jack the Ripper. The story goes that Lees dreamed of some of the murders before they happened, and clearly saw the face of the killer. One day, on a London bus, he suddenly recognised the 'Ripper' sitting opposite him. He followed him home, to a large house near Park Lane, then went to the police. They checked, and told him that the house belonged to a well known doctor who was connected with the royal family. They were so impressed by Lee's sincerity that they watched the house, and one night caught the doctor as he was setting out to prowl the East End, his knife concealed in a black bag. His wife admitted that her husband had been overworking, and had been behaving oddly recently. . . The doctor was incarcerated in a mental home in Islington, and Lees was rewarded with a pension from the Privy Purse. . .

There is, in fact, no evidence of a pension from the Privy Purse. But Queen Victoria *had* invited Lees to the palace on two occasions. It could have been because she was hoping to receive spirit messages from Prince Albert. It could, said Stowell, have been because there was some grain of truth in the story about Lees and Jack the Ripper. . . In fact, Caroline Acland had told him that a detective, accompanied by a medium, *had* visited their house at 74 Grosvenor Square (near Park Lane) and asked Lady Gull some impertinent questions that had infuriated her.

This made it sound as if Gull was Jack the Ripper. But that was impossible. Gull had had a stroke in 1887, the year before the murders, and had died three years later of a second stroke; he was in no condition to stalk around the East End. But there was an odd story in Gull's papers to the effect that Gull suffered from lapses of memory, and one day awoke with blood on his shirt. Somehow, Stowell inferred that Gull knew that Eddie, Duke of Clarence, was Jack the Ripper, and set out to shield him. He had probably got the blood on his shirt from examining Eddie after one of the murders. . .

It was all bewildering stuff, and I found it hard to take in. Stowell's own attitude puzzled me. He told me solemnly that he wanted the story kept secret in case it 'upset Her Majesty' — he told me this later, when I suggested writing about it — yet he gave me the impression that his 'secret' filled him with mischievous schoolboyish delight, and that he would not have been too worried if I had ignored his prohibition and published it.

I never met him again, but we corresponded, and some time later had a long talk on the telephone — by then he had retired to the south coast — during which he repeated much of what he had told me; I made notes as he talked. In retrospect, I get the feeling that he actually wanted me to publish the story — but against his express wishes, so to speak, so that he could feel completely absolved. But although I talked about his theory to various friends with an interest in "Ripperology" (a word I coined in a *Books and Bookmen* review), I stuck to my promise not to write about it. One of these friends was Nigel Morland, editor of *The Criminologist.* And, in 1970, Nigel persuaded Dr Stowell to tell his astonishing story for the benefit of his readers. The article — 'Jack the Ripper — A Solution', appeared in the issue for December 1970. The good doctor was still being coy. He declined to actually name his suspect, but dropped some very broad hints. *The Sunday Times* got wind of the revelation in November 1970, and rang up Donald McCormick (who worked for the newspaper) to ask if he had any idea of the identity of Stowell's suspect. He did, since I had told him; the result was an article stating that, according to Stowell, the Duke of Clarence was Jack the Ripper. The following evening, Kenneth Allsop questioned Stowell on the *'Twenty Four Hours'* programme on TV, and although Stowell declined to name his suspect, he made no objection when Allsop tacitly assumed it was Clarence. (Allsop was, in fact, another close friend whom I'd told about the theory years before).

Having let the cat out of the bag, I think Stowell was startled at the publicity he received. It was a piquant news item, and it went round the world within hours. A correspondent to the *Sunday Times* pointed out that Clarence had been on a world tour in 1889 — to which Stowell might have replied, had he been inclined, that he had already discussed that very point in his article. But a piece in *The Times* was more to the point; someone had checked on the Court Circular for 1888, and discovered that Eddie was at Balmoral in Scotland, on the day after the murders. Yet even this discovery was less conclusive than it looked, since the murders had taken place not long after midnight on Sunday, and the Duke was not in Scotland until Monday. Even in those days, British Rail was efficient enough to convey an heir to the throne from London to Scotland in twenty four

210

hours. (In fact, train times in those days were incredibly swift — only modern high speed trains have surpassed them.)

The sudden burst of publicity — and indignant criticism from royalists — was too much for Stowell, who died a few weeks after the article was published. His son seems to have become so bored with enquiries about his father's papers that he burned everything that related to the Ripper case.

It made no difference, of course, since Stowell had already told me everything. By way of preserving it while it was still fairly fresh in my mind, I wrote it all down in an article for my home-town newspaper, the *Leicester Chronicle,* and the bulk of this article was subsequently published as an appendix to my book *Order of Assassins.*

About a year after Stowell's death, I received a letter from an old friend, Michael Harrison, asking if he could quote my *Leicester Chronicle* article in a book he was writing — a biography of Eddie, the Duke of Clarence. In a postscript, he mentioned casually that he had now definitely established the Ripper's identity, and that he at present had a letter written by the Ripper lying on his desk. It was about six months later that I was allowed to see a proof copy, and finally learned the identity of Michael's suspect. Again, it was a man of whom I'd never heard. But in this case, at least, I was able to follow the chain of reasoning that had led to the identification.

From the beginning, Michael Harrison was convinced that Stowell's theory was absurd; Eddie was simply not the type of person to become a mass murderer. Let me, at this point, summarise the essence of Stowell's theory — based, let us recall, on what he had seen of the papers of Sir William Gull. According to Stowell, his suspect, whom he calls 'S', was an 'heir to power and wealth'. At the age of sixteen he went on a round the world cruise, and in the course of a 'gay party' in the West Indies, contracted syphilis. Stowell believed — although he does not say so in his article — that 'S' was homosexual, and that the syphilis was contracted from another man. It was the syphilis, according to Stowell, that gradually led to a softening of the brain, and to the Whitechapel murders. Immediately after the double murder, 'S' experi-

211

enced total collapse, and was confined at a mental home near Sandringham. By this time, the royal family was aware that he was Jack the Ripper, and had placed him under the care of Sir William Gull. In November, 'S' escaped and committed the final murder of Mary Kelly, after which he was again locked up. He recovered enough in the following year to go on a five month cruise, and to undertake a few public engagements. He even made short speeches. But he was now 'on the downward path from the manic stage of syphilis to the depression and dementia which in time must inevitably overtake him.' And when the final collapse came, his death was blamed on the flu epidemic.

As Michael Harrison read this account of the life of the Duke of Clarence (Stowell mentions in his article that 'S' was nicknamed 'Collar and Cuffs' — a name first applied to Eddie by the journalist Henry Labouchere, on account of 'the extravagance of his dress') he was puzzled by certain inconsistencies. For example, Stowell says that 'S' resigned his army commission at the age of twenty-four. But Eddie never resigned his commission. Stowell says that, according to Gull's papers, 'S' had another relapse towards the end of 1889, and then slid into the final stages of syphilis. But Eddie was in India in 1889, returning in March 1890, after which he appeared in public three times, making speeches on each occasion.

There was another interesting minor puzzle. Why on earth did Stowell choose to disguise Eddie under the initial 'S'?

Could it have been because Gull himself referred to some mysterious person as 'S' — and that Stowell *mistook* this for a reference to the Duke of Clarence?

In short, was there a real person, a friend of the Duke of Clarence, a patient of Sir William Gull, who *did* fit Stowell's description?

Indeed there was. His name was James Kenneth Stephen. He became Eddie's tutor and friend in the summer of 1883; He had been selected to 'look after' Eddie at Cambridge. Jim (or 'Jem') Stephen was ambitious; he saw himself as a future power behind the throne. But it was not to be. Eddie was not noted for brilliance; he didn't really enjoy mixing with the Stephen's decadent literary friends — like the homosexual Oscar Browning, a Fellow of Kings. Eddie spent only two years at Cambridge; during that time, theorises Mr Harrison, he and Jim Stephen became lovers. Then Eddie plunged into public life, and he and Stephen met only occasionally. In 1896, Stephen made the mistake of reining his horse under a windmill, and was knocked unconscious by a descending vane; this blow on the head produced an abcess on the brain which would finally undermine his sanity. He became a patient of Sir William Gull.

Michael Harrison believes that Jim Stephen was Jack the Ripper. He argues his case convincingly. In the summer of 1888, Stephen was appointed a Clerk of Assize for the South Wales Circuit, but he was in London on all the dates of the Ripper murders. Mr Harrison quotes two poems by Stephen that reveal a capacity for pathological hatred. He points out that both Stephen's father and his grandfather died insane. Stephen *was* confined for two years in a mental home — at Northampton — where he died in 1892.

If Mr Harrison is correct, then Sir William Gull knew that Stephen was Jack the Ripper, and said so in his papers, referring to him by his initial 'S'. He also knew that — to some extent at least — Stephen's illness was brought on by his frustrated attachment to Eddie, who now avoided all contact with his former tutor. His mysterious references to 'S', Eddie and Jack the Ripper were misconstrued by Stowell, who thought that 'S' referred to Eddie, and that Eddie was therefor the Ripper.

I have to admit that I am far from convinced. To begin with, I find it hard to swallow Harrison's theory that Stephen and Eddie had a homosexual affair, and that Stephen's insanity was triggered, to some extent, by sexual jealousy. In his book *The Cleveland Street Scandal,* H. Montgomery Hyde comments: 'There is no evidence that Eddie was homosexual or even bisexual. On the contrary, he formed several romantic attachments to women, of which the first was to Princess Alix of Hesse who turned him down for the future Tsar Nicholas II of Russia.' Neither is there any evidence that Stephen was homosexual, apart from his friendship with decadents like Oscar Browning. Michael Holroyd states in his biography of Lytton Strachey that not long before his death, Stephen made 'violent advances' to Virginia Woolf's half-sister Stella Duckworth. This, admittedly, proves nothing — Stephen could have been bisexual — but in the absence of any definite evidence of Stephen's homosexuality, it would surely be reasonable to regard it as unproven.

It remains true that Stephen became insane in the late 1880s, and that he *could* have committed the Ripper murders. If I remain unconvinced, it is largely because I find it hard to imagine a brilliant, languid young man-about-town becoming a mutilator of women. My own mental picture of the Ripper — compounded from a number of descriptions given by women who saw the victims in conversation with a man — is of someone with dark hair and complexion, more powerfully built than either Eddie or Stephen, and of a distinctly lower social class. He is good looking in a coarse, brutal way — rather like Severin Klosowski, alias George Chapman, the sadistic poisoner who was executed in 1903. (Readers who are curious will find photographs of him in the *Notable British Trials* volume). And he has never, at any time, had the slightest inclination to homosexuality.

Early in 1973, I received a letter from a BBC producer named Paul Bonner, asking me if I would be willing to act as a consultant on a series of programmes about Jack the Ripper. He had already contacted another friend, Donald Rumbelow, the policeman who had 'discovered' the original morgue photographs of the Ripper's victims, and who was later to include them in his own book on the subject.

I met Paul Bonner in a pub next door to New Scotland Yard. He explained that what he now intended to tell me must be treated as a secret, at least for the time being. The BBC research team had, it seems, come up with a completely new theory of the murders. Its origin, it seemed, was a painter named Joseph Sickert, son of the famous late Victorian painter Walter Sickert. Sickert claimed to know the full story behind the Ripper murders, and he claimed that it was told to him by his father, Walter Sickert, when he, Joseph was about fourteen.

The story was this. In the mid-1880s, Walter Sickert, a bohemian young painter living in Cleveland Street, Soho, became acquainted with Eddie, Duke of Clarence, a young man who loved wine, women and song. Eddie frequently visited Sickert at home. And it was in Sickert's studio that Eddie met a young shop-girl who modelled for him; her name was Annie Crook. Annie was a Catholic. On 18 April, 1885, she gave birth to Eddie's child, a girl who was named Alice Mary. Soon after this, Eddie went through a wedding ceremony with Annie Crook at a private chapel — Sickert was one of the witnesses. The other witness was another Irish Catholic girl who was the child's nanny — her name was Mary Jeanette Kelly.

Inevitably, the secret leaked back to the palace. The Prime Minister, the Marquess of Salisbury, was horrified. What was to be done? The heir presumptive had not only married a working class girl but a Catholic. Orders were given. One day, two coaches drove up to the house in Cleveland Street where Eddie lived with his wife. Eddie was dragged away in one, Annie in the other. Annie was certified insane, and confined in a mental home. Eddie, presumably, received a stern talking to from his grandmother, Queen Victoria, and had to promise never to see Annie again.

The child, Alice Mary, was taken away by her nanny, Mary Kelly, to live in the East End of London. She found her way back to Sickert, who eventually took her to Dieppe. When she grew up, she became Sickert's mistress, and the mother of Joseph Sickert.

Mary Kelly made the mistake of telling her story to some gin-sodden prostitutes, and decided that the royal family would be willing to pay for her silence. This was her downfall. More frantic counsels were taken, and Sir William Gull, the royal physician, was given the task of eliminating Kelly and her friends. He did it with the aid of a coach driver named Netley, who took him to and from Whitechapel. Gull was Jack the Ripper, and Mary Kelly's fellow blackmailers — Polly Nichols, Annie Chapman and Elizabeth Stride — were his victims; so finally, was Mary herself, in the room in Miller's Court.

Bonner's story struck me as preposterous, and I said so*. The heir to the throne might well have impregnated Annie Crook, but that he would marry her was surely unthinkable? But there *was* evidence, said Bonner. They had checked at the address in Cleveland Street; a girl named Annie *Cook* had lived there in 1885 (her name had obviously been mis-spelled in the rate book). They had located the birth certificate of Alice Crook; no father's name was given. They had discovered that there *was* a coachman named John Netley, who had died in an accident in 1903.

The story still sounded absurd to me. Nevertheless, it was used in the BBC television series 'The Ripper File', in which Barlow and Watt of 'Z Cars' discuss the case and re-examine all the evidence; Joseph Sickert appeared in the last of the series, repeating his story.

A young journalist, Stephen Knight, was so fascinated by Sickert that he made an extensive investigation into the case; the result was published in 1976 in a book entitled — with optimism — *Jack the Ripper — The Final Solution. Books and Bookmen* sent me a copy for review. I read it in a single sitting, found it absorbing and fascinating — and, in the last analysis, totally unconvincing. For when the Sickert story is set out at length, its implausibilities suddenly become glaring.

We are being asked to believe not only that the heir presumptive was sufficiently infatuated with Annie Crook to marry her — although he was terrified of his grandmother, and knew he would one day be king of England — but that the royal family then connived at a gruesome series of murders as the only way of hushing up the whole affair. But was this not, in itself, by far the most dangerous way to silence blackmailers? Mary Kelly and her friends might believe that one murder was a matter of chance; but when Annie Chapman was killed too, they would have realised what was happening, and told everybody in sight about the Prince Eddie scandal that someone was now trying to hush

Colin Wilson was correct in his assumption. The Sunday Times of June 18, 1976, carried an article in which Joseph Sickert was reported as saying, "It was a hoax: I made it all up." The only part he continued to stick to was his father's account of his mother's parentage.

up so horribly. And surely Mary Kelly would have been chosen as the first victim, not the last? How is Gull supposed to have located the women? Mary Kelly was the only one who could be easily found; the others used common lodging houses when they were in funds, and slept on the street (or backyards) when they were not. Mr Knight wrote '(Joseph Sickert) said the murderers (Gull and Netley) located their victims and . . . offered them a lift in their carriage. All but Stride were murdered in the vehicle as Netley jogged through the busy main streets . . .' But *how* did they locate their victims — women with no fixed addresses, wandering the streets of Whitechapel in the early hours of the morning? Mr Knight says that Netley 'made advance enquiries', but that is preposterous. If a man had been enquiring the whereabouts of the victims before the murders, plenty of witnesses would have been eager to say so. And even if Netley *had* been able to pinpoint where Polly Nichols, Annie Chapman and Elizabeth Stride would sleep that night, how would he have located them wandering the streets?

There is only one case in which this explanation is remotely plausible — that of Catherine Eddowes — a woman who, according to Sickert, was killed by mistake. Catherine Eddowes was in the Bishopsgate lock-up — for being drunk and disorderly — until one in the morning, when she was discharged. She had given her name to the sergeant in charge as Mary Ann Kelly, a name she also used. According to Sickert, the Assistant Commissioner of Police, Sir Robert Anderson, was also in the plot, and found out that a woman named Mary Kelly was being held at Bishopsgate. He knew what time she would be released, and sent the murderers hot foot to meet her . . . But how would Anderson have found out, in the days before the telephone (or at any rate, before it was in general use?) Did the sergeant in charge send a messenger rushing to his house at eleven o'clock at night. 'That Mary Kelly you've been enquiring about — we've got her in the lock-up now. . .' When, presumably, more messengers rushed off to try and locate Gull and Netley, who were already out hunting for Elizabeth Stride. . .

Another implausibility stands out like a spider on an

angel cake. Why was Annie Crook allowed to remain alive? According to Sickert, she was confined in Guy's Hospital for a hundred and fifty-six days after that day in April, 1888, when she and Eddie were snatched from their Cleveland Street address. Joseph Sickert suggests that Gull performed a brain operation to destroy memory; but would it not have been simpler to eliminate her, like the others? Instead, the records show that she spent the next thirty odd years in various workhouses, and died in 1920.

Finally, the most obvious question of all: why did Gull choose to disembowel his victims? His task was only to kill them. And no one suggested that Gull was insane. Mr Knight is convinced that the answer lies in the fact that all the principle plotters, including the Commissioner of Police, were Freemasons, and that the murders were committed according to 'Masonic ritual'. This, he explains, is the ritual method supposed to be used for killing Masons who have betrayed their oath of secrecy. But since none of the women were Masons, this seems irrelevant.

Gull had, of course, suffered a stroke in the year before the murders — a piece of information which, in most people's minds, would immediately rule him out as a candidate for Ripperhood. But according to Sickert (and Mr Knight), this partially disabled man chose an incredibly complicated way of disposing of four blackmailers, luring them into the coach, killing them according to Masonic ritual, then placing the mutilated bodies in carefully arranged positions: Polly Nichols lay with her legs together, her dress pulled down; Annie Chapman was carried down an entry into a backyard, then carefully laid out with her possessions arranged at her feet.

A final point. How did the painter Walter Sickert learn all these details, if he saw the last of Eddie and Mary Kelly in April 1888? Did the Palace take him into its confidence? No doubt he would recognise the last of the Ripper's victims as the nanny of Alice Crook, but how would he proceed from there to his apparently detailed knowledge of the murders? Faced with this problem, Mr Knight shows his customary audacity and ingenuity. Sickert, he believes, was a party to the whole plot — and, in fact, took part in the murders. So Sickert himself was also Jack the Ripper — or at least, one third of him. As an afterword to Mr Knight's book, Joseph Sickert admits reluctantly that Mr Knight could well be correct.

There are some readers who may object that there is no smoke without fire, and that if Prince Eddie's name is coupled with Jack the Ripper, there must be *some* foundation to the rumour. But in that case, what precisely is the 'fire'?

Here, it seems to me, we have a simple question of logical inference. The Sickert story must be dismissed on grounds of common sense; for even if it could be proved that Annie Crook bore Prince Eddie a child, this would in no way support the absurd story of a complicated Masonic plot to kill four women. Which seems to dispose of that particular connection between Eddie and the Ripper. But then, we must come back to the origin of the whole story — Thomas Stowell himself. I met Stowell; he did not strike me as the kind of person who would invent such a story, although the 'will to believe' might have led him to exaggerate something he really knew. And what did he know? Simply that Sir William Gull had made certain mysterious references connecting the Ripper and the Duke of Clarence. But what possible connection could there have been, in reality, assuming — as we do — that Eddie was not himself Jack the Ripper? The answer seems to me obvious. Jim Stephen was a close friend of Eddie; he was also a patient of Sir William Gull. He was also suffering from some disease of the brain after 1886, when he was struck on the head. He was, in any case, a member of a family in which there was a great deal of insanity. *Could* Jim Stephen have been the Ripper? I think not. In his biography of Virginia Woolf (Stephen's cousin), Quentin Bell describes his various eccentricities: 'One day he rushed upstairs to the nursery at 22 Hyde Park Gate, drew the blade from a sword stick and plunged it into the bread. On another occasion he carried Virginia and her mother off to his room in De Vere Gardens; Virginia was to pose for him. He had decided that he was a painter — a painter of genius. He was in a state of high euphoria and painted away like a man possessed, as indeed he was. He would drive up in a hansom cab to Hyde Park Gate — a hansom in which he had been driving about all day in a state of insane excitement. On another occasion he appeared at breakfast and announced, as though it were an amusing incident, that the doctors had told him that he would either die or go completely mad. . .'

None of this sounds like the cunning maniac of White-chapel. But it *does* emphasise that Stephen was a member of London's 'upper crust', the sort of young man who played cricket and went boating and had his portrait painted to hang in the Combination Room of his college. It is true that there is no reason why this type of person should not become a sadistic mass murderer. But a glance at the case histories of sex murderers — for example, in my own *Encyclopedia of Murder* — reveals the interesting fact that they tend to come from deprived backgrounds, often from slums. Vacher, Kurten, Haarmann, Grossmann, Denke, Christie, Whiteway, Albert Fish, Earle Nelson — not one comes from an upper, or even middle class background. Good-looking, monied young men like Jim Stephen do not seem to develop the kind of morbid obsession with sex that produces this type of crime.

But Stephen *was* drifting towards insanity in 1888, at the time he was under Gull's care. At a time when every-body in London was thinking and talking about the murders, he was undoubtedly no exception. Michael Harrison cites two of Stephen's poems that reveal a capacity for brooding venge-fulness. In one, he talks about a passenger on a train who stood on his foot, and ends:

'May fiends with glowing pincers rend thy brain,
And beetles batten on thy blackened face!'

The other describes how, walking along the Backs, he *'met a woman whom I did not like'.* He speaks of her shabby dress, shapeless boots, her dull and stupid face, and ends:

'I do not want to see that girl again:
I did not like her: and I should not mind
If she were done away with, killed or ploughed.
She did not seem to serve a useful end:
And certainly, she was not beautiful.'

These poems allow us a glimpse into Stephen's state of mind, and suggest that, if he discussed the Ripper murders, he expressed no sympathy for the victims. He probably told Gull that he thought the Ripper was a public benefactor, and that he wished there were more like him. And Gull must have wondered, perhaps quite seriously, whether his eccentric patient was the man the police were looking for. If so, he might also conceivably have worried about Stephen's other pet obsession, the Duke of Clarence.

All of which is, I agree, pure speculation. Yet it is speculation based on the one fact that seems to emerge fairly clearly from this welter of theory and hearsay: that Sir William Gull made notes in which he mentioned Jack the Ripper *and* the Duke of Clarence.

As to the question of the Ripper's identity, I have no favourite candidates. All seem to me thoroughly unlikely. But I have to concede, reluctantly, that the Duke of Clarence is the least likely of all. Why reluctantly? Because I enjoy allowing my fantasy to dwell on historical might-have-beens, and I can think of none more bizarre than the idea of Jack the Ripper being crowned in Westminster Abbey.